FLIGHT TESTING TO WIN

The Autobiography of a Test Pilot

by

Tony Blackman

ISBN 0-9553856-4-4

First Published October 2005
First Revision June 2007

Blackman Associates
24 Crowsport
Hamble
Southampton SO31 4HG

To Margaret, without whose ideas,
enormous help, and continuous
encouragement this book would never
have seen the light of day.

AND

To Jack Real, who sadly is no longer
with us. He was a great friend, an
aviation enthusiast, a great engineer
and he inspired me to write this book.

Anthony L Blackman OBE, M.A., F.R.Ae.S

About the Author

Tony Blackman was educated at Oundle School and Trinity College Cambridge, where he obtained an honours degree in Physics. He was called up to do National Service and taught Maths and Physics to student pilots and navigators in the Royal Air Force. He joined one the courses he was teaching, learnt to fly, spent three years in the 2nd Tactical Air Force in Germany and then was accepted to be trained as a test pilot at the Empire Test Pilots School. From there he tested the V Bombers at Boscombe Down and, as a result, Avro's asked him to join their team, at that time developing a supersonic bomber as well as the Vulcan. Tony spent 22 years at Avro's, becoming Chief Test Pilot. Besides developing the Vulcan and the Nimrod, he spent many years testing, developing and demonstrating the Avro 748 all round the World. He was appointed project pilot of the Hawker Siddeley 146 when it was first started and flew with the legendary Howard Hughes when Hughes was the owner of Hughes Air West.

Tony was an expert in aviation electronics and was invited by Smiths Industries to join their Aerospace Board, initially as Technical Operations Director. He helped develop the then new large Electronic Displays and the Flight Management Systems. He also help sell, and then, manage the Head up/Head Down display system for the British Aerospace Hawk.

After leaving Smiths Industries he was invited to join the Board of the UK Civil Aviation Authority as the Technical Member.

Tony is a Fellow of the American Society of Experimental Test Pilots and a Fellow of the Royal Institute of Navigation.

He now lives in Hamble writing books and spends his spare time designing and maintaining databases on the internet.

CONTENTS

Introduction

There is no such things as a safe aircraft. When we fly in an aircraft we are taking a risk and the rules for designing aircraft try to ensure that the risk being taken is sufficiently low to be 'acceptable'

During the time I was flying, the emphasis changed from the Government funding development costs for both military and civil projects to the aerospace companies having to take the financial risks. Military projects had to be bid for at fixed prices and civil projects had to be developed with private funding.

As firms took more and more of the financial risk in aeroplane development, it was necessary for pilots to realise that they had to be salesman as well test pilots. For some pilots it took a little time to realise that their livelihood depended not only on being good test pilots but also good marketing men. In addition, they had to learn that an aircraft only has to meet its safety requirements; making an aircraft pleasanter, and perhaps safer, to fly was counter productive to their firm's financial viability. This principle applies just as much to-day as it did then. There is no advantage in making an aircraft safer than the certification rules require since to do so will almost certainly make it uncompetitive.

Test flying was always thought to be the most demanding of flying tasks but we learnt that demonstrating an aircraft in the third world was just as demanding, if not more so, than most test flying. Very often far from civilization, the demonstration pilot had no back up team of engineers, the runways were invariably short, rough and very often surrounded by hills.

Test flying involves many tasks --- development and production testing, demonstrating aircraft at flying displays, demonstrating aircraft to customers at home and overseas, and training the customers' pilots. Test pilots are not all equal and tasks must be allocated according to interest and ability, as I discovered when I became Chief Test Pilot, but they must always remember that they are being employed to sell aircraft as well as to test them.

This book is about test flying and the aerospace industry in the latter half of the 20th Century spanning a lifetime in Aviation. It starts in the Royal Air Force going from National Service to learning to fly, then squadron flying, then test flying school and, finally, testing aircraft at Boscombe Down. The scene then shifts to industry and to Avro's in Manchester where the Vulcan and Shackleton were being built and tested. The Vulcan development is described, including the Vulcan Mk2 with automatic landing development and the SkyBolt Air Launched Ballistic Missile. Then there is a step change as Avro decided to build a small twin engined turboprop airliner for use all round the world to replace the ubiquitous DC3. The development and demonstration of this aircraft took more and more time as it played a vital part in the economic success of Avro and this work is described in some detail, especially the demonstration flying on some of the third world's worst airfields. In parallel with this work, Avro won the contract to convert the Victor Mk.2s from bombers to refuelling tankers and, vitally important, to replace the Shackleton with the Nimrod maritime aircraft, based on the Comet airliner.

Inevitably there are stories to be told including flying with the legendary Howard Hughes. This book gives an insight into what it takes to be a test pilot and spending a life in the aerospace industry.

The final part of the book is devoted to describing working in the Avionics Industry with Smiths Industries, selling electronics to the World's airplane manufacturers.

There is also an account of the time I spent as a Member of the Board of the UK Civil Aviation Authority, when I had to make the transfer from being regulated to being a regulator. In the last chapter there are some thoughts, reviewing the past and considering the future.

Prologue

"Vulcan Two, you are cleared for take-off."

The Farnborough air traffic controller had given us permission to go. With my right hand I moved the four small throttle levers on the central console between the two seats fully forward while pushing hard with my toes on the brake pedals to prevent the aircraft moving. The whole aircraft shuddered and slid slightly as the engines came up to full power. We could hear the incredible noise, even inside the cockpit.

This was the moment I had dreamed of when I had decided some years earlier, as a National Service Education Officer, to stay in the Royal Air Force and learn to fly. I looked out to the left at the serried white rows of chalets, one above the other and at the flags by the exhibition halls streaming in the breeze. Ted Hartley, my co-pilot, and I could see the thousands of spectators standing by the rails looking at us in the grey delta bomber. The professional photographers seemed very close in front of the barriers. The small aircraft which had just taken part in the Society of British Aerospace Constructors show ahead of us taxied clear of the runway and Jimmy Harrison, my boss, took off in the prototype Vulcan Mk2. Even now, as we were cleared to start our display, it was difficult to believe that my unlikely plans had actually come to fruition. Looking forward down the runway, the tarmac stretched clear before us towards the trees far in the distance.

I released the toe brakes and the aircraft leapt forward like a Formula One racing car in pole position at the start of a Grand Prix when all the red lights go out. The airspeed indicator needle started to move forward at lightning speed as Ted called out the numbers. I moved the rudders to keep the aircraft in the middle of the runway as the aircraft raced past the chalets.

"Rotate"

Ted called out as the airspeed reached 120 knots and I pulled the control column back with my left hand to get the aircraft into the air. As we left the ground I had to push the column forward immediately, with the speed building up very rapidly, in order to prevent the aircraft climbing. My right thumb pushed the button on the instrument panel to select the landing gear to retract. The push force on the control column was now getting very high. I moved my left thumb and pressed the electric trim knob on the top of the column forward continuously to trim the aircraft nose down and try to keep the stick force under control. I did not want the aircraft to climb at all, once the landing gear was up, so that the speed would build up as quickly as possible as we raced along the top of the runway.

"Pull up"

Ted called out as we reached 270 knots, 308 mph, just before the end of the runway. I released my push force on the control column and pulled the stick backwards. The aircraft reared up in the air and started to rotate rapidly upwards, pressing us into our seats.

"Three g"

Ted called out the normal acceleration that was driving us down and making the aircraft point at the sky. I released my pull force slightly and tried to maintain the three g as the aircraft, pointing skywards, rotated through the vertical, since three g was the maximum acceleration permitted for the aircraft structure without it starting to break up.

The speed was dropping rapidly now and I had to adjust the pull force to maintain three g but then, as the speed dropped, I slowly relaxed the pull force so the normal acceleration reduced, preventing the aircraft from stalling. I looked out of the tiny front windscreen but there was nothing to see except sky. I looked anxiously at the top of the screen for the horizon to appear, even though it was going to be upside down. At last it came into view. The aircraft was completely on its back , 3,000 ft above the onlookers at Farnborough. I allowed the Vulcan to continue to rotate for a second or two more before moving the control column all the way to the left to apply full aileron. The delta shaped plane, now flying just above the stalling speed, tried to yaw to the right and I had to apply full left rudder to prevent sideslip building up and thus enabling the aircraft to rotate.

The Vulcan seemed to roll interminably slowly, as the horizon rotated from the top of the screen to the bottom but, finally, after a few seconds, it was the right way up with the runway below. I pushed the control column forward and dived as steeply as I dared at the ground, slamming the throttles closed with my right hand. It was eerily silent except for the wind noise as the aircraft accelerated. The tents below rushed up to meet us and then, at 270kts once more, a few hundred feet above the ground, I rotated the aircraft upwards again to do another 'roll off the top'. I rolled out back to level flight as we finished the second roll off the top, but there was no time to relax. I searched for the runway and dived down, this time positioning the aircraft downwind for landing. The challenge now was to get my Vulcan on the ground as quickly as possible and not to interfere with Jimmy's first run and barrel roll in front of the crowd.

We lost height very rapidly, throttles closed all the way, doing a tight left hand turn on to finals. People often told me not fly the Vulcan like a fighter but I always explained that there was nothing else I could do. Why else did it have a fighter type control column? I let the speed of the Vulcan fall so that we were almost stalled as we approached the first few yards of tarmac. I pulled the two outboard throttle levers fully back and lifted them up over the closed gates so that the engines stopped as I made the final flare for landing. We touched down with the nose way up in the air like a praying mantis. The wheels rubbed gently on the ground and the aircraft slowed rapidly with the enormous aerodynamic drag. I gradually allowed the nosewheel to come down as the first runway turn off appeared and then engaged the nosewheel steering by pressing the button below the control column. I pushed the right rudder pedal and steered the aircraft off the runway, using the two remaining engines. We checked our watches. The whole flight had taken 3 minutes and 10 seconds, 5 seconds better than our rehearsal. It was all over. My first chance to demonstrate in front of the crowd. I was elated, but in reality the flight meant a lot more than that. My years of training had come to fruition. The work had been rewarded.

CHAPTER 1

Learning to Fly

Some people in life seem born to fly. They yearn, almost it seems from when they are born, to pilot an aircraft. It is their driving ambition and they are emotionally involved with everything involved with aviation. I was not one of those people. In my formative years at school, during the 1939/45 Second World War, the thought of flying an airplane never occurred to me. I watched with horror as some of the United States bombers returned damaged from Germany, emitting smoke, and landing on the many airfields surrounding my school at Oundle in Northamptonshire; the airfields are now deserted but some names I shall never forget --- Polebrook, Molesworth, and Deenethorpe. I still remember seeing the planes that did not make it, crashing in the countryside nearby, not really appreciating the terrible human tragedies that were occurring.

It is strange that though I eventually spent my whole working life in the aerospace industry, I was not the slightest bit interested in aviation whilst at school or college. My involvement with flying was purely an accident and I have often wondered what finally motivated me to get involved with aeroplanes. It might have been significant that every summer in the 1930s we spent our holidays at Westcliff-on-Sea in Essex. My mother got rid of me for the week by paying the local boatman, who made his living taking holiday makers sailing off the beach, the then not insignificant sum of two shillings and sixpence to take me on as his helper. I learnt about sheets, booms, anchors, tides and many other skills. More importantly, I learnt how to trim sails into the wind and how to steer a sailing boat. Sailing was my first experience of aerodynamics and the effect of wind and tide. I did not sail again until I was at College.

My prowess in matters educational, before I reached my 'teens, was abysmal. My local day school was evacuated to Devon twice, the first time in 1938 to a guest house in Dawlish when another World War seemed inevitable. The Prime Minister came back from Germany with a 'piece of paper' saying 'peace in our time' and so we all returned home. We went back to Devon again in 1939 to

Luscombe Manor when the war actually started. I can still remember listening to Neville Chamberlain's speeches both in '38 and again in '39 when he announced the invasion of Czechoslovakia and the declaration of war. To us at school the threat of war or even war itself meant very little. My parents tried very hard to find a school which would teach me properly and improve my education and in 1940 they sent me to an expensive private school, Downsend School in Leatherhead in Surrey. Here the teachers made serious efforts to educate us because, I realised some years later, it was vital to get good results to the so called Public Schools, actually privately run, in order to ensure that parents were willing to pay to send their children to the school. No sooner was I settled in Downsend than we were evacuated, this time to Hurstpierpoint Public School in Sussex, further from London but actually closer to the war and the enemy aircraft.

I loved being at Hurstpierpoint, set in the Sussex countryside with lots of Victorian and Edwardian buildings, housing the boys and the classrooms. There, at the age of eleven, I unexpectedly developed an obsessive interest in mathematics and this obsessive streak in my character has never left me, though the obsession drifted from mathematics into computing. Thanks to Mr Straker, the maths master at Downsend, I managed to get a major scholarship to Oundle. He introduced me to Lancelot Hogben's Mathematics for the Million and I was enthralled. His book taught me differential calculus at an early age and, like learning any language, the earlier one starts the easier it is to assimilate. Hogben followed his first book with Science for the Citizen and again he opened my eyes to concepts that I had never imagined. To this day they are still my favourite reference books, together with the three text books my maths master, G.W.Brewster, wrote at Oundle.

I remember my excitement as my mother bought all the clothes required by Oundle, listed in detail by the school's administration. Every article of clothing had to have a tag sewn on to it bearing my name and the 'house' where I would be accommodated whilst in the school. The war was causing shortages so things were not all that easy to obtain. The great day finally came; all the parents arrived at Euston with their offspring and off we went in a special train direct to the station at Oundle. I was in New House, one of eleven houses at the time and, of course, it was the oldest house in the school.

Oundle School was wonderful for me. Mr Brewster taught me for the four years I spent there and I enjoyed every minute of his lessons, much to the amazement of many of my school fellows. I was very fortunate that I was able to assimilate mathematics with incredible ease but, after two years, I decided to concentrate on Science as being a more practical discipline. I developed an interest in electronics which I found very demanding theoretically but which, I realise now, was very time wasting practically and, rather like a disease, it started to blunt my academic skills. Luckily the blunting proceeded slowly and, as the war ended in 1945, I went up to Trinity College, Cambridge with a major entrance scholarship to read Physics with my anticipated future quite clear; to get a good degree and do research as befitted a scholar. But somehow things did not work out as planned and I was called up into the Royal Air Force for two years National Service.

In October 1948 I went to Padgate near Liverpool, as many thousands of recruits before me had done, to do 'square bashing' and to learn how to be the R.A.F. equivalent of an Army private. Of course, for me and the others who were with me, it was a special situation because we had all been pre-selected to become officers in the Education branch. As we finished at Padgate we went on to the Officer Cadet Training Unit at Spitalgate in Lincolnshire to be trained as Officers. It was an interesting course and twelve weeks later we emerged as Pilot Officers ready to be trained as teachers. We went on to Wellesbourne Mountford, where the R.A.F. School of Education was based. The students on our course came from many disciplines but we all had to learn that just having a degree was not an immediate passport to becoming effective teachers. After twelve weeks we were judged ready to be let loose on our students; our training as teachers was, of course, rudimentary, but we managed because we had a depth of knowledge in our various subjects.

As the course came to a close our chief instructor discussed with us the various postings that needed to be filled. I cannot remember all the choices for the few science graduates on our course

17

but I was attracted to a post at Wittering since it was only 100 miles north of London and therefore convenient for my social activities. The job at Wittering was to teach mathematics and physics to students who were to become pilots and navigators but, at the time, this fact made no special impact on me. I asked to be sent to Wittering and, as luck would have it, my request was granted. I was posted to No. 1 Initial Training School to become an instructor, my first real job. So, in this casual way, my life and career was settled!

Wittering appealed to me. It was one of the R.A.F. stations built between the two world wars with standard buildings, hangars and an Officers Mess where all the unmarried officers lived. It was near my old school, near Cambridge and not too far from London. The place was on the Great North Road and, by modern standards, the traffic was very light. I was lucky enough to have an old second hand car so I was able to tour the area, though petrol rationing was still in force after the war so I could not go far. The airfield had been used during the war but there were no runways as such; however there was a grass strip nearly two miles long which was a magical place in many ways. I loved getting up early in the morning when I was going to London, harvesting the mushrooms from places where, twelve hours before as night fell, there was absolutely no sign of any; their speed of growth never ceased to amaze me. Unfortunately, due to the drive of technology, it was not many years later that an enormous 10,000 ft runway was constructed on the airfield with runway lights and approach lighting for the V bombers that I was later to test, but luckily at that time we had no inkling of what was going to happen. I often wonder whether the mushroom grounds are still there or whether they have been covered with concrete.

My job was to take over from a Flying Officer Hague, a National Serviceman like myself, to instruct in mathematics and physics pupils who had been selected to be trained as pilots or navigators. The pupils mainly came from volunteers who had the necessary academic qualifications and wanted to make the Royal Air Force a career. However, there were a few National Service pilots on the pilot courses who had already been trained in the University Air Squadrons. All the students had had to go to Hornchurch where they had been subjected to a battery of aptitude tests to determine their level of intelligence and to find out whether they would be suitable as pilots or navigators. I am not sure how effective the tests were or how much weight the R.A.F. accorded the results but, as I learnt later myself, the tests were very different from the normal academic exams I had been used to, requiring the student merely to select an answer from several choices. Such tests, which do not test the ability of the student to write coherently, are commonplace to-day but at the time they were very new.

Hague showed me the syllabus, sample lectures and the exams he was setting at the end of the course and, after listening to a few of his lessons, I started teaching some of the courses myself. I found that quite a few of the students did not have the necessary mathematics to be able to complete the course and I had to spend a lot of time teaching things like basic trigonometry. The academic range was very large on the courses and it was a challenge to keep the interest of the students who had either passed mathematics at Advanced Level at school, or had degrees. After I had completed the first few courses the lectures became routine but it was fascinating meeting all the different people and hearing their ambitions for the future. Most of them, obviously, wanting nothing more than to learn to fly.

Some of the other instructors at Wittering were ex-pilots and navigators and had joined the education branch because of a loss of medical category. In addition, there were some current pilots and navigators who were posted to Wittering to be in charge of the courses going through the system.

Airspeed Oxford

Occasionally an aircraft would land on the airfield and give the pupils air experience and I remember flying with a Flt. Lt. Bethell in an Airspeed Oxford, an ancient twin engined aircraft with a tail wheel and an appalling view from the flight deck. I don't think the event made a great impression on me one way or another. I certainly enjoyed looking down on the long green airfield as we slowly flew around the area, slowly being the operative word. It was at about this time that I began to wonder what the future held in store for me. My father had arranged for me to train as an accountant but the idea was not very appealing to say the least. For some reason my aptitude for mathematics did not spill over to managing money.

I cannot remember when exactly I decided to stay in the R.A.F. and become a pilot. I know that we had some visits from senior officers and some of the visitors suggested that I should convert from being an Education Officer and take a Permanent Commission. Unlikely as it seems, even at that time I realised that my training at University could be very valuable in helping me to become a test pilot, because most of the experienced and famous test pilots of the time had been trained in the war and had just not had the opportunity for academic training. This lack of training did not matter much then, but times were fast changing and I could see that aircraft design was moving rapidly from an art to a science and that test pilots needed to be able to talk the same language as the designers and engineers. Of course, though I did not know it at the time, the powers that be in the Royal Air Force had come to the same conclusion rather earlier, so that in 1943 the Empire Test Pilots School had been formed under the command of Sammy Wroath, an outstanding leader in the test piloting fraternity. Fifty years later, at the half century re-union of the Empire Test Pilots School Sammy, on the wrong side of eighty years old, gave the keynote speech without referring to any notes let alone the modern love affair with Powerpoint, an outstanding performance by any standard.

I considered my options and realised that I did not relish returning home and having to learn to be an accountant. I was enjoying my first job, earning some money and being able to decide what it was I really wanted to do. Somebody pointed out to me that if I did transfer to the General Duties branch and apply for a Permanent Commission I could enrol as if I had been a member of the University

Air Squadron, which meant that I would get accelerated promotion. I decided to take the plunge and I was sent to Hornchurch to check on my aptitude to be a pilot. Of course I was very lucky; I was born at the right time and, by chance, was in the right place to have the opportunity to fly and, moreover, something training could not supply, I had excellent eyesight and was physically fit. In due course I was informed that I would be accepted as a student pilot and so, at the beginning of 1950, I found that I was posted to No. 6 Flying Training School at R.A.F. Ternhill in Shropshire, to join one of the courses I had just finished instructing, No. 38 Pilots Course.

***

Ternhill was very different from Wittering. I was a pupil once again, albeit a privileged one, since I was the only member of the course who was already commissioned. I shared a room with another student officer pilot, Flying Officer Erik Bennett, who had joined No. 35 Pilots Course, the Ternhill course before ours. I had not met him before as he had been posted straight to Ternhill and had not been to Wittering. He had already gone solo and was mad keen on flying. He was also well connected locally and, together, we visited some of the local landowners in our spare time. He was very determined in everything he did, a trait that I have noticed in people who are not very tall. I was not surprised to discover in later years, long after I had left the R.A.F., that he had become an aide to King Hussein of Jordan. In fact Erik became a very senior and distinguished Air Force officer, specialising in the Middle East and finished his career as Chief of the Sultan of Oman's Air Force. To me he seemed very much in the mould of Lawrence of Arabia, quite rightly loved and respected by the senior rulers and airmen of the Gulf States.

Because I had not been a student on 38 Course at the Initial Training School, I had not received instruction on all the many subjects that needed to be learnt to become a pilot. It was necessary for me to catch up quickly with the rest of my course and learn about matters that had never previously interested me, like how an internal combustion engine worked, about navigation, about meteorology and a host of other matters. I thoroughly enjoyed exploring these practical subjects, though the knowledge I gained never really turned me into

21

an engineer; I always considered everything I did from an academic viewpoint and I was not used to putting precept into practice. Looking back, I probably asked too many questions but, like most people, the instructors responded to the challenge and my curiosity probably made their job more interesting.

In parallel with our Ground School we were introduced to our first aircraft, an ab-initio trainer, the Percival Prentice and to all the supporting services that were needed to be able to fly in the R.A.F. We soon learnt that there was no question of flying a working aircraft merely for enjoyment; in later years as Chief Test Pilot I had to remind some my staff of the same thing. Furthermore, we soon came to realise that safe flying is only possible if there is an infrastructure to support the aircraft. First and foremost an aircraft has to be maintained properly. It consists of many parts, the engine, the flying controls, the navigation and radio equipment, the instruments and, nowadays, many other systems. On the course, we learnt that a serviceable aircraft only happens as a result of a lot of hard work by the ground crews. Every day, the flying programme was put on the board with our names, our instructors and the aircraft, but without the hard work and skill of the ground crews, it would never have happened.

We needed to learn about the weather and the way the Meteorological Office provided all the data to help pilots determine whether it was safe to do the flight that was planned. We were introduced to miles of paper printout, which showed us the conditions at the airports all over the country and the synoptic charts that attempted to forecast what would happen next. We had to recognise when the weather forecast was likely to be correct and when the conditions made it much harder for the forecasters to be certain of the future. In our slow aircraft, winds were very important not only near the ground but also en-route and we had to be able to calculate the effect of the winds using a so called 'Dalton computer'. This was a device which could be strapped on one's knee, enabling graphical triangular solutions of drift and ground speed from estimated wind and airspeed. Rudimentary by modern standards possibly, but very effective.

It is not permissible now and it was not permissible then to just get into an aircraft and go. At a training airfield in particular there were hundreds of take-offs and landings a day and there was a control tower to watch over us. In fact we soon learnt that Air Traffic Control watched over us not only at Ternhill but wherever we were flying. We had to learn the Rules of the Air, how to behave in an airfield traffic pattern, how to navigate from one place to another and how to file a flight plan, when one was required, and how to keep air traffic informed of the destination of the aircraft. There was the operation of the radio to master so that we could tell the air traffic controllers of our immediate intentions or what had happened to us. Above all we had to learn to keep a good look out, whether we were on the ground or in the air. We also needed to watch the signals that the controllers had put next to the control tower to show, amongst other things, which way the aircraft had to fly around the circuit.

Percival Prentice

The Percival Prentice was the main ab initio trainer at the time in the R.A.F.; a low wing monoplane, non-retracting landing gear with a tail wheel and a de Haviland 292hp Gypsy Queen 32 inverted in-line piston engine. We were given the Prentice Pilots Notes to study. Each aircraft type in the R.A.F. had its own Pilots Notes and the Prentice was no exception. These excellent books were written by the R.A.F. Handling Squadron, then at Hullavingon, and I got to know the unit very well in later years when they moved to Boscombe Down. It seems incredible to-day, but the Prentice Pilots Notes had just twenty eight small pages and some illustrations. Not surprisingly it did not take us long to learn about the aircraft and its limitations; maximum dive speed 215 knots, maximum speed with flaps down 75 knots, maximum weight 4,200 lb., full fuel 20 gallons of petrol in each wing and no fire extinguisher if the engine caught fire.

The crew seating arrangement was side by side which was obviously good from a training viewpoint since the instructor could see what was going on and point things out to his student. However, I was reminded of a remark by Uffa Fox, a famous yachtsman of the time, whose books I used to enjoy reading. He pointed out that in building small boats it was difficult to absorb the space required by a yachtsman without distorting the aerodynamic design of the boat and, of course, the same is true for a small aircraft. For this reason, from a performance viewpoint, tandem seating is best in a small trainer but, of course, it is then difficult for the instructor to monitor the pupil properly since the pupil is out of sight. The Royal Air Force policy makers had decided in their wisdom that side by side seating was to be preferred and the Prentice was the first post-War example. The aircraft had had to be made very wide to accommodate the two seats and the result was that it was under powered, heavy, ungainly and slow since, not surprisingly, the engineers at Percivals had been unable to design the Prentice to escape from the limitations resulting from the design requirements. The Prentice was as uninspiring to the instructor as it was to the student though, as students, we did not then know any better. It was an enormous contrast to the famous biplane trainer, the Tiger Moth of pre war years, and the de Haviland Chipmunk, a relatively modern trainer aircraft at the time, not penalised commercially by the need to meet the R.A.F. requirement of side by side seating. The R.A.F. soon realised the shortcomings of the Prentice and specified a new trainer which resulted in the Percival Provost, another side by side seating aircraft, but with a much more powerful radial engine, the Alvis 550hp Leonides; the aircraft was able to be larger so that the side by side seating drag penalty could be partially absorbed by having a wider fuselage. The Provost started to replace the Prentice in 1953. I managed to fly it some years later - it was a delightful aircraft; I wish I had had the opportunity to train on it.

As the Prentice had a fixed undercarriage there was no need for a system to retract the landing gear. However, the wheel brakes were operated by pneumatics, a feature that seemed to have endeared itself to UK aircraft designers, unlike the United States manufacturers who preferred to use hydraulics. The Prentice brakes were operated by pressing a lever on the hand wheel. which slowed the aircraft down if the rudder was central. To turn the aircraft the brake lever was depressed with the rudder displaced, which introduced differential braking to the wheels and, therefore, altered the direction of movement of the aircraft on the ground. The pneumatic braking system did not work well on the Prentice, or on any other aircraft that I have flown for that matter, and it never ceased to amaze me how long it took before British designers finally faced up to the fact, which all pilots who had flown US aircraft knew very well, that hydraulic brakes were much more reliable and much easier for the pilot to use to control the aircraft.

Landing flaps were fitted to the Prentice, also operated by the pneumatic system. The flying controls, ailerons and elevators, were unremarkable, operated by a stick moving cables. The aircraft had one VHF four channel radio set, the frequencies being pre-set and controlled by crystals. This feature, which was standard about this time, meant that all flights had to be planned very carefully to ensure that it was possible to talk to the necessary airfields and navigation agencies. One of the arcane mathematical feats that all pilots had to master was the calculation to determine the frequency of the crystal required to be fitted in the set, to get the desired VHF frequency. If the calculation was incorrect, the only possibility was to talk on the international distress channel, 121.5 Mc/s as it was called then, now 121.5 Mhz, but this understandably was very much frowned upon unless, of course, there was a real problem. We had to learn what to do if our single radio set failed, how to alert the tower by waggling our wings and how to read the circuit instructions which were laid out next to the Control Tower. We relied on the Aldis light signals, red and green, to know when it was safe to land. It all seems prehistoric now but then it was absolutely normal, not worthy of comment.

The only other radio we had on board was an aid to help us to land in bad weather. It was called the Standard Beam Approach, SBA; though the system and technology seem archaic now, it was definitely

25

a vital bad weather approach tool at the time. The design principle was that there were two antennas on the ground, one transmitting dots and the other dashes; on the left hand side of the runway centre line on the approach you could hear dashes on the radio receiver and on the right hand side of the approach only dots. On the runway centre line the dots and dashes merged so that all the pilot could hear, in theory at any rate, was a steady note. However, the problem was that the sets were not very reliable and the tuning mechanism was extremely poor to say the least. Each airfield had a different frequency for transmitting the signals and there was a different morse code identifier for each airfield. The pilot had to crank a handle driving a very inefficient cable connected to the radio box and listen to the noises on his earphones; there was no reliable indication of tuned frequency since there was not much connection between the needle indication on the tuning indicator and the frequency being received, so it could take a long time to find the signal and check it came from the right airfield. The volume from the set was low and the range of the equipment was poor so it was always a nerve racking business getting tuned in, particularly when the weather was bad and the system was really needed.

The method of using the SBA was to get headings to steer from the control tower until the aircraft had passed over the airfield. The plane was then turned on a timed downwind leg until it was considered that it was six or seven miles away from the airfield. It could then be turned towards the beam and the pilot would listen to the dashes waiting for the noise to change as the dots would come in until a continuous note was heard, the dots merging with the dashes. The turns had to be judged from experience in order to reach and hold the centre line, allowing of course for the wind. If all had gone well a fan shaped beacon called the outer marker would be heard at about five miles out; altitude could then be reduced slowly down to an approved minimum height. The aircraft would be levelled off, the inner marker would be heard and then, hopefully, the runway would appear out of the gloom; if not the aircraft would be put into a climb and either another approach commenced or it would be diverted elsewhere. Old fashioned as the system was, it never ceased to surprise me how effective and useful the SBA was. I realise now that it only worked as an approach aid because the aircraft approach speeds were so slow.

Prentice Instrument Panel

The instruments on the Prentice were duplicated, one set for the instructor on the right and one set for the trainee in the left hand seat. The main instruments conformed to the standard layout at the time with the airspeed indicator on the left, artificial horizon central and the altimeter below the airspeed indicator; the vertical speed indicator was top right with the turn and slip indicator below. Interestingly, the standard layout changed in the next few years so that the altimeter and the vertical speed indicator changed places. The change was probably due to the fact that civil airliners had that layout and the Royal Air Force decided to conform.

The engine instruments were centrally located between the two sets of blind flying instruments. In those days the artificial horizon was driven by suction and the instrument could be 'toppled' or lose its orientation if the aircraft climbed or dived vertically when carrying out aerobatics. Consequently, it was important to know how to fly using just the turn and slip indicator. For training purposes the aircraft was fitted with blue screens which we could put up in front of the windscreens and we were able to practise instrument flying by wearing amber goggles. This trick enabled us to see the instruments but ensured that we could not see outside to get visual cues; the system was not perfect but it worked reasonably well.

Keeping the directional gyro pointing the right way was very important if you did not want to get lost. The problem was that all gyros, then and now, tend to drift partly due to the imperfections of

27

the gyro itself and partly due to the rotation of the earth, since the gyro axis of rotation is fixed in space. The only heading reference of the aircraft was the magnetic compass but the magnet, and the card that was fixed to it, only pointed at the magnetic north if the aircraft was flying level in un-accelerated flight. It was necessary to synchronise the directional gyro heading to the heading of the magnetic card every few minutes to ensure the heading being followed on the directional gyro was correct. Whilst on the ground, it was easy to turn the gyro control knob to the indicated heading of the magnetic card but, once in the air, the magnetic card would wander all over the place so precise flying was required to get an accurate heading from the magnetic card before updating the gyro. If one forgot to set the card then the aircraft would enter a large curve, taking the unwary pilot away from the desired destination.

As students we had so much to learn that it never really occurred to us that the Prentice left a lot to be desired. Our instructors knew that the aircraft was pedestrian but it did not worry us. We were immersed in learning everything that there was to know about it. Each time, before we got anywhere near flying, we had to walk round the aircraft to make certain that the control locks had been removed, that the control surfaces moved freely and that the pitot head cover had been taken off so that the airspeed indicator and altimeter would work. In winter we had to make certain that there was no ice or snow on the wings. When we had finished our external inspection we climbed aboard and connected our parachutes which we had had to carry out to the aircraft with us. It was many years before I had the luxury of flying in an aircraft which did not require a parachute and, though I accepted the need for it and carried out all the drills, thankfully only on the ground, I always felt that the perceived need for a parachute definitely spoilt the enjoyment of flying .

Once strapped in to the aircraft as well as the parachute, we had to look all round the cockpit checking that all the levers and switches were in the correct positions, working from a check list to make sure that nothing was forgotten. In fact we had a card with a list of checks to be carried out before starting up, taxiing, taking-off, after taking-off, before landing and after landing. These formal procedures ensured, then as now, that everything had been done that needed to be done so that the aircraft would be able to fly safely. When all was complete it was time to start the engine; the ground crewman supervising the start would give the thumbs up, meaning that nothing was in the way of the propeller or the rest of the aircraft. In the Prentice it was only necessary to turn the magneto switches on and press the starter button; after a few seconds with the propeller turning very slowly, the engine would fire and the propeller then rotated steadily at ground idling speed. The checks before taxiing were then carried out, the chocks in front of the wheels were waved away and the clamp on the brake lever was released. The throttle was opened and the aircraft was on its way.

On 4th February 1950 I had my first flight with my instructor, Flight Lieutenant Palmer. To ensure that everything that needed to be covered in the course would indeed be covered, every flying task was given a number and we had to complete thirteen of these exercises before we were allowed to go solo. On this first flight we did exercises 1 to 3, whatever they were. I hardly touched the controls since Palmer was demonstrating everything to me.

On the third flight, two days later, I was allowed to be in control of the aircraft. I got permission from the controller in the tower, opened the throttle gradually and taxied forward slowly, peering on either side of the engine and propeller which blocked my view. Once on the taxiway we moved steadily towards the runway in use, with all the other Prentices and Harvards, the advanced trainer on to which we would graduate, ahead and behind us. As the runway was approached it was necessary to stop, turn sideways to avoid damaging the aircraft behind and open the engine up to full power to check the magnetos, switching each off in turn, checking that there was no significant drop in engine r.p.m. and therefore power. In later years aircraft designers dreamt up the concept of 'fail-safe' for their designs which in effect meant that a single failure would not prejudice the safety of the aircraft, but the use of twin magnetos used the concept long before the system was given an esoteric name. Once the check was completed we taxied forward again, turned on to the runway when the controller had given permission, and then lined up with the runway for take-off. I released the brakes, pushed the throttle lever forward, the engine roared, the aircraft accelerated, and I kept it going straight down the runway by moving the rudders. When the correct speed was reached, I pulled back the control column and the plane took to the air. For me it was a thrilling moment.

During these few weeks we were taught how to control the aircraft not only when we could see the ground but also when we were in cloud and had to use our instruments. We were taught how to turn the aircraft without losing height, how to take-off safely and, much harder, how to get the aircraft back on the ground in a neat and tidy manner. It is often said that a good landing is one the pilot can walk away from but a rather higher criterion was set by the flying instructors at Ternhill. We also had our first introduction to aerobatics which, I realise now, was a vital part of learning to fly; not because aerobatics were needed at that stage of our flying career but because after looping and rolling an aircraft and recovering from the unusual attitudes, we found controlling the aircraft in straight and level flight and in the traffic pattern when taking-off and landing, much less demanding.

We had to learn that it was important to have enough speed at the start of a loop so that when we were upside down, at the top of the loop, there was still enough speed to avoid stalling and possibly inadvertently spinning. We also had to learn how to roll the aircraft so that the nose did not drop and cause the aircraft to start to go towards the ground when we were half way round, upside down. All these aerobatics were carried out several thousand feet above the ground to ensure that all manoeuvres could be completed safely.

We had to learn how to control the engine and the propeller it was driving. The propeller on the Prentice was a variable pitch propeller so that the blades rotated relative to the hub; consequently there was a propeller pitch control lever as well as a throttle lever. For full power, when the throttle was opened, the propeller pitch lever had to be fully forward to ensure that the propeller was in fine pitch and was rotating as quickly as possible, 2600 rpm for the Prentice. During the cruise, the pitch lever was moved rearwards so that the engine/propeller rotated more slowly at an economical speed. In addition there was yet another control, the mixture lever, on the left hand side only which the instructor could not reach, to reduce the fuel

,to the fuel/air mixture when cruising, for greater efficiency and to get the maximum air miles per gallon..

Before going solo we had to learn how to stall an aircraft and how to recover with a minimum loss of height. A stall is when the airflow cannot flow smoothly over the top surface of the wing; the flow breaks down because the wing is at too steep an angle to the airflow and, consequently, the lift from the airflow to keep the aircraft flying is lost. Any plane will stall if it is flown too slowly and the classic way to stall an aircraft is to throttle the engine and pull the stick steadily back. Aircraft designers always try to design aircraft which have an immaculate stall; that is as the wing reaches its critical angle of attack and loses lift, the elevators lose control and the aircraft nose drops evenly without one wing stalling before the other and causing the aircraft to bank. I was to spend many hours investigating aircraft stalling behaviour in later life but, at that time, it was just another exercise to be undertaken before I could be allowed to fly by myself. The Prentice in fact stalled very well with no sign of a wing drop so that all the pilot had to do when the nose dropped was to push the stick forward, apply power and then pull the stick back gently as the aircraft increased airspeed.

Learning to fly in England in the winter is not an ideal time. The weather is nearly always bad and early 1950 was no exception. Going solo for the first time is a psychological barrier for most people, like driving a car on one's own. Certainly I found it a barrier, exaggerated each day I had not gone solo and learning each evening that other members of my course had crossed that hurdle. I suppose Flt. Lt. Palmer was getting worried about my flying ability and got the chief flying instructor on our flight, Flight Lieutenant Briggs, to fly with me; a 'scrub check' I think it was called. I remember to this day Briggs giving me two pieces of advice when he realised that I was worried about going solo and feeling under confident. 'Get the aircraft somewhere near the ground, close the throttle and don't interfere, the aircraft will land itself'. The other pearl was 'Flying can't be very difficult, look at all the people who can do it'. I've always remembered that latter remark because not only is it very true but also because it is very helpful to people, like myself, who let their innate ability be overtaken by nervousness and who have an over critical attitude to personal performance. For me his advice solved the problem and I went solo on the next flight because of his sympathetic guidance. I've quoted his latter remark on many occasions, not about flying because I was never a flying instructor, but about many other activities in life from driving a car to operating a personal computer. It has been adopted as a standard saying in our family.

Aircraft these days are much easier to fly than fifty or more years ago. In the past, aircraft were always struggling for power so that the margin for error was very small. Furthermore, the power generator, the engine, was unreliable so that the pilot had to be good at landing the aircraft without any power on the nearest flat space. Flying controls were all manually operated and had to be aerodynamically balanced so that the pilot had the strength to move the controls once the aircraft was moving through the air. Control surface design to keep the operating forces low was not easy even on slow aircraft and on the faster aircraft the controls would often try to lock hard over in certain flight conditions, even on production aircraft; this required instant response from the pilot if disaster was to be avoided. Luckily, we did not have this problem on the Prentice.

Even though modern aircraft are easier to fly than their predecessors, the critical part of flying an aeroplane has not changed, that is the take-off and the landing. But there is no comparison between the skill and judgement required to land the early aircraft and the almost negligent ease with which a pilot can deposit a modern large airplane on the ground. When we were learning to fly, most aircraft had tail wheels which made them basically unstable on the ground. The very early aircraft did not have wheel brakes for directional control which, in some ways, was a good thing. However, the tail wheeled aircraft immediately after the second world war certainly did. This meant that if you put the brakes on when you were going quickly, either the back of the aircraft would try to overtake the front like a jack-knifing lorry with embarrassing results as the aircraft tried to do a 180° turn or else it would go over on its nose.

I realise now that the Prentice was completely unsuitable as a vehicle for learning to fly; the elderly Tiger Moth biplane, which I flew a few years later, would in many ways have been a much better trainer but its age and lack of radio equipments had forced the Royal Air

Force to change. As Briggs had pointed out, if you got anywhere near the ground in the Prentice and closed the throttle it would subside gratefully onto its wheels like a lazy duck. It did have a tail wheel, but it did not seem to matter. It did have a rudder, but the aircraft was so directionally stable it barely needed it. Briggs had let me into the secret of how to land the Prentice — 'don't interfere and it will all happen'. On 3rd March I went solo at a grass airfield called Chetwynd in Shropshire somewhere; I doubt that it is in use to-day. I flew for 20 minutes after having logged 14 hours 30 minutes dual in 17 flights. If I had not gone solo then I probably would have failed the course but, from that point, I never really looked back. Navigation had always been a hobby of mine and still is to-day. I had done a lot of sailing in small yachts and spherical trigonometry, using the sun, moon and the stars had made me quite adept with the sextant, not that much navigation skill was needed in the sort of flying we were doing. Nevertheless, for me it was a great adventure leaving Ternhill's airfield and setting course for a distant destination, though in reality only a few miles away.

In June we started to fly at night and I found this experience particularly enjoyable. I got the same feeling flying alone at night as I still do now when I am sailing, looking at all the lights and deciding which lights matter and which are of no significance. The Prentice, like most aircraft built for the R.A.F. at that time, had two sets of lights for illuminating the blind flying panel; there was a set of red lights and also a set of lights fitted with Ultra Violet screens. The instruments were coated with paint which glowed under UV light; the idea behind these UV lights was that the pilot could see the instruments without having his night vision spoilt by bright lighting, which would have prevented his being able to see out of the cockpit. The system worked very well. Going solo at night presented no problems for me and I was soon on my way, landing away at different R.A.F. training airfields such as Cottesmore in Rutland and Syerston near Nottingham, always checking I had the right airfield by deciphering the Morse code being illuminated by the lighthouse next to the tower. It was always very peaceful and quiet on the radio at night and I had time to think and enjoy the surroundings.

Probably the most critical manoeuvre we had to learn was recovering from a spin; that is when an aircraft stalls unevenly, drops a

33

wing and then rotates steadily out of control as height is lost rapidly. In fact, on the Prentice it was very difficult to get the aircraft to spin at all; full aileron and rudder had to be applied at the moment of stall and the controls held in the fully displaced position. The aircraft would reluctantly start to spin and, providing the number of turns was less than five, the student had merely to centralise the controls to stop the aircraft spinning and then recover from the nose down attitude. If more turns were carried out then getting out of the spin was a bit harder; full opposite rudder had to be applied, followed by a wait for another turn before the elevator was pushed fully forward. The aircraft would then stop turning but the recovery attitude was quite nose down. A straight pull out followed but care was necessary not to pull the stick back too vigorously before the speed had built up or the airplane would enter another spin.

We flew the Prentice for six months and towards the end of the period we took tests in instrument flying, navigation, aerobatics and general flying. By the end of July it was all over and I was declared fit to carry on and fly the Harvard. Unlike the Prentice, which was a British design, the Harvard was manufactured in the United States under the designation AT6. Apart from the radio, the aircraft had not been modified and was, basically, the same as the trainers used in the United States Air Force.with a Pratt & Whitney R-1340 590hp radial engine

Boulton Paul Balliol

I had one minor disappointment as I graduated from the basic to the advanced trainer. Training Command had just got a new advanced trainer, the Boulton Paul Balliol, which had been cleared by the Aircraft and Armament Experimental Establishment at Boscombe

Down for general use and it had been decided by the powers that be that Ternhill should be the first F.T.S. to try the new aircraft. Our course was going to be the first one to train pilots on the Balliol but there was only one available when we started and we could not all be trained on it. My name was not selected but I remember that one of my friends called Beaton, who had a phenomenally fast motor bike on which we used to travel together to London on the week-ends, was and I was very envious. It was a delightful looking aircraft, low wing monoplane with retracting undercarriage and it sounded spectacular, since it had a Rolls Royce Merlin engine of Spitfire fame with the same noise of crackling exhausts. The seating, of course, was side by side and because it was quite large the designers had easily absorbed the cockpit into the fuselage design without creating a lot of unnecessary drag. I was not able to fly it during the course but when I was at Boscombe Down some years later I did manage to fly the Sea Balliol, which was almost identical but had a hook attached, and it fulfilled my expectations with regard to handling and performance; Beaton was indeed a lucky student. But then I suppose so was I, even if I missed out on flying the Balliol.

Harvard Trainer

As usual the first thing one had to do when learning about a new aircraft was to understand all of its systems; the Pilots Notes were even shorter than the Prentice, this time twenty four small pages. The Harvard was faster than the Prentice, with a maximum speed of 260 kt. clean, 150 kt. with the landing gear down and 125 kt. with the flaps down. The cruise performance of the aircraft was included in the Notes so that the pilot could know the best combination of boost, engine rpm and mixture; 115 kt. was the best speed for range, but it was very difficult to fly at that speed without continually having to adjust the engine power to prevent the aircraft going too slowly.

We had a complication on the Harvard that we had not had on the Prentice and that was the undercarriage, or landing gear as our friends across the Atlantic called the retractable wheels; the legs folded into wings under the fuselage when the pilot selected the correct operating lever in the cockpit after becoming airborne. The pilot had to remember to select the landing gear up after take-off and, even more important, select down before landing. It is a truism that if something can go wrong it will go wrong and retractable landing gears gave us a real opportunity for making pilot errors and, in addition, occasionally there were aircraft malfunctions such as a failed hydraulic system. We all had to learn the correct procedures to follow if the aircraft systems failed; in the Harvard there was a hand pump to try to pump the gear down manually in the event of a hydraulic failure. Luckily, if the pilot forgot to put the wheels down before landing, despite the warning lights and horns in the cockpit and the warnings from the controllers in the tower, at least both legs would be up and, hopefully, only the propeller, the engine and the pilot's pride would be damaged.

A landing gear malfunction which resulted in only one main landing leg going down was likely to be much more serious; the preferred option in this case was retract the 'good' leg so that the landing was made completely wheels up. If the landing had to be made with only one leg down then the plane was liable to spin round and round once the aircraft was going so slowly that the flying controls had become ineffective; the wing tip on the side without the landing gear down would dig into the ground and the pilot was then unable to influence the future course of events. I think this happened once during the year we were at Ternhill but luckily the pilot was uninjured, though it was not considered worthwhile repairing the airplane.

We had to know how to deal with the engine should it go on fire and how to abandon the aircraft in the air. I am not sure if it was possible to abandon the Prentice in the air, with its side by side seating and entrance door arrangements, but there was no doubt that it was necessary to know how to leave the Harvard. In fact it was not at all easy to get out of the aircraft, even if it was controllable, without hitting the tailplane or rudder but, luckily, I never had to try. The last ditch method of escaping was to fly the aircraft upside down, trim the elevator fully nose down, slide back the hood, release the safety straps and then, hopefully, drop out as the aircraft zoomed temporarily upwards. It sounded easy but there were a lot of doubters on the course. Fortunately we did not have an engine fire while we were at Ternhill and I don't believe that there was a case in Flying Training Command or I would surely have remembered.

We were duly tested on our knowledge of the Harvard and its systems before we were allowed to try to fly it. Unlike the Prentice, the Harvard had tandem seating so we could not see the instructor, who had to communicate with his student over the headphones. Much more significant was the fact that, once settled in the seat, it became quite impossible to see ahead; the nose of the Harvard, with the tail wheel on the ground, obscured all forward view unlike the Prentice, which really had quite a good forward view despite also having a tail wheel. The aircraft had basically the same radio fit as the Prentice, the chief difference that I remember being the toe brakes which were hydraulically operated. It was a good system but trying to apply brake with some rudder already deflected occasionally produced dramatic results; if you were lucky only the Harvard's wing tip would be damaged as the wing scraped along the ground before the pilot had time to recover the situation but occasionally the wing would dig in and a 'ground loop' would result usually resulting in the undercarriage collapsing. Luckily, I was able to avoid these excitements though I think there were one or two scraped wing tips on the course.

Engine starting was unusual. The pilot in the front seat pressed a switch which operated a flywheel. Gradually the starter motor would accelerate the flywheel and the pilot could hear an ever increasing whine. At the moment juste, the pilot moved the switch the opposite way which turned the starter motor off and caused the rotating flywheel to be connected to the engine; the propeller would rotate very slowly and, hopefully before the flywheel had slowed down, the cylinders would fire. On 11th August I had my first flight in the Harvard; I managed to get the engine started and my instructor,

Flt. Lt. Williams, taxied out turning first one way and then the other; how he managed to see what he was doing amazed me since his view at the back was much worse than mine but, somehow, he got the aircraft to the runway and took-off. The noise was appalling even with our excellent helmets which deadened the sound. All of a sudden the tail wheel came up, the nose dropped and I could see where we were going. Williams pulled the stick back and the aircraft leapt in the air; for me it was a great moment.

Erik Bennett, with his one Course seniority, took great delight in telling me all about the Harvard, not minimising in any way its reputation for rubbing its wings on the ground and ground looping through 360°. In fact, I found the Harvard quite easy to fly in spite of its incredibly noisy engine compared with the insignificant growl of the Prentice's Gypsy Queen. From being one of the slowest to go solo on my course for the Prentice, I was the fastest on the Harvard, going solo after five flights and a solo check. It seemed a delightful aircraft with crisp controls and lots of power. I flew it some years later when I was a test pilot at Boscombe Down and it seemed underpowered, requiring much larger movements of the stick than I remembered to get a fast response from the aircraft. Like many things, it is all a matter of where one was coming from, but there is no doubt in my mind that the Harvard was a wonderful aircraft on which to learn to fly.

Aerobatics in the Harvard was a joy compared with the Prentice. Lots of power and crisp controls. However, stalling and spinning was much more demanding. For a start the Harvard did not usually stall with the wings level though careful use of ailerons would help. If one was at all vigorous entering the stall the wing was liable to drop sharply, so that an immediate and fast forward movement of the stick was required to prevent a spin. The most exhilarating manoeuvre was to apply rudder and back elevator at the stall; the aircraft would immediately enter a fast spin, or at any rate it seemed fast to us who knew only the Prentice. Another good way of entering the spin was to let the speed fall off rapidly in a steep turn. Recovery could be effected by applying opposite rudder, though the spin would increase speed slightly at first, followed by a very firm and forward movement of the stick. It says a lot for the excellence of the Harvard as a trainer that all the students were sent off to spin the aircraft by themselves and we all returned to tell our tales.

Of course we had to learn instrument and bad weather flying on the Harvard, which was much more demanding than the Prentice. We still had only rudimentary navigation and landing aids and yet we were sent off in some appalling weather. During our time at Ternhill the runway had to be resurfaced and we flew from a normally disused airfield down the road called Eccleshall. I can remember to this day being sent off to do bad weather approaches at Ternhill and then having to fly back about five or six miles down the road hoping to be able to find the airfield and position oneself to land. It certainly would not be allowed these days, which I think is a pity, because it gave us a lot of confidence in our own ability.

Flying at night was even better in the Harvard than the Prentice. We were higher and faster and somehow I felt more alone, a feeling I enjoyed. We always did it on clear nights and, compared with the Prentice, I felt I could see all the lights of England at once. Instrument flying was absolutely vital if one was to survive at night and, of course, in cloud. Like the Prentice, the basic instruments were the airspeed indicator, the altimeter and the rate of turn indicator and, to get one's wings, one had to be able to recover from 'unusual positions'. The instructor would make the student cover his artificial horizon, put the aircraft in some unlikely attitude and then the student had to be able to recover back to normal flight. It was quite a severe test of one's instrument flying ability and certainly set the Adrenalin flowing, not that I knew about Adrenalin in those days.

When recovering the aircraft as the instructor announced 'you have control', it was necessary first to look at the rate of turn indicator; the ailerons had to be moved to stop the aircraft turning and bring the wings level. Once this had been done, and it had to be done very quickly, the airspeed indicator was inspected to see if the speed was increasing or decreasing; if it was going up then it was necessary to bring the control column back to apply up elevator and pull the nose of the aircraft back to level flight. Of course after a bit the instructor would try to confuse the situation even more by, for example, giving the student control with the aircraft pointing skywards and on its back; however, I suspect he chose his students carefully for that sort of manoeuvre; I often wondered in the Harvard whether the instructor could see if the student actually did cover the horizon. These exercises gave the students great confidence though,

39

with the advent of artificial horizons that could not be toppled, the importance of these manoeuvres declined.

1951 came to an end and at the end of January I took my final handling test. In early February I finally got my wings but, to my disgust, I did not get the best pilot award which went to someone called Diamond; I can't remember his first name. However, I did get an 'above the average' endorsement in my log book for flying, a prize for being the best overall student on the course and I was rated top of the course for ground school but then so I should have, bearing in mind I had been their instructor. The award I received for being the best student was called after the donor, Eustace Broke, but inevitably the trophy, of which I still have a miniature, was dubbed the 'Useless Bloke'.

It had been a magnificent year at Ternhill and I enjoyed every minute of it. We played rugger, explored Shropshire and learnt how to do drill like other officers and airmen. In fact being the only officer on the course at the time, I was in charge of the passing out parade. There didn't seem an awful lot of room on the parade ground to carry out all the manoeuvres required, including marching past the reviewing officer on the saluting base; it was all a little bit unnerving trying to keep everybody on the tarmac, moving around without going on the grass. We were all very proud on being given our wings and we said our good-byes, vowing to keep in touch but alas I lost touch with the rest of the course. However, I did manage to keep in touch with some of the students who were at Ternhill but not on my course.

We left expecting to go to an Advanced Flying School to be trained on the operational aircraft we were going to fly, but life is always unpredictable and there was a splendid surprise for some of us as things definitely did not work out as expected

CHAPTER 2

2nd Tactical Air Force, Wunstorf

When leaving the Flying Training School it was normal for pilots who had just finished training and received their wings to go to an Advanced Flying School to learn to fly the type of aircraft they were going to use on their first operational unit, be it transport aircraft, bombers or fighters. For some reason the powers that be decided that they needed to experiment and see if pilots straight from training at the FTS could be trained on operational squadrons. I think the reason must have been that if pilots were needed in a hurry it would have taken far too long for them to have to go through the standard training scheme that existed at the time. Consequently, a few of us from Ternhill were chosen to go straight to Germany to be trained on Vampire jet fighter/ground attack aircraft by the squadrons themselves, rather than to receive further training in England.

I was delighted by this twist of fate and in just over two weeks after leaving Ternhill in March 1952, I found myself at Liverpool Street station to catch a train bound for Harwich. I met up with one or two other pilots and we took the night ferry to the Hook of Holland. The next morning we caught a train to Hanover where there was transport to take us to Wunstorf. Everything seemed very strange on the journey, in spite of the German they had tried to teach me at school. West Germany was still recovering from the effects of losing the war but there seemed to be plenty of building taking place.

Wunstorf was an old Luftwaffe base and, in some ways, was not dissimilar to the standard pre-war R.A.F. stations, except that there was a cellar in the Officers Mess with a bowling alley. The airfield was situated on the Saxony plain and the ground was flat from Holland in the west, round the North Sea Coast to Denmark in the north east, thence to the Baltic and East Germany. The cold war was at its height and just sixty miles to the east of Wunstorf lay the Iron Curtain. Consequently, Wunstorf had been used by the Allies a few years earlier as one of the key airfields to support the Berlin Airlift when Russia had decided to test the West's resolve to keep Berlin as a neutral territory separate but within East Germany. The end of the

Airlift was clearly an anti-climax for Wunstorf and this could still be felt on the station itself, even though there were three very active fighter/ground attack squadrons on the base. Instead of the continuous noise of aircraft, twenty four hours a day, penetrating the station, there were just the few sporadic movements of Vampires and Meteors.

North Germany

Wunstorf was a an excellent place for new pilots to be posted. Apart from the flat ground which always makes flying that much safer, the airfield was close to Hanover and also close to a large recreational lake called Steinhuder Meer, which not only was good for sailing in the Summer but also for ice yachting in the winter when the lake froze over, which it normally did. Not that we had much time to think of anything else on our arrival except flying, since the Wing was clearly determined to see how quickly they could get us trained and onto a squadron. Two of the squadron pilots, who were also qualified flying training instructors, had been given the task of training us to fly jets and everything seemed to happen very quickly.

Each squadron had its own Meteor 7 for general training, instrument flying and communication work and it was on this aircraft that we were to get our initial flying on jet aircraft since the squadron Vampires were single seat aircraft. As usual, we first had to study the Pilots Notes; the Meteor book was still small by modern standards but the number of pages had gone up from the Harvard's 24 to a magnificent 41.

Gloster Meteor 7

This was not at all surprising bearing in mind that the aircraft flew twice as fast and twice as high. The Meteor was a mid wing monoplane with two pilots seated in tandem, a configuration which had clearly been chosen to keep the drag down. It had two Rolls Royce Derwent engines of 3,500 lb. each. There were 162 gallons of fuel in each wing, a 180 gallon optional ventral tank and two, even more optional, 100 gallon drop tanks under the wings. The landing gear, flaps and air brakes were operated hydraulically but there was only one hydraulic pump, fitted to the starboard engine, which was very important to remember if there was an engine failure. The wheel brakes were pneumatic, operated by a 450 lb./sq. in pneumatic system, the pump being on the port engine. There was a hand lever on the stick and rudder had to be applied to get differential braking, just like the Prentice and not a patch on the Harvard's hydraulic braking system. Thankfully, the Meteor had two 24 volt generators, one on each engine, to keep all the electric services and radios going in the event of an engine failure. The VHF radio was similar to ones we had used before except that we now had eight channels which made the choice of crystals a lot easier; there was still no stand-by set which meant that we had to be very careful when flying in bad weather. There were no radio sets devoted to navigation and we were very much at the mercy of the homing and radar equipment being operated by the air traffic controllers on the ground. There was an IFF set, Identification Friend or Foe, which helped the ground radar controllers identify the aircraft by marking the radar blips on their screen.

The instruments were still in the form of a basic T but we had a new instrument, the machmeter, stuffed untidily beneath the coaming and above the airspeed indicator, to tell the speed relative to the speed of sound. The primary heading indicator was still the gyro but there was a fluxvalve compass to help keep the gyro and the aircraft pointing the right way; this compass was much better damped than the magnetic compass card which was just as well, bearing in mind the much greater accelerations ever present in a jet aircraft. Nevertheless, there was still a small standby magnetic compass which was used normally only on the ground to check that the fluxvalve system was functioning correctly. The artificial horizon and the directional gyro still required vacuum pressure but luckily there were two pumps, one for each engine.

We were given some ground training before we flew the Meteor. We had to learn about the speed of sound, the compressibility of air and the effect this had on the flying of aircraft generally, and on the Meteor and the Vampire in particular. In 1951 there were no aircraft in squadron service in the R.A.F. capable of supersonic flight in a dive let alone in level flight, though there were British aircraft just being developed. A decision had been taken just after the war by the Chief Scientist at the time that it was too dangerous to try to fly supersonically and that tests should be carried out with models only. Our allies in the USA had no such inhibitions at the time and, after Chuck Yaeger's first supersonic flight in the Bell X1, they were developing supersonic test aircraft as fast as they could go. Looking back I wonder whether the UK decision was taken partly for political reasons because of the much greater cost of developing real aircraft.

The Meteor and Vampire were limited to .80 and .78 of the speed of sound, respectively, .80 mach or .80M for short. The reason for these limitations was that at these speeds the local accelerated airflow at the top of the wing, which was very thick by modern fighter standards, was already just about supersonic. This had the effect of causing a shock wave and killing the lift of the wing, at the same time creating a large amount of turbulence and buffet. Furthermore, the aileron controls at the back of the wing were in a very bad airflow so that their effectiveness was reduced significantly. Luckily, the air over the tailplane and elevators of the Meteor and the Vampire was still subsonic, so that control in pitch was not generally a problem as the limiting speed was approached.

An associated part of our ground training was concerned with the effect of altitude and the drop of barometric pressure with height. So far in our flying we had not flown above 8,000 ft and had never had to use oxygen. From now on we would always have to check that we carried enough oxygen and that the supply to our mask through the oxygen tube was working; failure to receive oxygen at altitude was an almost certain killer. In addition we had to learn that the speed of sound dropped with altitude as the pressure reduced, so that as height was gained, even though the indicated airspeed dropped, the mach number would start to climb. We were soon to learn that at the maximum altitudes for these aircraft, there was quite a small range between the maximum permitted mach number and the minimum

45

stalling speed, though it took a very long time to climb up to reach this condition.

On 9th March 1952 only 29 days after my last flight at Ternhill, I walked out with Flying Officer Farley to have my first flight in the Meteor. I walked round the aircraft and it seemed much larger than anything I had been used to. There was no question of removing the external locks to the elevators, they were way out of reach. The days of the ejection seat had not yet arrived so the ground crews stood on the wing and took our parachutes and put them in our seats. Without ejection seats, the escape procedures in an emergency for both the Meteor and Vampire were extremely hazardous as had been confirmed by actual and attempted escapes in real emergencies. The recommended procedure was to fly very slowly, jettison the hood or canopy, trim the aircraft fully nose down, release the harness and let go of the stick; hopefully one would escape cleanly without hitting the back of the aircraft but we were all aware of the very high fin and rudder of the Meteor. If the aircraft was uncontrollable and going at high speed the chances of escape were very small. But, to be honest, we were not all that concerned at the time. Most pilots always believe that it will never happen to them though, hopefully, they are always prepared in case it does.

I climbed up into the front seat and strapped myself in. At last I was sitting in an aircraft with a nose wheel and could see what was going on all around. The ground crew helped to close the lid of the Meteor, a large tunnel of metal and glass which hinged on the right hand side and covered both pilots. I did all the checks and got ready to start my first jet engine. The battery pack was plugged in and I got permission to start up. I pressed the starter button and instead of the usual groaning and banging there was a smooth whine and the rpm indicator started to whirl round; when it was going at about 2,000 rpm I opened the high pressure fuel cock to admit fuel into the combustion chambers where the igniters were firing in expectation and there was a rumble from the left engine. The needle of the jet pipe temperature gauge came rapidly off its stop and headed ominously towards its limit but then suddenly slowed down and stabilised. The rpm continued to climb and then steadied at about 3,500 rpm. The first engine was running and I repeated the operation for the starboard engine. With both engines running I turned on the engine generators and waved the battery away. The instruments seemed to be running correctly and after reference to the fluxvalve and the small spherical stand-by compass I set the correct heading on the gyro. Air Traffic gave permission to taxi, the chocks were removed and we were free to go, another particularly exciting moment.

Slowly I opened both throttles and the engines increased their discreet whine; the noise was so much quieter than the piston engines at Ternhill it was unbelievable. However, not much else happened. This was my first experience of the lag associated with jet engines at low engine speed, in the air as well as on the ground. We soon learnt that the time taken for jet engines to accelerate and produce thrust is a lot longer than for a piston engine driving a propeller. After a few seconds the engines finally began to produce some thrust and the aircraft started to roll forward. We were being trained to fly the single engined Vampire so I kept the two throttles together and started the aircraft turning by applying the brake lever and the rudder. The Meteor was straightforward to taxi on the ground and we were soon on the taxiway on the way to the take-off point. There was no need to run up the engines and we did the vital actions, putting the flaps down, as we approached the holding point. We were cleared to line up and ready to go.

I opened the throttles completely with the brakes off and the engines made a very satisfactory roar. I checked that the rpm and jet pipe temperatures were within limits. The acceleration seemed stupendous and I eased the stick back slightly to get the nose wheel in the air. The rotation speed was soon reached and a firm backward movement of the stick caused the aircraft to leave the ground. It was necessary to work quickly to select the undercarriage up followed almost immediately by the flaps to avoid exceeding their limiting speeds when not retracted. The stick needed what seemed like a very firm pull to get the aircraft pointing skywards to maintain the desired climbing speed of 290 kt.. To me, with no experience of jet aircraft, the angle of climb seemed to be taking us out of this world.

The excitement continued but a lot of work had to be done to keep to the flight plan and the training that needed to be done. The landing gear warning lights had gone out and the flap gauges showed that the flaps were fully retracted. We climbed rapidly up to 25,000 ft, reducing speed to 230 kt., and everything below seemed to shrink to insignificance. The mach number had been climbing steadily and it was time to go to maximum speed. The buffet increased as we reached .80M but not much else happened; lateral control was still just there and the elevator worked well. We did a maximum speed descent using the air brakes, a new and very necessary additional control for jet aircraft since there was no drag from the propeller when an engine was throttled. The Meteor air brakes were like combs on the inboard top surface of the wing and very effective; the Gloster aircraft company who made the Meteor seemed to be very good at making air brakes as I discovered when I flew their delta Javelin night fighter some years later. The dive angle was impressive and we soon got down to about 10,000 ft. We did some aerobatics, loops and rolls and, unlike the piston engined aircraft, there was lots of power in reserve. There was no worry about running out of airspeed at the top of a loop. However, the normal acceleration required in these manoeuvres forced us very firmly into our seats as the aircraft rotated in space, g in common parlance, was much greater than we were used to. I think on that we day we used about 3.5 g at the start of the pull-up for the loop and again on the way down to get the aircraft back to horizontal flight.

I found the thing that took a little time to get used to was the amount of g necessary to turn the aircraft. It is a fact of life that all aircraft have the same amount of normal acceleration in a steady level banked turn; for example at 60° bank the acceleration is 2g whether you are in a glider or a Boeing 747. For a slow aircraft this produces a very rapid rate of turn and the aircraft may be near the stall. For a fast aircraft the rate of turn will be very slow so that for a fighter aircraft that needs to turn very quickly the angle of bank will need to be nearly vertical and the g may be at the pilot's and aircraft's permitted limit. This is why fighter pilots in modern aircraft have to wear g suits to keep the pressure on the lower abdomen so there is enough blood to go to the head and stop the pilot blacking out. Anyway on this, my first flight in a jet aircraft, there was no doubt that the amount of g I experienced just to make the aircraft go where I wanted was much more than I was expecting.

At 12,000 ft we started to do some stalls prior to practising some landings. In fact the stalls were very gentlemanly without any wing drops or sign of any spinning tendency. We retraced our steps back to the airfield. The Meteor was straightforward in the circuit, on two engines let it be said, though heavy to control. The view was impressive and I managed without much difficulty to land smoothly at about the right airspeed. After touch-down I re-trimmed the elevator, retracted the flap to the take-off position and opened the throttles; we soon accelerated back in the air for another circuit. After about three circuits we taxied in. I am sure I must have got out of the aircraft absolutely radiant from the experience.

We had another flight in the afternoon and started to practice Ground Controlled Approaches, GCAs, to make certain that we would be able to land safely if the weather got bad. The good thing about the jets was that one usually climbed through the clouds quickly and was above the weather; the bad news was that it was frequently necessary to let down through the clouds to get back to the airfield. The Meteor did not have any modern landing systems so that good instrument flying following the instructions from the ground was imperative for survival. A GCA required two radar controllers, one tracked the aircraft laterally and transmitted the required course corrections to reach and maintain the runway centre line; the other controller, with a vertically aligned radar, tracked the aircraft down the glide slope so that any error by the pilot holding the glide slope was transmitted to the first controller, who not only had to keep the aircraft lined up but also tell the pilot whether he was above or below the glide slope. Ideally, when the pilot was told to commence his descent he would immediately adjust the power and hold the airspeed so that the aircraft would descend on the glide slope. In fact this was quite difficult to do since even if the pilot flew perfectly the wind, over which no one has control, affected the aircraft very significantly.

By and large GCAs worked very well for many years until airfields were fitted with the Instrument Landing System, ILS. With ILS, the instrument on the aircraft could detect and display the displacements from the centre line and glide slope on a deviation indicator; the pilot was then able to make the necessary adjustments to the approach path to hold the centre lines without help from the ground. One of the weaknesses with the GCA was that in certain

49

weather conditions with heavy rain the radar which the 'tracker' used on the glide slope was not able to separate the aircraft from the weather.

Three days later I had a short check flight with Fg. Off. Greenfield and then came my chance at last to fly the Vampire which had a very unusual design having a central fuselage barely large enough to contain the pilot, the guns and the engine. There were two booms on either side connecting the tailplane/elevator to the wings. As usual I had studied the Pilots Notes, all 44 pages, and was ready to go. In later years we would have been trained on the two seat Vampires but in 1951 we had to rely on our Meteor flying.

De Haviland Vampire 5

The Vampire was a much smaller aircraft than the Meteor and the cockpit therefore was very neat. Once seated on the parachute there was no room for anything else. If the view from the Meteor seemed good, the view from the Vampire was fantastic through the bubble canopy. I squeezed in and looked slowly round to check everything. In fact to do this it was necessary to bend the neck down and peer around, since there was nothing very high up at all. After carrying out all the pre-flight checks, I started the de Haviland Goblin engine, put the aircraft power on and waved the battery and the chocks away. Taxiing out I immediately felt some slight anticlimax since, after the Meteor, the aircraft felt like a kitty car very close to the ground. I had to remind myself that unlike the Meteor I was flying a fighter aircraft with four .5 inch Aden guns and the capability of carrying air to ground rockets.

The tower gave permission to go, I pushed the throttle lever forward with my left hand and the aircraft accelerated, albeit slowly compared with the Meteor. However, as the aircraft became airborne I rapidly realised that the controls were much more precise and lighter than the Meteor and I felt almost part of the aircraft. I went to a clear area climbing steadily and then did all the normal exercises of flying to maximum mach number, maximum airspeed of about 455 knots and maximum descent with the air brakes out, not that the air brakes were much good, being two small plates which rotated at the back of the wings instead of the large above wing fences on the Meteor.

Aerobatics were very straightforward and I returned to do some landings which were probably easier than in the Meteor though the undercarriage was less flattering, a characteristic, I was to find out later, of most de Haviland aircraft; as the wheels touched the runway, the whole aircraft invariably shook, there was no smooth feeling of the wheels spinning up as the aircraft touched down. I was back on the ground in only 35 minutes but, as I was to learn when I started test flying, you can get through a lot in a jet aircraft in a very short time. Flying hours per se mean little, it is what is done in the time that is important.

For the next few days I alternated my flying between the Meteor and the Vampire learning about formation flying, more instrument flying and then formating on aircraft that were doing the instrument flying so that I could formate in cloud. Formation flying was never really one of my strong points though I did many hours of formation flying in the three years I was in Germany. I was fine formating straight and level but not very good during aerobatics; my imagination was always running riot and I was always subconsciously looking at external references instead of blindly following the aircraft on which I was formating, probably because I have never been very good at following instructions. I also had a habit of introducing a small amount of rudder and sideslip, very disconcerting to anyone formating on me at the same time. However, as a leader of a formation, which is an art in itself requiring smooth flying and anticipation of the future course of the flight, I think I was probably better than most.

Vampire 5 Instrument Panel

After only two weeks, instead of probably six months had we gone to an Advanced Flying School, our formal training in the Meteor was over and I was released to join 11 Squadron to fly with B Flight, commanded by Flight Lieutenant Doug Chandler, a good disciplinarian and a good Flight Commander. Even though I was now on the strength of the squadron I was very much a trainee. The Squadron was composed of two Flights, eight aircraft per flight, and was very much a team, everybody in the team working together. The Squadron was as strong as the weakest part and so the three new boys definitely needed training very quickly. We started with close formation because fighters always flew as pairs, at the very minimum, to defend each other and to provide another pair of eyes. Our first formation flying was done in clear weather but, once we had demonstrated that we could formate reliably, we practised climbing and descending through cloud. It was not long before we were doing the whole flight in formation from take-off to touch-down.

The squadron often operated as fours, flights of eight or occasionally as a whole with all sixteen aircraft. The weather was seldom completely clear and so good formation flying was absolutely key. We would take-off as pairs and then formate as fours. Generally, the formation leader would execute a turn so that the fours could form up quickly, following a shorter track turning inside the leader. If it was cloudy then we would climb through cloud as fours and form up as a squadron above cloud, assuming that the leaders of the fours could see one another above cloud, not always easy if the cloud had been thick. If the cloud was very thick and very low at take-off the chances of a squadron joining up above cloud were pretty remote without the help of the ground radar controllers.

I did not take part in these large formations for some time until I had practised formation flying in pairs. I had to fly sortie after sortie in the beginning, formating on one of the senior members of the flight; I gradually came to realise that to lead a formation needs smooth flying and that my various formation leaders were not equally good. Sometimes this was due to just poor flying ability and sometimes because they had been up too late the night before. Slowly I learnt to cope with all my leaders, good or bad, so that I could stay with them whatever the weather.

Acquiring the necessary skill in formation at low altitude was not too difficult, but things became much harder at 30,000ft. At altitude the air is thin, the amount of excess power to catch up with the leader is small and throttling back the engine does not cause an increase in drag, as in a propeller driven aircraft. At altitude we did not fly in tight formation but flew further apart in a battle formation, either a pair or four aircraft shaped like an asymmetric arrow, so that we all could keep a good look out, unlike in close formation when one could only look at the leader or a collision would occur. Strangely, flying loosely made matters worse for keeping in formation, not better, because it was necessary to pick up the first signs of overtaking or falling behind one's leader immediately in order to get the necessary power corrections on in time; the further one was apart, the harder it was to spot changes of airspeed. The problem was compounded by the fact that the more one pumped the throttle or used the air brakes, the more fuel one used compared with the leaders, so that on a long

53

mission the bad 'number twos' were always biting their finger nails wondering if they were going to run out of fuel before getting home.

Later on when I started to lead pairs and fours, I appreciated the problems and the skill required. Leading the four smoothly and only making small movements of the throttle was sometimes very difficult, particularly if we were flying as a squadron. Sometimes we operated with three squadrons in a wing and that was always a nightmare. Above cloud it was necessary to join one's own four with the rest of the squadron and spotting small aircraft in the vast sky is not an easy sport. We all used to peer ahead trying to see the target we were trying to catch up so that we could form up with it in battle formation. At last someone in the formation would spot them giving a clock reference 'ten o'clock high', minute specks in the distance, invariably into sun. Full power would be applied to catch up and then, just at the last moment, the formation ahead would change from being insignificant dots to Vampires increasing in size at an alarming and unstoppable rate; there was no way to prevent the formation sliding past, throttles closed, air brakes out in full view of the leader. Some leaders saved their comments until the debriefing, others made their thoughts very clear over the radio.

After a few weeks trying to acquire the necessary skills, Tom Seaton our Squadron Commander flew with me in the Meteor 7 to see what my flying was like. Tom was ambitious and very well known in the fighter/ground attack world, not only in the 2nd Tactical Air Force but also at the Central Fighter Establishment at West Raynham in Norfolk. He tried hard to get us all to fly at a high standard and I respected his flying ability. Being a good squadron commander, he would ask us back to his home and I got to know his wife and young children quite well.

The Vampire squadrons and wings of 2nd T.A.F. flew in two very different modes; firstly we tried to act as fighter interceptors being watched by radars which covered the whole of Western Germany, and, I suspect, by the East German radars as well. The second mode was as ground attack aircraft attacking targets, normally pre-selected before take-off. As a fighter the Vampire was clearly past it, rapidly being destined for a place in the Science Museum; the

R.A.F. used Meteor Mk8s in the UK as interceptors, augmented by F.86s imported from the United States. Nevertheless, we flew many hours in the fighter mode climbing up to 30,000 ft intercepting targets which had been sent up by the planners. We learnt to attack the targets either in fours or pairs and, of course, once we had been split off from the flight or squadron we rarely saw them again until after we had landed. It took us all our time to stay together as a pair or a four. Good eyesight was a wonderful asset and the excited 'twelve o'clock high' or some other clock references, shouted over the radio was a real stimulant.

After about six weeks we started to be trained in rocket firing. There was a range close by the airfield where we could fire live rockets but without any lethal charges in the nose. Firing rockets proved to be one of the more enjoyable exercises that we did. The Vampire was able to carry two rockets under each wing. The modus operandi was to approach the target at low level, pull up and roll over to manoeuvre the aircraft so that it was pointing at the target on the ground, and then firing the rockets with the aid of the gun sight. There were some brave range safety officers who observed the target and noted where our rockets landed, faithfully recording the score. I admired these people enormously, not that they had any choice but to obey their orders, because in the early days our rockets might have landed anywhere in Germany; in fact the safest place to be to avoid being hit would probably have been the target itself. It took me quite a few months to get the measure of this task but in the end I used to get quite reasonable scores. It was also my introduction to how careful one had to be with live munitions. As we taxied out for take-off some poor armament mechanic would have to rush out and plug in the pigtails to make the rockets live. Nevertheless, it was amazing how often rockets would get launched across the airfield or into the hanger. Courts of Inquiry seemed always to be in progress despite all the care that was taken.

I learnt a valuable skill at Wunstorf which proved to be very useful later in my flying career and that was operating from airfields which did not have paved runways. Obviously, this seemed very important at the time for a tactical air force reliving the last war. Every few months the squadron would be sent to operate for a week or so from a strip of grass, sometimes covered with pierced steel planking.

Appropriately enough, my first tented detachment to an unprepared strip was on Luneburg Heath where the surrender of the German forces took place. The strip was made of pierced steel planking laid on grass and we soon discovered that it was very slippery when the ground was wet. I encountered steel planking again in southern Columbia and it was just as slippery there as it was in Germany. For take-off, it was necessary to get the nose wheel in the air as early as possible to remove the ground drag off the nosewheel and to try to partially rotate the aircraft to get the weight off the main wheels. The aircraft would then be hauled in the air as soon as it would fly and accelerated to a safe speed close to the ground.

For landing, it was necessary to get one's approach speed really low so that when the throttle was closed and the flare commenced, the speed would drop rapidly and the aircraft would have no alternative but to drop on the ground, hopefully near but just after the beginning of the landing strip, thus ensuring that only minimum braking was required. The way to become really unpopular with ground crew was to land too fast and have to apply a lot of braking. The brakes of the Vampire consisted of inflatable bags which, when the pilot pulled the brake lever, would expand and press pads surrounding the bags against the brake drum and everything would get very hot. If the pilot braked hard the inflatable bag could not stand the heat and would burst or start to leak and the ground crew would have to jack the aircraft up, take the wheels off and change the bags. It was a nasty enough job in the hangar but on detachment, when it was invariably raining, it was a very thankless task. Despite the brakes, I enjoyed these trips to unprepared landing strips enormously; the squadron was very much a team, there were no distractions, everyone lived in tents and, as a bonus, they taught me a lot about precise speed control in the circuit and landing.

Besides rockets our other offensive armament was the set of four Aden guns fitted right underneath the pilot's seat with the ammunition just behind the back. Every six months we would go to the island of Sylt, renowned for nudist bathing. There, at Westerland, we learnt the art of firing our guns. But first we had to learn about gun sights, aiming off and all the other delights of trying to hit a target with guns. It may sound simple but even when the target is co-operating it is very difficult to hit anything. Nowadays, we have
56

intelligent missiles which tell the pilot when they are locked on to the target, but in those days we had to judge when to turn in to make an attack and try to judge, with the aid of a gyroscopically controlled gun sight, where to put the nose of the aircraft with the four aden guns fitted underneath. In order to try and help the training situation, the aircraft carried a camera in the nose and when we pressed the trigger the camera would record the position of the target. We would go off in pairs and attack one another using the camera to record our attacks. I remember that Flying Officer Smith, a very forthright Geordie, was our weapons specialist; he was probably the best pilot on the squadron and, understandably, a great favourite with Tom Seaton. We used to have a de-briefing presided over by Smith when the films had been developed showing how we had done attacking one another and, certainly at first, we hardly covered ourselves with glory. Smith was very sarcastic, particularly when there was nothing to be seen, or more commonly, the target aircraft was a minute speck, barely visible and quite out of range.

We gradually improved and it was with great excitement that we set course on our first visit to Westerland. The month was July, which was perfect for flying as well as for the bathers. Tom Seaton, who was justifiably proud of his squadron, took us up all together so that we arrived for a 'stream' landing, one aircraft behind the other but to make things slightly easier, landing on alternate sides of the wide runway. It was necessary to keep very alert when this was going on to ensure that one was not too close to the man in front and not so far back that you would get told off at the de-briefing for spreading out too far. I know that on one of these landings I had to break very hard to avoid a collision on the runway but luckily no-one seemed to notice apart from the poor old crew chief who discovered on the following morning's pre-flight check that one of the bags was leaking and had to spend half a day replacing it.

At Westerland there were a lot of target towing Tempests which used to pull target flags up and down the coast for us to attack. The ammunition was painted with four different colours and the theory of the thing was that four aircraft, each with different coloured ammunitioh, would take turns to make attacks on a flag. The idea was to approach the flag turning very hard so that one had as broad a view of the flag as possible. The gun sight would be aimed ahead of the flag

57

by a notional amount and then the guns would be fired. It normally took several attacks on the flag to use up all one's ammunition.

The aircraft would return as quickly as possible to be prepared for the next pilot to have a go whilst the Tempest pilot, after four pilots with different coloured ammunition had done their sorties, would take the flag back and drop it on the airfield. The flag would then be examined for holes and, in theory, each hole would be coloured by paint from the bullets. The holes for each coloured paint were counted up and the score phoned through to the squadron. Nobody ever believed the scores since the colour of the paint was very difficult to judge, but it was a wonderful way to spend three weeks.

De Haviland Mosquito

I was lucky enough to have a demonstration of how to attack the flag in a de Haviland Mosquito Mk 3. As always when I flew in these old aircraft, I was amazed at the reputation they were said to have had at the time; in the case of the Mosquito I assumed it was the relatively high airspeed that caught the imagination. For me, it was the handling of an old aircraft that mattered and the Mosquito didn't rate very highly in my book. The aircraft had two Rolls Royce Merlin engines and the noise on take-off was delightful and clearly very satisfying to a Spitfire aficionado. We lumbered into the air, found the flag, and I watched while the Mosquito pilot made a few spasmodic passes. We then returned for the highlight of the trip as far as I was concerned, the landing. It confirmed my view, then and now, that modern pilots have an easy time getting their aircraft on the ground; I well remember the curved approach to get a decent view, the lack of drag before touch down, the float for the three point landing and the fierce braking to make the contraption stop. Altogether the whole flight was an interesting experience but I don't think it affected the number of bullets that I put through the flags.

Shortly after our return from Sylt I managed get myself checked out to fly the Meteor in command. This time I had to learn about asymmetric flying, practising for a possible engine failure. The Meteor was very demanding when flying on one engine, as the rudder forces were very high when trying to keep the aircraft straight at low speed with a lot of power on the live engine. Looking back on my check flight, it was not nearly rigorous enough and I learnt a lot more about the Meteor when I went to test pilots' school. Unfortunately, there were many fatal Meteor accidents with pilots practising flying on one engine; in fact the engine very rarely failed and when it did the pilot normally got away with it. The problem was that at rotation speed there was not sufficient rudder control to keep the aircraft straight should one engine fail; a few seconds later the speed was high enough to have full control but if an engine failed before this safety speed was reached then great skill was necessary to prevent disaster. More pilots got killed practising asymmetric flying than those having real failures and stories were legion of Meteor pilots being discovered in the wreckage with the Pilots Notes held in their hands.

I am reminded of a fatal accident which happened to a friend of mine on the squadron who was at school with me, Flt Lt Swash. He had taken a Permanent Commission like myself but had been on the squadron a year or so longer than I had since he had been in the University Squadron and did not become an education officer first. On this particular day he was flying the Meteor and was taking up a member of the ground crew in the back of the aircraft for air experience. He took off and climbed through the overcast and lost complete contact on the radio. He crashed on the plain after about an hour and a half, presumably running out of fuel. I can't remember what was the verdict of the court of enquiry but on all Meteors there was an instructor's mute switch in the back seat so that the instructor could switch off all incoming radio signals if he needed to talk to the pupil. However, I remember that on this aircraft the switch was not spring loaded and it was my theory that the crewman in the back inadvertently knocked the switch into the mute position. I still don't know why Swash was unable to break cloud and find his way home, since the weather was not all that bad at the time but perhaps he left his let down too late and could not recognise were he was. Accidents are always difficult to understand and becoming more so as safety in aircraft design is increased. One thing is for sure, and that is that accidents will continue to happen whatever precautions are taken. I knew the family vaguely from school and he had a younger brother, also at school. They all came out for the funeral and it was a difficult time for all concerned.

The Meteor was to test me a few months later. Our squadron aircraft needed a modification at R.A.F. Lyneham at about Christmas time and I managed to be authorised to take it, stay over the entire holidays and bring the aircraft back after modification. I flew to Tangmere to clear customs, dropped a passenger off, Flt Lt Yeardley our training captain, and flew on to Lyneham. I returned on 1st January to find the aircraft was not ready and I stayed the night in the mess. The following day I made an air test to check everything out, refuelled and took off for Wunstorf. The forecast weather en route was appalling, low cloud and snow, but Wunstorf was meant to be satisfactory. It was very quiet at 30,000 ft and suddenly I could not hear anybody on the radio. The heating system seemed to have failed and I was getting very cold. I called all my favourite frequencies without any luck. I had calculated the flight as best I could and at the due time I decided I had better start my descent. The whole of the aircraft canopy iced up on the descent and then to my intense relief I heard a faint radio call, which as I got closer, was indeed Wunstorf. The controller managed to home me overhead and I continued the descent whilst I struggled to clear the inside of the canopy without much effect. I broke cloud at about 3,000 ft but could still see very little. I had to make a GCA approach scraping the ice away all the time and just managed to land satisfactorily, almost completely blind. As I slowed down and then opened the canopy everything returned to normal and it was difficult to describe to anyone afterwards the loneliness and fright at altitude when I was all alone. Even the icing of the canopy during the descent was not really believed. All my friends knew was that I had got away with what our United States friends call a boondoggle over the Christmas holidays and, predictably, I got precious little sympathy from them that night in the bar.

Author and his Vampire 5

In July 1952 three things happened. Firstly I had my annual assessment from Tom Seaton who classified me as a good average as pilot/navigator but only average as a fighter/ground attack pilot and a weak average in air gunnery which he later changed, probably as a result of my remonstrances, to average. In fact all the assessments were fair but my grand plan was to be trained as a test pilot and that needed an above the average assessment, so I had a problem.

The second happening in July was the arrival of a Tiger Moth for the pilots on the base to fly. Why it was there I shall never know but I had no intention of not getting the experience of flying it and a new type in my log book. The Tiger Moth or the DH82A as de Haviland, the manufacturers, designated it was a propeller driven dual tandem seat bi-plane with a de Haviland Gypsy Moth engine. It was a classic design and used for many years before the war by the Royal Air

Force as its ab initio trainer. It was a fabric coated aircraft and it needed a lot of maintenance; I was surprised that we had the necessary skills at Wunstorf. I certainly never thought that I would have such an opportunity to fly the aircraft and I leapt at the chance. I managed to get the agreement of Tom Seaton that I could fly it and he checked me out one clear and calm summer's day.

De Haviland Tiger Moth

We strapped in and as usual on this sort of aircraft all I could see was the top of the engine and the propeller; goodness knows what Tom could have seen. The engine was started by swinging the propeller; a potentially dangerous thing to do but we all learnt to do it. After a couple of pulls from the ground crew I turned the magnetos on and the engine spluttered into life. There were no brakes and it was important not to rev up the engine too early or the aircraft would have gone over on its nose, possibly impaling the brave man who had swung the propeller. In the event all was well; I waved the chocks away and taxied slowly out. There were no brakes so the aircraft was kept straight during taxiing by using the rudder and revving up the engine; there was a tail skid that moved sympathetically with the rudder but I never believed that it did much good. In fact one never taxied straight but swung the nose from side to side so that a good look out could be kept at all times.

There was no radio and the aircraft operated from the grass, so having told the control tower what we planned to do, we operated by the classic method of watching an Aldis light in the control tower, hopefully flashing greens rather than reds. I looked out very carefully, crossed the taxiway and then lined up into wind. I opened the throttle and the aircraft became alive as the slipstream washed over the rudder and elevator; it accelerated quite quickly and I needed to be very gentle with the controls to avoid over controlling. The tail came up and vision was restored. I pulled the stick back very gently and we were airborne, responding to every gust of wind that was about. Everything happened very slowly so that a full circuit of the airfield seemed to take forever. For the first time since I had been at Wunstorf, I was able to look down and inspect carefully the airfield signals square, the buildings, the motor cars, the people, the local village, the lake; it was a great experience.

The Tiger Moth could do aerobatics but unlike modern jet aircraft, or even the trainers I had been brought up on, the loops and rolls had to be flown all the time since there was very little reserve power available. We climbed up and did a stall and then a spin which in the Tiger Moth was a very pleasant manoeuvre with very simple recovery, so that it was possible to do what good aerobatic pilots do during displays and stop the aircraft spinning pointing the desired way.

On all single engined aircraft pilots are taught to keep an eye open at all times for fields where they can land if the engine stopped. Luckily engines generally were very reliable but in the Tiger Moth I felt very exposed. In fact the aircraft had a very slow rate of descent with the throttles closed so there was plenty of time to select one's field, though of course the field had to be close.

Finally we returned to the circuit and I did my first landing. There were no flaps and the trick was to close the throttle in plenty of time and then pull the stick back very gently as the speed fell off. The aircraft had a very low wing loading and would glide for a long time with the elevators remaining responsive all the time. However, eventually it would subside on the ground in a three point attitude. There was plenty of scope for error, such as hitting the main wheels first and ballooning into the air; the only real solution to this embarrassing event was to open the throttle and go around again.

63

Clever pilots could arrest the potential kangarooing but that was just not one of my skills. Anyway, Tom seemed satisfied and let me go off solo for 30 minutes. I did a few more landings and taxied in very pleased. It was clearly an aircraft that could only be flown in light winds. I never flew it again; I don't know why but I suspect some other pilot bent it and I count myself very lucky to have had the opportunity just once.

The last happening in July was important. The squadron was being re-equipped with the de Haviland Venom Mk.1, a very similar aircraft to the Vampire aerodynamically with its twin booms and bubble fuselage in the middle, but the engine power had been increased from the Goblins 3,500 lb. to the Ghost's 4,850 lb. In addition the wing design had been changed to permit the maximum speed to be increased from .78M to .86M. I am sure No. 11 Squadron had been selected to be the first squadron to have the Venom because of Tom Seaton's influence but, of course, there was a downside to being first since the squadron lost its operational capability. The sixteen plus aircraft that we required did not arrive all at once; they were delivered piecemeal one at a time over a period of some months. Furthermore, being new they were all of different modification standards.

The first few aircraft had large red bands painted on the wing since they were restricted in the amount of g we were allowed to apply. Structural tests at the factory had discovered a weakness in design at the undercarriage bay cut-out and early aircraft could not be modified. In some ways the fault was not dissimilar to the fault on the first civil de Haviland Comet passenger aircraft, which had crashed from pressurisation fatigue failure; the undercarriage bay had square cut-outs in the same way that the Comet windows were originally rectangular. Stress was concentrated at the corner intersection of the straight lines and the metal gradually weakened. Later Venom aircraft came with modified curved undercarriage bays and were also fitted with ejector seats which we felt were really needed, bearing in mind the increased performance of the aircraft.

photo *Alan R Lane*

De Haviland Venom

In fact I was away in July sailing in the Baltic so I did not have my first flight in the Venom until 8th August. The Pilots Notes were still in draft form but the aircraft cockpit and systems were almost identical with the Vampire including the unsatisfactory airbags for the brakes. However, starting the engine was different; instead of having to wind up the engine with a starter motor, the Ghost had a cartridge starter, so that to start the engine the pilot turned on the electrical power, opened the fuel cocks and pressed the firing button. There was a hiss and a roar and if all went well a few seconds later the engine would be idling. However, if the pilot had forgotten to open one of the fuel cocks there would be a nasty silence as the engine ran down after the explosion from the cartridge. Luckily, the starter held two cartridges but one had to wait for the engine to stop rotating before trying again.

The Venom's equipment was significantly better than the Vampire's. The Compass was the all electric Mk 4F with a rotating card; all the pilot had to do was to check occasionally that the dot/cross annunciator flag was flickering, showing that the card was synchronised to magnetic north. We finally had an electric untoppleable artificial horizon and a powerful 1.5 kW 24 volts DC Generator. The flying controls were different from the Vampire in that instead of having conventional gear tabs to help move the

65

controls, the Venom had spring tabs to give a better balance at the higher speeds. The oxygen system was changed to allow for unpressurised flying at high altitude; a pressurised breathing system had been fitted and the pilot had only to push down a lever on the front of the oxygen mask to clamp the mask to the face; this allowed a small amount of positive oxygen pressure to be forced into the lungs when above 38,000ft.

I still remember my first flight in the Venom. The aircraft had an exciting smell like a new car. When I opened up the throttle and released the brakes the aircraft leapt forward in a way I had not experienced before and the angle of climb seemed fantastic. I soon got up to 40,000 ft, an undreamed of height for the Vampire, and I could see the curvature of the earth against the horizon. I tried going up to maximum mach number very gingerly at first since the aircraft had a new characteristic compared with the Vampire. At about the maximum mach number of .86 when the buffet was getting quite severe, the ailerons would lose all their effectiveness and if the wing dropped then the aircraft would be uncontrollable. The aircraft would dive down and it was necessary to close the throttle completely; if all went well about 10,000 ft. lower down the mach number would have dropped sufficiently so that the ailerons would start to work again and level flight could be regained but, if the aircraft attitude was steep, a lot more height could be lost, not an ideal feature for a fighter.

By October we were nearly fully equipped and 2 TAF was expanding. New airfields were being commissioned further west at Wildenrath, Wahn, Brucken and north at Jever. At Wunstorf, 26 Squadron left for Wildenrath and a new squadron was formed No 266. I was promoted to Flight Lieutenant because of my seniority from accelerated promotion and to my surprise suddenly found myself posted to No 5 Squadron as a Flight Commander but, of course, back to Vampires. Tom Seaton reassessed my flying skills on posting and kindly rated me above average as a pilot navigator and a good average for air gunnery and as a fighter/ground attack pilot. My test pilot future still seemed possible.

***

No 5 Squadron commander was Squadron Leader Daw, a delightful and cultured man, but not, in my opinion, a wartime leader of a squadron. The other flight commander was Prince Nicky Varanand, a member of the Siamese Royal Family and might have become King of Thailand, but for some unforeseen family circumstances which I did not understand. Nicky was not like any other Air Force officer I ever knew, then or since. He did not suffer from the financial privations that were a never ending source of strain and topic of conversation for most of us in the Mess. When he arrived in Germany he naturally ordered a new car from Mercedes, one rather superior to the Commander-in-Chief's. He understandably did not want it delivered but drove down to Stuttgart to collect it. He had married an English girl, had started a family and I imagine that this was one of the reasons why he did not return to Thailand. His rank and age suggested that he was not destined to be a very senior officer in the RAF, quite apart from the 'handicap' of his birth.

I met Nicky years later when I was visiting Bangkok on a marketing trip to Bangkok. He was even smoother and more urbane than when he was in Germany. To save embarrassment he introduced me straightaway to a beautiful Thai lady "You have not met my wife — she is not the one you knew in Germany". He was running the Mercedes Agency in Thailand and clearly wasn't suffering any deprivation that I could see. We sat down to dinner with the head German Mercedes representative in the Far East. Nicky was conversing in English, German and Thai as required and explaining some finer nuances of language in French; I may have been a better mathematician than he was but I envied his complete fluency in languages.

We slowly started to train up the squadron; there was a mixture of seasoned 'veterans', mostly Sergeant Pilots, new officers with short service commissions and some national service pilots from the university air squadrons. I knew a lot of the more experienced pilots because they had been on the courses I had instructed at Wittering. John Horrell was a graduate and later became a Group Captain and Arab specialist. Tony George, son of a famous very senior air attaché in Paris, left the service and spent his life in the airline industry. There was also John Crossley who was very much a lateral thinker and could not be relied upon to react to responses as

67

other people would. He left after his National Service, joined an auxiliary squadron and also the Central Electricity Generating Board. He had the distinction of connecting a stationary generator to the National Grid. Unfortunately, he died failing to finish an illicit slow roll under the Clifton Suspension bridge.

Another colleague and friend was Keith Sturt. He had the misfortune or luck to fall in love and eventually marry the wife of one of the other squadron commanders at Wunstorf, which effectively meant that his air force career was likely to be limited. I met him some years later when he was a test pilot for Rolls Royce but more of that later. It was just as well that we could not tell what the future held in store for us.

The Squadron re-equipped with Venoms in January, this time without red bands but with ejector seats. They soon proved their usefulness with an ex-Cranwell graduate, who had a reputation for causing flying accidents. He managed to fire at least one rocket into a hangar and later, when he was firing rockets at the range at Fassberg, had to eject when the left wing folded at the critical wing undercarriage cut-out during a pull-out after firing a rocket.

Sadly, in March 1953 Squadron Leader Daw was killed when he was on the Central Fighter Establishment's Course at West Raynham. The course was famous for long sorties using every fluid ounce of fuel and Daw ran out of fuel and ditched somewhere in the Wash. It was very sad. He was rapidly replaced by Sqn. Ldr West, definitely a more experienced pilot and he seemed a more purposeful leader.

The R.A.F. was being reviewed by the Queen in her coronation year 1953, 50 years after the Service was formed, and every unit in the Service was going to fly over Buckingham Palace. This was a very complicated exercise bearing in mind the number of flying units that had to take part, many flying at different speeds arriving from all over the United Kingdom. The squadrons from overseas had to be based in the UK for the occasion. It was just as well no war was brewing that summer since the whole of the operational resources of the R.A.F. were devoted to planning the fly-past. Once the plan had been prepared it was necessary to have quite a few dummy runs with the formation leaders taking part without their formations in order to check on routing, timing and ironing out the inevitable difficulties that occur on an exercise of that nature. I can't remember when the phrase Mission Impossible entered the English Language but, had it been around then, the phrase would have been used to describe the fly-past.

For some reason I never discovered, Arty Shaw our Wing Commander Flying did not want to take part in the practices and he deputed me to take his place. Of course as a Wing Commander he did not get a lot of flying and the Venom was still relatively new, certainly to him. I wondered why the powers that be allowed the substitution but his reluctance was my good fortune. I think I was chosen because of my understanding of the performance of the Venom and the likely fuel usage in what could well prove to be a marginal exercise from an endurance viewpoint. I duly got all the operation orders and timings etc. At first the practice was just within the 2 TAF aircraft and I managed to find the other wing leaders with the help of ground radar. After each practice there would be signals coming in the evening detailing what we had all done wrong and encouraging us to do better next time. I did one final practice in the UK with all the units operating from Wildenrath, flying over London and landing at Manston to refuel. I then flew on to Wattisham where we were to be based for the big day.

By the time I reached Wattisham the whole wing had arrived led by Arty Shaw and full of stories of the inevitable problems that had occurred when every aircraft that could fly had been pushed into the air and flown by pilots with a very wide range of skills and experience. I was reminded of Wellington's comment reviewing his army before Waterloo 'I don't know if they will frighten the enemy, but by God they terrify me.'

During the next two days the R.A.F. had two full rehearsals and every evening we were buried by reports of good and bad timings, who got it right and who had better get it right next time. On the great day 15th July 1953 the weather was good and we all excelled ourselves including Arty Shaw. I even managed to get a quick look down at

Buckingham Palace myself as we flew overhead. I don't know what the whole exercise must have cost but we all improved our formation flying.

Vampire Trainer

Throughout that summer the squadron trained in rocketry, air to air firing and fighter interceptions. One very good training aid arrived in the shape of the twin seated Vampire 11. This aircraft enabled the junior pilots to be trained much more effectively and we could get a much better feel of the skill of the people with whom we were flying. We could use it for gunnery instead of the Mosquito and we could also carry out spinning, something we did not do in the Meteor.

Squadron Leader West had to go to CFE for training and I was left in charge. For some reason we had been talking in the pilots room of formation patterns and I decided that we should fly over the airfield in a figure 5. This was not a trivial exercise since it required eleven aircraft to get the desired shape. It took us several flights before I was prepared to fly over the airfield but in the end we all felt pleased with ourselves, including the tail-end charlies at the end of the figure five, who were much closer to the ground than I was and had to put up with the whiplash effect generated by the inevitable cumulative effect of not perfect leading on my part, and the slight imperfections of formation flying by the people between me and the pilots at the back. For some reason it was always the inexperienced people who had to fly at the back where, sometimes, the formation flying is the hardest. Certainly when I used to do it I invariably finished up wringing wet with perspiration.

The author leading 5 Squadron

I only have one rather poor photo of the formation taken from the ground which is in my log book. The photo is opposite my flying assessment by Sqn. Ldr West and luckily he had given me an above average assessment for my flying in all categories. My memory seems to tell me that I had discussed the need for him to do this if I was going to get to the test pilots school and he decided to co-operate. Consequently, armed with this assessment I applied to go on the next course at Farnborough when the 'advertisement' appeared in Air Ministry Orders and was duly called for interview. On the interview board were Sammy Wroath, Wg. Cdr Sewell the Chief Flying Instructor and Wayson Turner the Chief Ground Instructor, though Wayson was going to Boscombe Down to join the bomber test squadron, B Squadron. I can't remember much of the interview except I recall having several technical discussions with Wayson whom I got to know very well in later years. I enjoyed myself at the interview even if the rest of board was bored and returned home.

When I got back to Wunstorf I discovered that all Squadron and Flight Commanders in the tactical air force had been called to headquarters in Wildenrath to receive a harangue on the unacceptable level of flying accidents. We returned suitably chagrined. As bad luck would have it, the very next day I had my first flying accident. I was leading a formation take-off with Flying Officer Schlesinger as my number two. It was a funny day with thunderstorms all around us. We accelerated up the runway and I rotated in the normal way. Suddenly, the whole aircraft buffeted like mad and the Venom would not climb. I decided to abandon the take-off, throttled back, stopped the engine, selected undercarriage up on the ground and came to an ignominious stop beyond the end of the runway.

Schlesinger watched me get into difficulties, had time to wonder what the problem was, and then he too was overtaken by buffet. He too realised that he had to abandon his take-off but he was in a much worse situation than I had been since he was higher and had travelled further before he lost control of his aircraft. He received some burns and broke some bones as he came to rest well beyond the airfield.

A court of enquiry was called and a de Haviland test pilot who I got to know well later on in my career, John Wilson, was sent out to advise. He discovered that the aircraft was ballasted outside the aft limit because the ammunition containers were full and so everybody assumed that I had rotated the aircraft too early because of being outside the permitted centre of gravity range. However, like all accidents the true explanation was probably more complicated. The Venom wing was like the original Comet wing before it was modified; it had a symmetrical wing section and there was hysteresis in the stalling behaviour in that, once the wing was stalled, it was necessary to reduce the angle of attack quite a long way before the wing would unstall. After the Comet had had some take-off accidents, the wing profile was changed to try to remove the stall hysteresis effect, but not unfortunately on the Venom.

I am not convinced to this day that I did rotate too early but, understandably, nobody believed me at the time. I realise now that the meteorological conditions existing on the airfield were consistent with the down draught wind shear phenomena that has caused numerous accidents in recent years, but such conditions were not understood in those days. The explanation, with the advantage of hindsight, was that I almost certainly rotated in the normal way at the correct speed and then hit the down draught so that my speed dropped violently and the wings stalled; being a Venom with its symmetrical wing and there being no height to play with, the take-off had to be abandoned. As I learnt later, accidents are usually a combination of unlikely occurrences.

My chief worry, while all this investigation was going on, was whether as a result of the accident I would not be selected for the Empire Test Pilots School. Luckily, there could not have been any connection between my accident and my being chosen for the course since I was selected to join No. 13 E.T.P.S. Course starting in February 1954, probably because of my academic training since I don't believe they had had any graduates on the course up to that time.

I had got quite friendly with Arty Shaw and, for some reason I can't remember, there was a trip required to Colerne. Shaw was coming to the end of his tour at Wunstorf and asked me to take some bottles for him to West Raynham. Being an ambitious officer trying to please, I agreed but was rather bothered to find that about twelve bottles of booze if not more had been put in the wings of my Venom. I filed my flight plan to Tangmere which was the appointed port of entry for customs clearance but I was afraid that if I flew at altitude to get there, the bottles might crack and on landing alcohol would drip steadily out of the wing instead of the fuel or oil the customs officers and ground crew were used to. I therefore dreamt up a pressurisation failure and diverted to Manston after only a 30 minute flight. I cleared customs and flew on to West Raynham. That evening three Air Force Officers, Wing Commander Bird Wilson, who I had got to know in

Germany and who was a very famous fighter pilot at the time, Tom Seaton who had returned to be stationed at West Raynham and myself unscrewed the inspection panels underneath my Venom and took out the bottles. Not an experience I was particularly proud of and I was very relieved that it had all gone without any problems. The next day I managed to get my hands on a single seater Meteor Mk 8 fighter fitted with the latest gyro gunsight. I was getting quite knowledgeable on gunsights and so this was a useful trip besides getting a new type in my log book.

The Car

1954 started and I was definitely getting ready to leave 2 TAF and Germany. I was forced to sell my faithful car. It was a magnificent pre-war Auto Union with an enormous straight six cylinder engine which seemed to stretch for miles under a very long bonnet. The effect was exaggerated by the gear box being positioned in front of the engine with the drive going to the two front wheels. The gear operating lever was in the middle of the dash board and the operating rod went the whole length of the bonnet over the engine and then dropped somehow through a collection of levers into the gear box. Finding the right gears was a challenge but generally I was successful without disrupting the traffic. I had bought the car from a Sgt. Pilot

74

on 11 Squadron and I was a bit worried a few months later when he was charged with some rather heinous financial offence which involved trading with the local population. Luckily the car transaction was not a target of the ensuing Court Martial and I was able to keep it for the whole of my time in Germany. Unfortunately I sold the car for a song; I should have kept it and sold it to a Museum; it would now be worth a fortune.

Flamingo, still sailing 2005

At Wunstorf I had learnt an enormous amount about flying and had spent every other spare moment sailing on Steinhuder Meer or cruising in the Baltic. The R.A.F. Yacht Club in Kiel had taken over the Club House and sailing yachts of the Luftwaffe Yacht Club. There were 50 and 100 sq. meter. yachts and I concentrated on sailing the larger yachts, Kranich and Flamingo; they were about 55 ft. long and I was very fortunate to be able to skipper these boats at a comparatively young age. We had many cruises round Denmark and Sweden which were idyllic, inevitably visiting the flesh pots of Copenhagen and the harbour by Hamlet's Helsingor Castle. In addition we raced Kranich to Visby in Gotland, raced round the Island and then on to Stockholm. We even managed to take part in the Fastnet race, though we did not distinguish ourselves. It was the first race that started westward from Cowes through the Needles and, as luck would have it, the wind was a South Westerley Force 6. With a full flood tide taking us into the wind, the sea was very unpleasant and it took us sometime after going through the Needles to recover.

Most week-ends we raced the dinghies on Steinhuder Meer and learnt ice yachting in the cold German Winters usually finishing up drinking and eating in the local pub. However, I regret very much to this day that despite doing German at school up to A level standard I did not take advantage of the marvellous opportunities to learn to speak German. On 4th February 1954 I had my last flight in a Venom with the squadron and entered into a new world.

CHAPTER 3

Test Flying in the Royal Air Force

I never ceased to be amazed at how quickly in the R.A.F. one's whole working life could change. One moment I was a significant player in the 2nd Tactical Air Force. In less than two weeks, on the 18th February 1954, I was back at school achieving what, for me, had always seemed the desirable but unlikely goal of becoming a test pilot. There were thirty four of us on No. 13 Empire Test Pilots Course when we started. We came from the R.A.F., from the Royal Navy, and from the services in Australia, Canada, Denmark France, Italy, Netherlands, Norway, USA and Thailand. We had all volunteered to come to be trained at a school which had a very high reputation throughout the aerospace world for producing excellent test pilots. Our expectations were high.

Those of us who were not married lived in the E.T.P.S. Officers Mess just opposite the famous Queen's Hotel, as it was called then, on the Aldershot Road. Very conveniently, just over 150 yards away was the actual school itself within the airfield boundary. There were quite a few of us living in the mess and the friendships we struck up then have lasted throughout our lives, refreshed every five years when the School holds its re-unions. Regrettably, not everybody survived though we were taught at the school the importance of conducting flight tests in such a way as to minimise risk. Of course, however carefully tests are planned there are always some circumstances which do not yield to the scientific approach and, in these cases, risks have to be taken. Inevitably therefore, some members of the course died while they were carrying out their jobs but everybody knew the chances they were taking when they volunteered, never really believing it could happen to them.

Of course in those days flight simulators, on which the flight characteristics of a new aircraft could be checked on the ground before being experienced in the air, were unheard of so that it was not possible for the pilot to practise flying the critical tests in the comfort of a laboratory environment and for the engineers then to look at the test results. Nowadays, with modern computers receiving thousands of data channels from the aircraft in flight, accidents should not happen due to faults in design. However, sometimes the aircraft structure does not stand up to the tests that have to be carried out; sometimes the tests find aerodynamic features which make the aircraft uncontrollable and, sometimes, the actual systems of the aircraft are poorly designed and the designers and aircrew are caught by surprise. Test flying therefore always has an element of risk; technology may have changed the type of accident but not the fact that accidents will always occur. Accidents, when they happen and happen they will, are very important, not just because, invariably, they are so tragic but because there are always lessons to be learnt from accidents that must be applied to prevent similar accidents in the future.

With great expectation, we students walked over to the School for the first time and had welcoming messages from Sammy Wroath, the Commandant, 'Pop' Sewell the chief Flying Instructor and Jimmy Lang, the new Chief Ground Instructor who had taken over from Wayson Turner. From that point onwards we started a daily routine which went on throughout the year until the beginning of December when we graduated. The ground school time-tables were put up on the board, week by week and every afternoon the flying programme went up for the following day. Of course, flying in the test flying environment is particularly difficult to plan. Aircraft are always checked for serviceability but, in the case of the School, they were always being fitted with new equipment and, in addition, the instrumentation always needed checking. The situation was not helped by the fact that the aircraft at the School tended to be fairly elderly and, therefore, not very reliable from a maintenance viewpoint. New aircraft were a luxury since they were needed by the operational squadrons. We students had to learn our lessons on the old hack aircraft with all their bad features. In fact these bad features were welcomed by the instructors to see if we discovered them, to see how we dealt with them and to study how we reported them. If we were lucky we were allowed to sample the new aircraft on a pre-view basis towards the end of the course, when we were allowed one flight to give our opinions on the excellence or not of the Royal Air Force's latest aircraft.

Most of us on the course had come from fighter aircraft and were, therefore, not used to flying with other people. Consequently, it

78

had been rarely possible for people to comment on our landings unless some unfortunate incident had taken place like a burst tyre or a very heavy landing. Now we had to get used to fellow travellers, experiencing or savouring the delights of our varied arrivals. I am reminded of this inescapable fact because the first transport aircraft I was introduced to was the Vickers Valetta. If my memory serves me aright it was called the 'Flying Pig' and it certainly had a striking resemblance to one being fairly short in length and very fat; in fact some Valettas had hemispherical side windows used for observation by student navigators, which looked like teats and heightened the comparison.

Vickers Valetta

The Valetta had a tail wheel undercarriage and two Bristol Hercules 230 1,650hp radial piston engines and 48 pages of Pilots Notes. After opening the throttles for take-off there was not much else to do but wait. The good news was that close inspection of the airspeed indicator showed the aircraft was accelerating; the bad news was that the take-off was clearly going to take a long time. During the early part of this operation the rudders had very little effect and it was necessary to squeeze the brake lever on the control wheel and push the rudders from side to side in the desired direction to try to keep the aircraft within the confines of the runway. At some stage of the take-off, depending on the wind, the rudders became effective which made the take-off more predictable and, finally, it was possible to lift the whole contraption into the air at about 95 kt.

Not unexpectedly, getting the aircraft back on the ground was challenging. The Valetta did not have a lot of drag, even with the landing flaps down, and consequently had a tendency to float. People used to tell me that the way to land the aircraft was to try to get the main wheels on the ground while the aircraft still had flying speed and then stuff the control column forward to keep it on the ground. Like a fool I tried to take this advice but unfortunately I had no idea when the wheels were going to touch and by the time the wheels had touched and I had pushed the control column forward we were airborne again. Consequently the Valetta started kangarooing down the runway uncontrollably and, remembering that discretion was the better part of valour, I applied full power and went round for another try. Amazingly the tutor, Squadron Leader 'Spud' Murphy, made no comment but I expect he had seen it all before. Next time I landed the aircraft the way I eventually learnt to land all aircraft from the Tiger Moth to the Concorde, keep pulling the stick back with the throttles closed and inevitably the aircraft will hit the ground. There is unfortunately one problem with this method and that is that you have to have the aircraft somewhere near the ground when closing the throttles or it is likely to be damaged together with the pilot's ego. Still, for me it worked most of the time and my fellow crewmen did not complain too much.

The Valetta, like many piston twin engined aircraft, was actually a very demanding aircraft to be able to fly safely on one engine. The Pilots Notes announced that the required safety speed to keep directional control was 120 kt. so there was definitely a twilight zone during take-off when, if one of the engines failed, it was necessary to get the aircraft back on the ground as quickly as possible. Even if both engines were working correctly it was necessary to adjust the pneumatically controlled engine cowlings the whole time to keep the cylinder head temperatures under control. If an engine failed, the propeller had to be feathered to cut the adverse drag and there was very little excess power to climb on the other engine; furthermore significant rudder and aileron forces were required to keep it in trim when maximum power was applied. Luckily, flying the aircraft in

England at Farnborough was not as critical as when operating at high weight and at the extremes of temperature experienced overseas. The Valetta may have been useful as a light transport or a trainer for navigators, but it certainly was not an aircraft people fought over to fly, except of course to get the type in one's log book or to get home for the week-end.

Hawker Sea Fury

The next aircraft I was allowed to attack was the Sea Fury. This was a single seater, single piston engined aircraft, fitted with the radial engined Bristol Centaurus XVIII and a large five bladed propeller. As I strapped myself into this machine I began to wonder if I had been a bit over confident in my flying abilities when I applied to go on the ETPS course. The view from the cockpit while taxiing out was virtually non-existent and it was necessary to 'snake' from side to side the whole time to see what lay ahead. I had read the Pilots notes carefully and it said that it was necessary to wind on full right rudder trim before take-off. I soon found out why; I opened the throttle lever and the noise was stupendous. The aircraft was determined to turn left immediately and bring the whole take-off to a premature conclusion, somewhere in the middle of the airfield. I pushed my right foot forward as hard as I could as I was being sucked forward remorselessly by the propeller. I managed to avoid the aircraft's self-destruct tendency as we accelerated and eventually I was able to pull the stick back to get the plane into the air. It proved to be a really delightful experience. The Sea Fury's performance was not far short of the Vampire, its maximum speed being almost identical. However, it required a lot more attention to keeping the aircraft in trim directionally, with frequent rudder application to keep the slip ball in the middle and the wings level. Landing the aircraft was actually fairly straightforward in spite of the tail wheel. My standard landing technique worked fairly well and the aircraft was prepared to stay on the runway without a struggle after hitting the ground.

Vickers Varsity

My next aircraft was a Vickers Varsity. This was a Valetta with a nose wheel, but with a lot more equipment. It had the latest radio equipment, full of acronyms; a UHF (Ultra High Frequency) radio as well as a VHF set and it had an ILS receiver, IFF, Decca and TACAN (TACtical Air Navigation) for navigation. There was a G4B compass and an autopilot Mk 9. The Pilots Notes were of a new type, very comprehensive, and had 113 pages describing the systems and the equipment. The Bristol Hercules engines were 264s with 1,950hp, more powerful than on the Valetta but not powerful enough. Flying the aircraft was quite uneventful except that it seemed even more underpowered than its tail wheeled predecessor but, luckily, the aircraft had been fitted with nose wheel steering and toe brakes so that taxiing and taking-off was a much more controlled operation. The only confusing factor was the introduction of a flight fine pitch stop to ensure that should an engine fail at high speed, the failed prop did not produce too much drag; this was a good safety feature but just another device to go wrong and which needed careful watching. Modern jet pilots don't know how lucky they are not having to cope with large propeller driven piston engined aircraft.

Another new aircraft which I was looking forward to flying was the English Electric Canberra T.4 which was a great aircraft for testing. It had the performance to get to high altitude, well above 40,000 ft, and had some systems to test. It was the first aircraft in which I used the Instrument Landing System on which I was to spend many years in different aircraft, tailoring the aircraft controls and the auto-pilot to get the best out of the ILS/aircraft combination when flying in poor weather. The Canberra in some ways was not an easy aircraft to fly. The ailerons were fundamentally heavy since, unlike later Canberra variants, it did not have power controls. The design of the ailerons had, therefore, been a challenge to the design engineers at Warton. Their solution was to use special balancing tabs called spring tabs, similar to the Venom, but the ailerons were still poor and could be frighteningly heavy at high speed, low altitude, if the tabs were not rigged correctly, as I discovered later at Boscombe Down.

The Canberra's elevator also felt heavy and this was my first experience of an aircraft which had a moveable tailplane to trim the control column pitch forces. In my previous aircraft, the push and pull forces to control the aircraft were adjusted by moving a tab at the back of the elevator; in the Canberra the elevator floated freely behind the moving tailplane which, like most of the systems in the aircraft, was controlled electrically. The system worked well but the electrical control proved to be problem a year or two later when I was at Boscombe Down testing the Mk 8 version. One feature of the early Canberras was the poor view out of the aircraft, because the canopy was very flat to keep the drag down; it was necessary to fly wearing the standard protective helmet which meant that we were always pressing the helmet against the canopy to avoid missing anything.

Canberra T4

The rest of the aircraft in the fleet were fairly mundane and definitely not in their first flush of youth. There was the Percival Proctor which made no lasting impression at all. Then I had the chance to fly in the Airspeed Oxford again, this time at the controls. The Pilots Notes had only seven pages, a record as far as I was concerned. The propellers were fixed pitch and the 335hp Cheetah engines used magnetos for starting instead of the more modern booster coils. It suffered like all the older aircraft from a tail wheel and light wing loading, so that there seemed to be an air of reluctance in getting it back on the ground, but by using my technique it did not put up too much of a fight. Getting airborne required care since it had a tendency to swing to the right and at low speed the only way of keeping straight, initially until the airspeed built up, was to use the throttles differentially. The aircraft got into the air at less than 65 mph but the Notes warned that if a lot of buffet was felt, due to badly fitting panels, the speed should be allowed to go up to 85 mph before leaving the ground. If an engine failed, the good throttle should be pushed through the gate 'providing the speed was above 85 mph, else land straight ahead'.

Of the slightly younger vintage there was the de Haviland Chipmunk tandem seat trainer with a 145hp Gypsy Major Mk 8; it was used by University Air Squadrons and, in my view, would have been far superior for my training than the Prentice. We used it for glider towing which I used to enjoy. It handled beautifully, aerobatics, stalling, spinning and was a delight in the circuit; de Haviland had a flair at that time for making aircraft which handled well and, unlike some of the other aircraft they made, it did not seem to have any structural problems. We also had two types of communication aircraft which we also used for trying out some of our tests. There was the de Haviland Devon, a twin engined low wing monoplane with two inverted de Haviland Gypsy Queen Engines, and a military version of the Dove. It was an honest aircraft, reliable and did not have any particular alarming characteristics that I can remember; I flew it regularly in later years and it never it let me down.

The other communication aircraft was the Percival Pembroke, a twin engined high wing monoplane fitted with 550 BHP Alvis Leonides. My memory of this aircraft was that it was underpowered and had very poor controls. Furthermore, it had pneumatic systems controlling the landing gear, the flaps, nosewheel steering, engine air intakes, fuel cut-off, the brakes and the Sperry auto-pilot. Perhaps for this reason it was not very serviceable and one never knew whether it was going to available for flight. Unfortunately, we had a very nasty flying accident with one of the Pembroke's on the course. Wing Commander Sewell was flying the aircraft when one of its engines caught fire and he was unable to get the aircraft back on the ground; sadly Sewell and two others were lost.

Percival Pembroke   **De Haviland Dove**

There was the piston engined Percival Provost, the new delightful ab initio pilot trainer. The controls were crisp and, like the Chipmunk, very nice for all manoeuvres. Being a side by side trainer there was plenty of room in the cockpit, particularly useful when, as so often happened, I was flying the aircraft by myself doing tests.

De Haviland Chipmunk   Percival Provost

The rest of the fleet were aircraft types which I had already flown, Meteor 8s, Venom Mk1s and a Vampire 5. They were all excellent aircraft for carrying out the various tests we were given to do. Of course, we all wanted newer aircraft and during the course we were given our own Hunter 1 and, later, a Hunter 2. This gave us all a chance to experience the thrill of going supersonic, about 1.05M or so being the maximum speed of the Hunter. The controls of these early Hunters were boosted power controls with manual reversion; the challenge before take-off was to get the power boosters correctly engaged as indicated by a black indication on a black/white magnetic dolls eye. This required rapid movement of the controls until the indicators went black which could be a bit of a hit and miss operation. However, once one had managed to get the power boosters correctly engaged, the controls were a delight; the tailplane was trimmed with an electrical switch on the stick and the supply could be isolated with a circuit breaker, a wise precaution against electrical failure. The ailerons were fully powered, with spring feel with no airspeed modulation. The aircraft had a super performance, wonderful view and seemed to be free of any vices. Hawkers then, like de Havilands in the past, had learnt how to design aircraft that handled really well. The aircraft had two VHF sets, IFF and Distance Measuring Equipment, DME, which, at long last, gave the pilot a chance of being able to navigate accurately, very necessary when one considered how little fuel the aircraft carried, 334 gallons.

Kinch in the Hawker Hunter

In fact I did not have to wait for the Hunter to arrive before going supersonic. There were quite a few on our course from other air forces who had flown the North American F86, or Sabre as the R.A.F. called them, my friend Kinch, Captain Kincheloe of the USAF being one of them. The aircraft was battle proven in the Korean war and the R.A.F. had had to order a whole batch of them in order to keep the fighter squadrons operational before the later Hunters were fully developed and ready for production. I was fed up being talked down to because I had not flown the Sabre but luckily Tom Seaton was now on the staff at West Raynham; in September I arranged to spend the week-end with Tom and on the Monday he organised a Sabre 4 for me to fly.

Author in North American Sabre/F86

The briefing was detailed but I had read the Pilots Notes over the week-end, still very thin by modern standards, 74 pages, and was soon authorised and strapped in. I noticed with relief that unlike most R.A.F. fighter aircraft there was an ADF (Automatic Direction Finder) radio homing receiver as an emergency navigation aid. In fact I suspect that the ADF was only fitted because all the R.A.F. Sabres had had to be ferried across the Atlantic in Operation Beechers Brook; this Operation was initiated to enable all the R.A.F. Sabres to be built and test flown in Canada and then flown across the Atlantic without having to be 'shipped' and rebuilt, which would have wasted a lot of time and money. The range of the Sabre was insufficient to cross the Atlantic without refuelling and so the aircraft were ferried via Narsassuaq, Bluie West One, on the southern tip of Greenland and Keflavik in Iceland. The only means of navigation at the time was to use the aircraft ADF receiver listening to the very powerful radio beacons at Goose Bay in Newfoundland, in Greenland and in Iceland, beacons with which I became very familiar in later years when I was crossing the Atlantic. In the UK and Germany, the aircraft were either controlled by ground radar or the aircraft used TACAN but, at the time I flew the Sabre, TACAN beacons were not very numerous in the UK so ADF was very welcome for homing to the airfield.

It was an exciting moment for me to have this opportunity to fly the Sabre. Like a lot of United States aircraft there were a lot of switches and not too many levers in the cockpit. The engine started up without any problem and I taxied by pressing a small button at the bottom of the stick which engaged the nose wheel steering; this made ground manoeuvring so easy I immediately wondered why we did not do this in the UK. I was soon at the take-off point and accelerating down the runway. I can remember to this day my surprise and pleasure as the aircraft left the ground and I felt the response of the ailerons. The controls were fully powered, not boosted, and the artificial feel was superb. I felt supremely confident from that moment onwards and the rest of the flight was a dream, the climb to altitude, the supersonic dive to about 1.1M or so, the aerobatics and the return to the circuit for landings which were incredibly flattering of one's flying skill. The maximum speed of the aircraft was 600 kt. below 15,000ft; above that height there was no speed limitation! This aircraft was the first one I flew where the tailplane/elevator combination moved together, was fully powered and not trimmed by external tabs. I thanked Tom and drove away on cloud nine. I must have been the biggest bore in the School when I got back to the bar the following day.

The Ground School under Jimmy Lang was the constant thread throughout the Course. The serviceability of the ancient and revered fleet of aircraft was as unpredictable as the weather, so we never knew from one day to another what we were actually going to achieve in the flying programme, but the ground school time-table was inviolate. We knew that first thing every day after breakfast we would be exposed to all the technical background that we needed to learn and all the testing techniques that we had to employ in order to become effective test pilots. The real test of whether we had completed the ground school satisfactorily was not whether we passed the exam but whether we would be able to analyse the test results and discuss them with the design engineers. However, there was no escaping the need to pass the ground school examinations if we were going to graduate.

We all came from a very wide variety of backgrounds. Some were engineers by training, some had already done some form of test flying, some had degrees but not all were ready to go back to the classroom. It was necessary for Jimmy to assume some level of mathematical skill and some of the course had to revise to reach this minimum standard; in a way it reminded me of the similar problems I had had when I was instructing at Wittering and the difficulty I had had in choosing an assumed level of knowledge from the students. In fact, if my memory serves me right, I used to help some of the course members when Jimmy Lang had finished, explaining the mathematics required. However, even though I was fortunate in having the basic mathematical tools and though I was a physicist by training, I still had a lot of new disciplines to learn. Jimmy taught us aerodynamics, engine and aircraft performance; the tutors had to teach us the application of these subjects to the actual testing of the aircraft.

We learnt that test flying could broadly be divided into two distinct categories; firstly, the evaluation of the way the aircraft responded to the pilot's controls, the aircraft handling, and, secondly, the measurement of performance. It was no use having an aircraft that flew beautifully if it could not carry out its task. Conversely, it was no use having an aircraft that could fly at the maximum design speed, or fly to the maximum designed altitude with the maximum payload if, in doing so, it required an exceptional pilot to get to these corners of the flight envelope and bring the aircraft back safely. In addition, the aircraft had to be able to take off and land without requiring an exceptionally long airfield and, furthermore, for a multi-engined aircraft, it was necessary for it to be able to climb away safely if an engine failed during the take-off. In summary, the test pilot always has to check both the handling and performance of an aircraft.

Of course the decision as to whether an aircraft was satisfactory was not up to the whim of the test pilot. There were rules to be followed, standards to be met. The purchasing authority always told the manufacturer what rule had to be followed; in the case of the Royal Air Force the rules were laid down in the military publication

Aviation Publication 970. For example, this book laid down in detail how the aircraft had to respond when it was stalled; it sounded simple, but the aircraft had to be stalled throughout the weight range of the aircraft, at the forward and aft centre of gravity limits, in straight flight and in turning flight, at low altitude and at high altitudes. Even if the aircraft handled perfectly in the stall, without a wing drop, without spinning, without shaking itself to pieces, without any undesirable but unspecified vices, it would still be necessary to make hundreds of stalls in all these different configuration before its stalling behaviour was declared acceptable. But most aircraft did not behave perfectly at the stall, since the designer was trying to get the ultimate performance out of it and this often affected the stalling performance adversely. The aerodynamics frequently had to be fine tuned to get acceptable stalling performance and, of course, this could affect the overall performance. We learnt that the customer buys an aircraft for its performance and trusts that the designer will be able to make the aircraft's handling good enough so that it can be handled by the worst pilot likely to fly it.

All aircraft had to be tested at the maximum speed as well as the minimum speed for acceptable handling. The aircraft had to be stable or, depending on the flight conditions, neutrally stable in pitch if the speed changed; this meant that it was unacceptable for an aircraft to try to dive as the speed was increased. In other words if the aircraft was put into a dive, the pilot would have to push to keep the speed increasing.

Longitudinally, if the stick was pulled back to apply normal acceleration at constant speed, the stick force for a given amount of 'g' had to be positive and meet the required level, depending on whether the aircraft was a fighter or a bomber/transport aircraft; again it was not acceptable for the aircraft to 'tighten' into a turn or a manoeuvre. Directionally, an aircraft had to be stable or possibly neutrally stable in certain flight conditions and not try to 'change ends' as the rudder was applied. The response of the aircraft in roll to the pilot's controls had to meet the requirements for the type of aircraft and the design specification. All these tests had to cover the complete flight envelope. In addition a new training aircraft had to be able to be spun by the students. This meant that the test pilot had to test the aircraft in the spin with all the variables that applied to the stall, centre of gravity range, weight range, altitude range etc. No wonder that test flying an aircraft took a lot of time and effort. The test pilots and engineers had to be certain that the aircraft had no unexpected vices, whether they were the firm's pilots or the acceptance pilots, and it was not unusual for there to be a difference of opinion on the result of some of the tests which had to be resolved.

The School also taught us how to measure performance and this part of test flying seemed deadly dull. In fact I was to find in later years that it was not really dull, just very time consuming. Cruise performance was incredibly difficult to measure because the atmosphere was very rarely stable. We were taught how to measure performance 'non-dimensionally', how the aircraft had to climb at constant mach number to allow for its reducing weight. We had to establish a carpet of performance by measuring a large number of points. We soon learnt that performance flying required patience.

For all aircraft, performance was all about speed, height, weight and fuel consumption. For a civil aircraft, the airfield performance was particularly important. Civil Aircraft were tested against the British Civil Airworthiness Requirements, BCARs now JARs (Joint Airworthiness Requirements), which included airfield performance requirements as well as handling. At the school we did not carry out these airfield tests because the instrumentation support requirements and ensuing analysis would have been enormous. I discovered later that these performance tests could be very exacting when I started to test the Avro 748 later in my career.

The ground school, therefore, prepared us for all the handling and performance tests that we were called upon to do at the School and, hopefully, when we had graduated. This meant that we had to study in some detail aerodynamics, stability and control. We also had to absorb enough knowledge to ensure that we were up to date with modern transonic and supersonic aircraft. We learnt that AP 970 and BCARs were always behind the real world. Technology never stands still and tests are always having to be devised to test aircraft in ways that have not been specified. In those days, for example, decisions had to be made on how an aircraft behaved as it went through the speed of sound. If an aircraft had fully powered controls, what standards were required should a manual reversion occur? The Concorde required a completely new set of requirements, as did fly-by-wire controls and artificial stability.

In those days we did not have access to computers and copying machines. In fact, only a few of us had typewriters at our disposal. There were no pocket calculators; calculations had to be done with slide rules and books of logarithms. Copying was done with carbon papers, lecture notes and examination papers were prepared using gelatine. We had to think and continually improve the draft, before typing reports instead of using the now ubiquitous computer with the capability for making numerous drafts.

The marking system that was used on the course for our post flight test reports was clearly subjective and depended very much on the particular tutor. All the students had their own 'pigeon holes' for receiving papers and mail. This meant that since our marked reports were put in our pigeon holes they were available to the other students, should they decide to look into someone else's box. Mike Beeching, a fellow R.A.F. officer, was getting pretty fed up with some of the marks he had been receiving and decided to copy one of mine which had received good marks; the test report in question was called 'turns on one control' and was particularly uninspiring. I had typed my report as was my usual habit but Mike used long hand. We both had the same tutor, who shall be nameless, but his report was panned, quite rightly, as mine should have been. I don't know whether the news of this happening got widespread coverage but I suspect Mike was not over popular with the establishment.

Armed with the knowledge we had acquired in the ground school we carried out tests on the aircraft in the fleet. Generally, these test were uneventful because the aircraft had been cleared by the Ministry of Defence acceptance authority, the Aircraft and Armament Experimental Establishment at Boscombe Down. The only unusual event I remember was when I went up to carry out asymmetric handling on the Meteor Mk 8. I knew, from my time in Germany, that the pedal forces of the Meteor to keep the aircraft under control on one engine were very high so I was very circumspect when preparing for the tests.

The briefing was at about 5,000 ft. to apply take-off power with the aircraft at safety speed in the take-off configuration, landing gear down and flap in the take-off position; engine failure would then be simulated by throttling back an engine. However, in order to try to approximate to a real failure when the pilot would not be expecting any problems, the procedure was to wait two seconds before recovery action was commenced. I duly set up the conditions, throttled the engine and waited two seconds; however before the two seconds had elapsed, or so it seemed to me, the aircraft seemed to change ends and I found myself staring vertically down at the ground below 5,000ft. There was no way that I could recover without hitting the ground but every time I applied power and tried to change the attitude of the aircraft, it made another uncontrollable manoeuvre. After several attempts, I managed to get the aircraft to recover in a reasonable attitude and I was able to apply power on both engines and gain flying speed.

I tentatively carried out some more tests and returned slowly to Farnborough. The most likely explanation of the problem I experienced was that the fin had stalled due to the build-up of an excessive amount of sideslip and my later attempts at recovery were made difficult by being very close to the stall. I had the wit to realise that I would get no marks from the tutors for describing my incident; they would be most unhappy if the prescribed test proved to be unflyable since it would suggest they had not done the tests properly themselves. I therefore 'assumed' to myself that I had waited longer than two seconds. I wrote up the tests and I seem to remember I got a good mark. As far as I know no one else had the same problem as I did so perhaps it really was my fault for waiting too long.

One of the best features of the ground school was the visits we had from outside lecturers. We particularly liked talks from the famous test pilots of the time telling us about the new aircraft they were testing in house. I remember we had talks from Neville Duke of Hawkers where the P1052 and the Hunter were being developed. We heard from Brian Trubshaw of Vickers where the Valiant was about to go to Boscombe Down to start acceptance. 'Hazel' Hazelden of Handley Page told us about the Victor and Roly Falk described the work on the Vulcan and the one third scale model Vulcans, the Avro 707s. Beamont of English Electric told us about the Lightning and Peter Twiss about the FD2. These talks were fascinating not only in the subject matter but also in the method of delivery; some speakers were clear and analytical, others were a bit rambling. However, not surprisingly, all the speakers were at their best when responding to questions. I suppose all of us on the course had ambitions to one day step into the shoes of these famous people; we did not realise that the days of an abundance of prototypes in the UK aircraft industry were coming to an end and that the Country would not be able to afford to carry on funding a plethora of developments. Aircraft firms were going to reduce in number, programmes were going to be cut and the need for test pilots in the aircraft industry was going to diminish.

One thing we did appreciate from the talks from these famous test pilots was the complexity of the new aircraft compared with the aircraft we were flying. Military aircraft were becoming weapons systems and the new aircraft were composed of many sub-systems, hydraulics, electrical, pneumatic, pressurisation, navigation and many more. These systems had to be able to continue to operate if failures occurred within the system and, in order to fly these new aircraft safely, the pilots had to understand all the systems and the possible failures. The days of the thin blue Pilots Notes were numbered; the books expanded into two or even three volumes and an examination was required before a pilot was allowed to fly the aircraft. In addition, if a simulator was available then the pilot would have to get familiar with the aircraft on the ground.

There was a tradition at the School for the Courses to visit selected firms in the aircraft industry and these visits had an awesome reputation for the students misbehaving in the evening. Hotels which had been hosts during these visits never wished to repeat the experience. In fact when Sammy Wroath had made his introductory speech to us in February he spent an inordinate amount of time telling us that we would have to behave ourselves on visits to the Industry and misbehaviour would result in being dismissed summarily from the course. We were a bit puzzled by such a welcoming speech but after a few days the tutors and staff told us about the incidents that had happened in the past. In fact our Course was well behaved, perhaps as a result of Sammy Wroath's strictures, though there was one pugilistic incident between a rather pugnacious tutor and an overseas student, due we all believed from an over indulgence of alcohol by both protagonists, which unfortunately and perhaps unfairly, resulted in the student having to leave the course.

Our first visit was to the Blackpool illuminations where we stayed in the Norbreck Hydro; this was my first visit to 'the North' and at the time I did not really relish the experience. We went to English Electric to look at the Lightning, the Canberra and have our first taste of that well known ritual, walking the factory floor. Speaking for myself, these walks around the assembly lines were not particularly helpful and the only bits I ever remembered were the sheds where the aircraft were pretty well complete. In fact it was only after I left the airframe manufacturing part of the aerospace industry and went into the component industry that I learnt the importance of walking around a factory. A judgement of an organisation can be made by looking at the types and age of the machines being used, seeing the organisation of the production floor and viewing all the other facets that make up a production line, be it a large sub-assembly or the aircraft itself.

Hawker Hurricane

The best visit we had was to Hawkers at their famous airfield Dunsfold set in the idyllic Sussex countryside. We listened to their exciting aircraft development in the morning and then, in the afternoon, the firm made available for us to fly a choice of the Hawker Hart, the Hawker Fury and the Hawker Hurricane. For some reason I wanted to fly in the pre-war Hart but had to settle for the Hurricane.

Those of us who were due to fly the Hurricane queued up in turn to read the skeleton Pilots notes and then I seem to remember we changed seats with the Rolls Royce Merlin aircraft still running, ticking over gently. I got in and taxied away on the grass. I opened the throttle and the aircraft accelerated very sedately forward. Any comparison with the Sea Fury would be completely misleading. There was no torque trying to twist the aircraft off the runway and I remember after getting airborne that it was necessary to change hands, fly with the left hand, and then operate the hydraulic controls like a car gear change lever to raise the undercarriage. There was only time for a very large circuit of the airfield and then I put the Hurricane gently back on the grass.

I felt then, and still feel now, thrilled with having flown the Hurricane. It seemed incredibly underpowered and yet it used the same engine as the world renowned Spitfire. Surely an interesting comparison of the designer's art. Unfortunately, I believe that we were probably the last course to receive Hawker's incredibly generous flying hospitality. It must have been difficult to justify the expense of keeping the aircraft in flying condition. I think the aircraft went to the Shuttleworth Trust near Bedford and I hope, like Anna Sewell's horse Black Beauty, that they are having a happy time out to grass.

Ours was the first course which had Helicopter training, the object being to produce much needed helicopter test pilots for the helicopter test squadron, D Squadron, at Boscombe Down. There was understandably not a rush of volunteers to be selected for this work and, by intent, I did not prove to be one of the star helicopter pilots. I can't remember whether any of the course went solo on the ETPS helicopter but, thankfully, I know I never did. In later years I regretted my inability to come to terms with these non-instinctive heavier than air machines. I should have remembered the advice my flying instructor had given me when I was trying go solo for the first time; 'it can't be very difficult, look at the people who can do it'. Instinctively I felt that helicopters were not as safe as fixed wing aircraft; there was always the fear of mechanical failure of the blades or transmission which would produce catastrophic results. In addition, it seemed much harder to deal with an engine failure than on a conventional single-engined aircraft which would glide the moment the power was lost. On a single engined helicopter it was necessary for the pilot to get the blades to auto-rotate quickly the moment power was lost, that is to get the air to drive the blades round, rather than the other way round, so that the machine could in effect 'glide' to the ground and could be flared for touch down. It was the view on our course that the pilots who were selected for D Squadron had in some way got on the wrong side of the staff of the school. Whether that was true or not I don't know, but Mike Beeching and David Price were the ones who went to D Squadron. I suspect in David's case he was too nice a guy to make a fuss.

Looking at my log book for the period, I am reminded that I flew the prone piloted Desford Meteor. The front of the aircraft had been modified to accommodate a pilot lying on his stomach and the pilot could just look forward to see where he was going. The theory of the thing was that since the pilot's head was roughly level with his heart, he would have a high tolerance to the effects of g. There was of course another pilot in charge of the aircraft sitting in the normal Meteor's pilot seat. The tests were under the auspices of the Institute of Aviation Medicine and one of their doctors who also had been through a pilot's course would be in charge of the flight. The students on the Course were all used as guinea pigs and somehow we clambered into this device from which we would have had no chance of escape if anything had gone wrong. To be honest I can't remember too much about the flight which I did. I think the flying controls were something like a bicycle handlebars instead of the conventional stick. We carried out loops and rolls but the real excitement was in trying to land the device. In fact, I believe that the safety pilot was always required to avert catastrophe, certainly in my case. I don't believe the experiment contributed much to our store of knowledge though it kept the pilot doctors in the Institute of Aviation Medicine gainfully employed.

Besides our formal work on the course we had the opportunity to go gliding at week-ends at Lasham close by and, though I didn't care all that much for gliding, I used to like flying the Chipmunk which the school used for towing the gliders into the air. It was a very pleasant way of spending a Summer's day. We operated from Lasham at the same time as the flourishing civilian gliding establishment under the control of the very famous lady Ann Welch, who started her flying career as a ferry pilot during the second world War, became a famous gliding pilot and instructor, then an administrator and then an enthusiast for hang gliding and microlights.. I never met her at Lasham but luckily my wife and I had the privilege of meeting her many years later at a historical gathering at Shoreham, some months before she died.

On the way to Kiel in Kinch's taxi

There was one break in the middle of the course and Kinch and I went sailing in Denmark. Kinch had bought an old London taxi and we filled it up with all our junk and drove to Harwich. We crossed to Esjberg and then drove in fine weather to Kiel. The boat we had chartered from the RAF yacht club there was my much loved 100 square metre Flamingo which I had sailed so many times while based in Germany. We did the normal tour to Sonderborg, Kolby Kass, Helsingor, the Copenhagen breweries and back round to Kiel. We got back into our taxi and drove home. A memorable trip.

Whilst we were on the course Kinch met some American girls through mutual friends in the States and he went on later to marry one of them, Dorothy, when he got home. They started a family and then tragically Kinch was killed taking off in a Lockheed 104. He had by then become a very famous United States Air Force test pilot and was the first pilot to exceed 100,000 ft. achieving 126,000 ft. in the rocket propelled X2. After his tragic death he had both a USAF base and the star annual prize of the United States Society of Experimental Test Pilots named after him. Later I became a Fellow of the Society and so had the pleasure of seeing the prize presented several times at the Annual Banquets in Los Angeles by Dotty, his wife.

In November we had our exams. I had to do 'preview' handling on the Varsity with Squadron Leader 'Titch' Crozier and then we had the ground school exam. I managed to be top in the ground school examinations, graduating overall with a distinguished pass. I would have liked to have got the top prize, the McKenna Trophy, but that went to Vin Hill of the Royal Australian Air Force. The other distinguished pass went to Ted Mellor, also in the Royal Air Force with me; he was posted to R.A.E. Farnborough on Aeroflight and I was posted to 'B' Squadron, Boscombe Down where the new bomber and transport aircraft for the Royal Air Force were being tested. I had wanted to go to 'A' squadron where the fighters were tested but, in my heart of hearts, I knew that I would be better on the big aircraft, developing not only the flying characteristics of the aircraft but the systems that went in them.

It had been a wonderful year. I had been able to apply all the training I had received at school and Cambridge, just as I had planned, to the science of flight testing and, luckily, my flying skills had been adequate for the required work. I looked forward to the next step, applying all that I had learnt to new aircraft, rather than the hacks at the School.

***

A day or so after graduating from No 13 Course of the Empire Test Pilots School I was on my way to my next posting at Boscombe Down in Wiltshire. It was very different geographically from Farnborough; the airfield lay in the Wiltshire plain with its large fields and rolling countryside. The plain was the home of the Army; training and operational establishments were everywhere. My first view of the place was driving along the A303 in my new black Austin A40 and, looking across to the left as I coasted down towards Amesbury, I could see the large Weighbridge Hangar and the very long and wide runways close-by. Beyond was Salisbury and the tall Cathedral spire. It was an exciting moment as I drove up the hill to the airfield and reported to the security gate; they directed me to the Officers Mess which, in those days, was outside the security fence but very close to the Technical Block which had an access gate into the building and thence onto the airfield. I signed in for the first time and was allocated a room overlooking the airfield where, very conveniently, I could watch all the new types of aircraft, and the not so new, taking off and landing.

I unpacked and drove back to the gate to get passes for myself and the car and then found my way to 'B' Squadron. Conveniently, the crew room and flight operations were on the side of a hangar and looked across the very large ramp which was mostly filled with elderly B Squadron aircraft.

Boscombe Down was divided into four squadrons, A Squadron to test fighters, B Squadron to test bombers and transport aircraft, C Squadron to test naval aircraft and D Squadron to test helicopters. The four squadrons were supported by the Ministry of Defence technical staff and the Establishment was headed by the Chief Superintendent. In my time the Superintendent was a serving R.A.F. Officer, Air Commodore Wheeler when I arrived but was shortly to be replaced by Air Commodore Ramsey-Rae. There were two other flying units at Boscombe, the Civil Development Flying Unit which used to specialise in testing advanced navigation aids and the Royal Air Force Handling Squadron which wrote all the Pilots Notes, obviously an ideal location because they could see and describe the new aircraft before they got their own aircraft to work on.

The Commanding Officer of B Squadron was Wing Commander Roy Max who in fact was not a graduate of ETPS but was a very experienced pilot and he introduced me to Tommy

Tomlinson and Paddy Harper, his two flight commanders, who were both from No 11 Course. Graham Moreau who was on 13 Course with me was also joining B Squadron and we met Tom Frost from No 11 Course and Geoff Fletcher from No 12. There were quite a few others including, of course, the very important flight engineers who looked after the aircraft systems not available to the pilot on the flight deck; typically these controls were all the fuel tank cocks and the electrical generator switches including bus bar controls. Of course aircraft system design has changed significantly and modern day pilots are able to control pretty well all the aircraft systems including dealing with emergencies so that, in the Services, the role of the flight engineer has changed or has been shared out to other crew members. In civil airplanes the flight engineer has disappeared completely.

B Squadron was going through a slack time when we arrived. The three new types of V Bombers were on their way; they had all had preview handling at the manufacturers' airfields and the first production Valiants were expected fairly soon. Production Vulcans and Victors were not expected until the following year. Consequently, B Squadron's fleet was pretty uninspiring, consisting mainly of aircraft that were used for supporting overseas hot weather and cold weather trials for all the four test squadrons. In addition, we had a communication aircraft or two and a hack Canberra for weapon clearances.

Avro Anson

Every new weapon like, for example a bomb, had to be checked by Boscombe Down to make certain that the carriage of the weapons did not adversely affect the handling quality of the carrying aircraft unacceptably. Nevertheless, most of the aircraft were new types as far as we were concerned and new types in the log book were always worth having to broaden one's flying experience or just to get a new type in the log book if one was a type hog.

I started off by flying the Avro Anson which was a metal low wing monoplane with two Cheetah engines. There was nothing very remarkable about the aircraft and, in fact, I flew in the Anson a lot when I joined A.V.Roe. Its asymmetric handling was quite good, which was not too surprising since there was not a lot of engine power about, but this meant that the single engined performance did not meet the civil regulations. However, it took us all over the Country with a fair degree of reliability and the engines never let me down; however the Anson was not renowned for its speed.

Avro York

A much more interesting aircraft was the York transport, another product from the Avro stable. The York was a four engined high wing monoplane using the Rolls Royce Merlin engine. The York wing had come from the Lancaster bomber and the fuselage was a box for carrying things and had been added on underneath the wing. It had done a really excellent job during the Berlin airlift and we used it on B Squadron for carrying spares and people to the overseas sites where the new Service aircraft were subjected to tropical and cold weather conditions. The York was a really splendid aircraft. The throttles were between the pilots but the levers instead of being attached conventionally to a central pedestal, were suspended from the roof. The flight engineer would stand between the two pilots during landing and the captain would demand imperiously 'give me a slow cut' and at some stage the flight engineer, who was always vastly more experienced than the pilot, would then decide when to close the throttles and bring the aircraft safely and smoothly onto the tarmac. The York was one of the few tail wheeled aircraft I flew which never seemed to cause any ground handling problem. I grabbed every chance I could of flying it, which wasn't very often, and towards the end I managed to persuade the flight engineer to let me grasp the throttles during landing, which seemed to work out quite well.

Handley Page Hastings

The next aircraft I got my hands on, and both feet, was the Handley Page Hastings. In fact, I had had a brief flight in one at Farnborough but I had a chance to learn a lot more about it during my stay at Boscombe. It was incredibly heavy on the elevator due, we new pilots used to say, to the prodigious strength of 'Hazel' Hazeldene, the legendary Chief Test Pilot of Handley Page. The only way I, and I suspect many others like me, ever learnt to land the aircraft was to keep on trimming the elevator nose up during the flare so that the force required for the final round out was within one's capability; the situation was compounded by the nose down pitch when the throttles were closed for touch-down.

Unfortunately, the Hastings' heavy elevator forces caused the most horrendous accident at Boscombe whilst I was there. I was flying a Canberra on a beautiful summer's day when I saw a pall of smoke rising from the middle of the airfield. A Hastings had taken off, risen very steeply and crashed. The accident investigation found that the elevator trim wheel was trimmed fully up; the wheel should have been central for take-off and it was assumed that the pilot had not done the pre take-off checks which are required to be carried out for every type of aircraft. The terrifying sequence would have been that the pilot had opened the throttles and the aircraft would have started to roll down the runway. The pilot would then have found that he needed two hands to stop the aircraft going prematurely into the air and there would be no way he could takes his hands off the wheel and move the elevator trimmer nose down before the aircraft rose up and stalled.

Bristol Freighter

The other transport aircraft I remember was a Bristol Freighter, designed primarily to carry cars across the English Channel. It had a tail wheel, two Hercules piston engines and the most terrible landing habits. In fact, it was not too bad when it was heavy but when it was light the approach speed was so slow that the controls would lose effectiveness. If the speed was increased to counteract this shortcoming, the aircraft would behave like a glider a few feet above the ground. Luckily, I had had some related experience in bringing large sailing yachts alongside the quay, when it was not unusual to lose rudder control whilst the yacht was moving too quickly for the crew to be able to stop the boat. Judgement was required as to when it was safe to close the throttles and lose all control effectiveness but, unlike a boat, there was no crew to shout at when the manoeuvre was going out of control.

Blackburn Beverley

We did, as it turned out, actually have one new transport aircraft being tested in the Squadron; the Blackburn Beverley. It had four Bristol Centaurus engines, a nosewheel, thank goodness, and a very capacious fuselage to carry the many requirements of the R.A.F. The Blackburn company was famous through the years for their capacity to build aircraft that were incredibly strong and with the gliding characteristics of a brick. The Beverley was no exception. My chief memory of that aircraft was the ability to taxi it backwards and the splendid nose-wheel steering tiller. I did some testing on it with Geoff Fletcher, handling at the forward centre of gravity limit, and it was impossibly heavy on the controls. In retrospect, the Beverley was at the end of the line for large aircraft with manually powered flying controls since powered actuators were becoming available which could be fitted to aircraft without penalising their performance.

Besides the York, which I tended to regard as a vintage aircraft, I managed to fly an Avro Lincoln which was a Lancaster with a developed wing. It was owned by the Civil flight and normally flown by a civilian pilot 'Doc' Purvis, but for some reason we were allowed to fly it occasionally. My memory tells me that the controls were reasonably light and the aircraft landed quite well in spite of still being a tail wheeled aircraft. I suppose I should include the Avro Shackleton as a vintage aircraft, though it was still being used by Coastal Command; this aircraft again was developed from the Lancaster. In fact, it was a current aircraft on B Squadron because of new weapons and navigation fits and again it was a type I got to know very well at Avro's. It carried on flying for over 30 years providing the early warning system for NATO until the Boeing AWACS came along..

Avro Lincoln

The current B Squadron aircraft included the Canberra 2 and a brand new Canberra 7, which I collected from English Electric at Warton, two days after I arrived. Because we were short of work, we had been given some menial 'A' squadron tasks, so that there was a night fighter Meteor 13 with its very long nose housing the latest radars, a Vampire 10 night fighter and a Venom Mk 1. Graham and I were given the Venom to extend some bombing clearances on the range near Lyme Bay and we all helped fly the night fighters, while the boffins developed and tested the radars. This was my first introduction to testing systems and equipment, not a very glamorous job but an absolutely essential part of test flying. In fact, test flying in some ways has not changed; it consisted then and consists now of mostly very routine flying. The art of good development flying is to move in slow safe steps; rapid development flying, rushing through the work, can easily lead to disaster. Of course, nowadays, it is possible to make progress much faster because, as has been mentioned, aircraft are not only fitted with instrumentation but the data can be transmitted to the ground where it can be analysed in real time by computers, so that engineers on the ground can judge whether to proceed with planned tests, knowing the results of the last tests straightaway.

Gloster Javelin

While we were not too busy we looked around for other aircraft to fly. It was very rare for pilots in 'B' Squadron to be able to fly the fighter aircraft in 'A' Squadron but I must have been very persuasive, because I was allowed a flight in a Javelin twin engined delta night fighter with a high tailplane and elevator. The aircraft was unkindly called the 'drag master'. All I remember about my one flight were the airbrakes; they were the evaluation test pilot's dream; no trim change, very little buffet and the most enormous amount of drag. To this day, I have a memory of pointing the aircraft vertically down, throttles closed, airbrakes out and seeming to be suspended in space. In fact the Javelin had some very unpleasant and unforgiving stalling and spinning habits, but I kept well clear of the edges of the flight envelope. Dicky Martin, who joined us later at A.V.Roe, was Chief Test Pilot of Glosters at the time and I was thankful I did not have his incredibly demanding job of making the aircraft fit for squadron service.

Another aircraft I managed to fly was the Vickers Supermarine Swift. This, like the Javelin, was another not very successful R.A.F. fighter aircraft. It was renowned for pitching up during stalling manoeuvres and as often as not going into a spin, not a good feature for a fighter. It flew reasonably well but was not a patch on the Hunter, its chief competitor. In fact, viewed dispassionately, the R.A.F. procurement programme at that time funded a large number of poor aircraft produced by the UK aircraft industry. There were a few exceptions, such as Hawkers with the Hunter series and English Electric with some of the Canberra variants. In later years, the European joint programmes produced some excellent workhorses like the Jaguar and Tornado; it could of course be argued, that without the earlier work this would not have been possible.

Supermarine Swift

Through my No 13 Course colleague, Nigel Ducker who was on C Squadron, I managed to fly the predecessor of the Hunter, the Sea Hawk which was a very honest straight mid wing jet aircraft using the Avon. I also managed to fly the Sea Gannet, an incredible twin engined Armstrong Siddeley Mamba turbo propeller driven aircraft carrying specialist radar.

Fairy Gannet

Shorts Sea Mew

The Sea Mew, a single engined Mamba turboprop, was another unlikely flying machine being tested by C Squadron . Great care was needed on these turboprop aircraft to handle the propeller pitch controls correctly, particularly on the ground, to avoid burning out the jet engine. My great disappointment was not having a chance to land on a carrier. C Squadron had a Sea Balliol and thanks to the new angled deck carriers and the angle of approach lights, deck landings had become a lot easier. It was agreed that Graham Moreau and myself could do some real deck landings. We did some simulated carrier landings at Boscombe and the great day approached.

110

Unfortunately Graham left the oil dilution switch on during one of his flights and the engine was ruined as well as our chances of doing deck landings.

Roy Max left B Squadron early in 1955 and Clive Saxelby took over. Sax was a graduate of No 9 Course and had a very clear thinking intellectual approach to his work. He allocated Tommy Tomlinson and Graham to the Victor program and Paddy Harper and myself to the Vulcan, so we were able to start preparing ourselves for the first previews. Meanwhile the Valiant had arrived for acceptance.

Tommy Frost was the chief 'B' squadron Valiant pilot working with Brian Trubshaw, the Chief Test Pilot at Vickers, and the other test pilots at Wisley. The Valiant was a very conventional aircraft in many ways, featuring the standard UK engine configuration of two engines per side buried in the wing roots. The wings were set high on the fuselage with not much sweepback. The main feature of the aircraft that I remember was that the undercarriage and flaps were electrically operated; unfortunately the inevitable result of this design decision meant that there were large, heavy electric motors spread throughout the airframe and that each engine had a big 112 Volt DC generator to provide the necessary power. Furthermore, the aircraft had a lot of heavy cables connecting everything up. The power controls were fully powered with very heavy manual reversion should the power control system fail; the artificial feel system was provided by springs, their strength being modulated by large airspeed levers connected to pitot air filled 'dustbins'. It was my first introduction to a complicated systems aircraft and I remember that the Pilots Notes were no longer slim and elegant.

I flew the Valiant with the designated B Squadron test pilots and it ploughed on steadily towards acceptance with no particular perturbations. In due course the first squadron was formed, its operational role being to carry nuclear stores of some type. Aircraft of the complication of the Valiant could not be cleared for squadron service in one go. There would first be a handling release and then slowly navigation and radio systems would be added followed by the weapons clearance. This was no hardship for the Services since the pilots first needed to be trained to fly the aircraft before they started training operationally.

The tradition in B Squadron was that the prime acceptance pilots for a new aircraft carried out the handling tests, and then the other pilots on the squadron got checked out on the type to fly the more mundane tests of cruise performance and the addition of the radio/navigation systems. One day, Graham Moreau and myself took a Valiant to R.A.F. Gaydon for ILS approaches in rather poor weather, with visibility at the minimum limit, to advise on the recommended minima to be used in the initial ILS service release. In the Valiant, the pilot had to follow the raw ILS deflection of the two needles in the indicator which showed deviation signals from the centre line of the runway and the centre line of the glide slope; there were no on-board computed indicators to enable the pilot to hold the centre lines, as was being used in the USA at the time. This meant that a lot of skill, and therefore training, was needed by the pilot to fly the aircraft manually and keep it in the centre of the beams since the beams were becoming physically narrower and narrower as the airfield was approached.

The situation was made more complicated since the planned aim of the R.A.F., quite understandably, was to be able to carry out automatic landings in bad weather and their experts had advised the operations branch that automatic landing would not be possible using an ILS beam alone; it would be necessary to supplement the guidance close to the runway with a 'leader cable' buried in the ground. This meant not only that extra equipment had to be installed on the airfield and in the aircraft, but that the ILS beam had to be at an angle with the runway centre line since the ILS ground installation and the leader cable could not physically be co-located. The effect of all this was that the aircraft having locked onto the lateral ILS beam, directionally called the localiser, suddenly at short finals the automatic steering would change to the leader cable and the aircraft would have to turn to line up with the runway.

Our Valiant did not have a leader cable receiver, since the leader cable was still being developed at the Blind Landing Experimental Unit at Martlesham Heath. Consequently, Graham and I had to peer into the murk and we only just had time to see the approach lights and turn to touch down on the runway. After each touch-down we opened the throttles to go round for another approach. It was difficult work and we were justifiably quite pleased with ourselves when we finally returned to Boscombe. Our pleasure was spoilt somewhat when we got out of the aircraft to discover that one of us, probably me, had scrubbed all the tyres by touching down on one of our approaches with the brakes on. Incidentally, I never could discover why R.A.F. aircraft were fitted with maxaret brakes which prevented the pilots scrubbing the tyres when on the runway braking but which made no provision to prevent damage if the aircraft was landed with the brakes already on, a not uncommon happening.

Vickers Valiant

The leader cable concept was abandoned in due course, when it was realised that it was possible after all for an ILS beam to give adequate guidance for automatic landings. However, there was no way that the MOD were going to pay to move the localiser antenna to the airplane centre line and so, for all the V Bombers, the ILS localiser antenna remained in the wing tip. This meant that on an airfield with the localiser lined up with the runway, the normal case except for a few bomber command airfields, the aircraft would always be displaced from the runway centre line by the width of the wing.

The Valiant did not last very long in the R.A.F. as, not long after it went into service, the crew of a Boscombe Down Valiant Aircraft heard a loud bang as they were flying along not actually doing any tests; Flt Lt Milt Cottee of the RAAF was in command and he returned, very gently, to base. A very large fatigue crack was discovered in the wing and the design change required to strengthen the Valiant wing was so great that it was not cost effective to modify all the Valiant wings. The whole fleet was grounded fairly soon afterwards.

While waiting for the Vulcan to arrive I was given my first project to organise and fly. The R.A.F. had bought a new version of the Canberra, the Canberra BI Mk 8 attack aircraft which had a single pilot, a bubble canopy, and a navigator seated behind the pilot. This revolutionised the Canberra since for the first time it was possible to see out properly. The ailerons were fully powered and the tailplane was trimmed electrically with a switch on the fighter type grip. It was a delightful aircraft and I thoroughly enjoyed the programme.

Canberra BI Mk8

Not long after we had given the aircraft its full release, a fatal accident occurred to a Canberra Mk8 which could only be explained by an electric malfunction of the tailplane trimmer. Investigation showed that there was no proper protection at the time for welded contacts on the actuator, so that it was possible for the pilot to start the tailplane moving trying to trim the aircraft and then the actuator would carry on travelling by itself to full travel, possibly breaking the aircraft on its way, depending on its speed. In retrospect, perhaps we should have found the weakness in design before we gave the aircraft it's clearance. The problem was solved by putting in a back-up safety circuit automatically operated by the pilot as he tried to trim the elevator. This was my introduction to the need for safety assessments in systems and, fortunately, the lesson had been learnt at Avro's by the time the Vulcan came along.

There was an enormous competition between Handley Page with the Victor and Avro's with the Vulcan, to see who would get their aircraft to Boscombe first and this was just part of a long battle between the two firms to prove that their V Bomber was the better aircraft. Avro's won the first round and Vulcan XA889 arrived in March 1956. It was a great moment for everybody concerned with the project. Compared with the Victor, the Vulcan was a more unconventional aircraft aerodynamically, having a delta wing. It looked like a praying mantis with its long nosewheel undercarriage, particularly when landing, and I can remember the first time I climbed up the ladder into the rear crew compartment thinking the cockpit was a long way up. There were three seats for the two navigators and the air electronics officer who controlled the all important electricity generation system on the aircraft. These crew members faced aft and sat on their parachutes. In the event of an emergency escape the crew had to open the entrance door and slide down the chute; furthermore the nose undercarriage had to be up since the door was in front of the undercarriage leg. The whole rear compartment was very claustrophobic.

To get up to the flight deck it was necessary to climb up another ladder and slide onto one of the two ejector seats. The compartment was very cramped with a forward view that failed to meet any sensible design requirement. I could not believe at first that it was possible to see out for take-off and landing. The designers solved the lack of space on the flight deck by fitting a control column for each pilot, instead of the more conventional control wheel normally used in large aircraft. There was no problem controlling the aircraft since the controls were fully powered, with no manual reversion and there was fully modulated artificial feel. The effect of only having a stick was that the pilot in command in the left hand seat had to fly with his left hand and operate the four tiny centrally located throttle levers with his right hand. Some people found this difficult to get used to but I was left handed and so at last I had an aircraft that seemed to be designed for me.

Vulcan Mk.1 XA891

The Vulcan Mk 1 had four trailing edge elevators and four trailing edge ailerons, unlike the later Mk2 which had a clever mechanical mixer so that all eight surfaces, the elevons, could be used in both pitch and roll. The control surfaces were operated by individual electrically operated hydraulic motors so that the safety of the aircraft was bound up inextricably with the need for immaculate operation of the electrical system. The Mk 1 had an 112 Volt DC power system like the Valiant, with four generators paralleled on the system but the landing gear was operated hydraulically.

My first flight in the Vulcan was in the right hand seat with Sax in command. We gingerly taxied out peering through the front windscreen's letter box slits at the front, and the portholes on the side. When we reached the runway and opened the throttles the aircraft hurtled forward and climbed very rapidly up to 40,000ft. The view was still poor and we slowly became used to flying on our instruments even when the visibility was unlimited. Returning to the circuit was a challenge and at first we relied heavily on radar to position us for a straight in approach. We peered out, but the problem was that as we slowed down the attitude of the aircraft became more and more nose up so our forward view was very poor. Luckily Boscombe had a long runway and we carried a tail parachute; the undercarriage on the main wheels had trailing bogies which were very flattering for touchdowns

116

and we made some smooth touchdowns finishing with a full stop, streaming our tail parachute to avoid excessive wheel braking.

I flew my second flight with Paddy Harper and finally on my third flight I sat in the left hand seat with Sax in the right. We started to explore the handling characteristics of the aircraft. The Vulcan was like the Venom in one way; at high speed it was uncontrollable. In the case of the Vulcan, the aircraft developed a strong nose down pitch above .9 mach number and it was quite impossible for the elevators to stop this nose down tendency. The solution adopted by A.V.Roe, the manufacturers of the aircraft, was to move the elevators up automatically as speed was increased, but by more than was necessary to counteract the inherent pitching down moment, so that the effect to the pilot was that the aircraft pitched up as the speed increased. In this way stability was restored artificially and the pilot had to push the stick forward to accelerate. The snag of course was that once the limited authority of the mach trimmer had been reached and the elevators were fully up, there was only one way for the aircraft to go and that was down. A.V.Roe and ourselves had to decide whether the system as presented to Boscombe Down for certification was good enough for release to the R.A.F.

In retrospect is was amazing that we never lost control at high mach number and dived into the ground. We accepted the mach trimmer and our judgement must have been right because I don't think any of the R.A.F. Vulcans ever lost control when flying at high mach number. I was reminded of that film made soon after the war, the Sound Barrier, about the mythical first supersonic flights in the United Kingdom. The final solution, as the plane dived nose down out of control and got faster and faster, was to push the stick forward to regain control; it might have been all right at Pinewood Studios but we were never brave enough to try it.

The Vulcan had some other interesting aerodynamic characteristics. At high mach number, above about .88M, the aircraft would develop a short period pitching oscillation but, luckily, it was of such a short period the pilot could not join in and, luckily again, the oscillations were not divergent. Anyway, A.V.Roe introduced a pitch damper which was very effective in dealing with the oscillation. In fact, I am not sure whether it was really necessary to have the pitch damper since the pitching oscillation was outside the normal operating environment and even if the pilot did experience the effect, it was not dangerous. I mention this because it is a good example of how the R.A.F. and the manufacturers raised modifications which in many cases were desirable but not essential. It was some years before the concept of 'good enough' and 'fit for purpose' permeated the military test flying environment.

The Vulcan was badly damped directionally and a 'dutch roll' would develop so that the aircraft corkscrewed through the sky. In this case the yaw damper, which the firm had introduced was definitely required in order to make the aircraft a stable bombing platform.

Another feature of the Mk1 was a strong nose down pitch when the bomb doors were open. The auto-pilot could not cope with the change and Bill Stableford at A.V.Roe, a very clever mechanical design engineer with whom I worked a lot later on, arranged for the elevators to be applied upward by just the right amount as the doors opened. Interestingly, when the Mk1A went into service with a bulbous tail to accommodate the latest electronic counter measures, the effect disappeared, despite the forecast by our head of flight test that the tail would make no difference. The modification had to be removed as fast as it was introduced.

Gradually, I got used to flying the Vulcan in the circuit. One adapted to the fact that the view was terrible and learnt to cope. Of course at Boscombe the runway was 11,500ft long so no finesse was required to make a landing. I never really mastered landing the aircraft, instead of it landing me, until I flew regularly at Avro's airfield at Woodford, 7,500ft long with poor approaches.

The Vulcan acceptance programme at Boscombe proceeded smoothly and we got another aircraft, XA 890 for navigation clearances. Unlike XA 889, it still had a straight leading edge which meant that it buffeted at high mach number. This had been a serious problem for Avro's until they discovered the cure which was to fit a cranked leading edge towards the tip. This had been done on XA 889 in time for the acceptance tests and it gave us a chance to compare the two aircraft.

The Victor program was running a few months behind the Vulcan but the Victor Mk 1 did appear at Boscombe towards the end of my time there. I got to know the Victor Mk 2 very well a few years later, but I did not have an opportunity to fly the Mk.1 at Boscombe. It was clearly a much easier aircraft than the Vulcan in many ways and both aircraft had their proponents; there was great rivalry between the pilots, both at Boscombe and at the manufacturers. Looking back I suppose I was fortunate to have done test work on all the three V Bombers

Handley Page Victor

I managed to fly the Comet at handling squadron which proved useful later on when Avro's started the Nimrod. More useful were my flights on the Valiant and Canberra auto-pilots coupled to the ILS beams and my experience with the new Sperry Zero Reader. These flights started to give me the necessary experience I needed at Avro's to install instrument and auto-pilot systems and prepared me for my career with Smiths Industries many years later, by which time I had become fairly knowledgeable in the area of automatic flight control.

Whilst all this flying was going on, the R.A.F. Operations Requirements branch had specified the need for a supersonic bomber and the final bids from industry were being reviewed at MOD Headquarters in London, by the R.A.E. at Farnborough and by us at Boscombe Down. We came to the conclusion that the solution proposed by A.V.Roe was the best with the unusual feature of having no direct look out at all but using a TV camera and screen instead for take-off and landing. The aircraft was called at the time the Avro 730 and, like the small aircraft Avro 707s which had been produced before the Vulcan first flew, there were going to be 'man flown' one third scale models designated the Avro 731. In retrospect, it all seems ridiculous but at the time we were taking it very seriously. So seriously indeed that Avro's decided that they needed another test pilot to join their team. Roly Falk and Jimmy Harrison, his number two, had got to know me pretty well as a result of my Vulcan acceptance flying at Boscombe and they decided that I would probably be a desirable recruit.

On my side I had decided I wanted to get married and leave the R.A.F. My wife to be, Margaret, was an Education Officer in the Women's Royal Air Force based at Boscombe Down and neither of us wanted to stay in the Services. It had always been part of my plan to join Industry and so when Roly made me the offer I agreed in principle. Of course there were a lot of negotiations required; I needed to get the R.A.F. to agree I could resign after only 20 months productive test flying and I needed to get Roy Dobson, who was still the legendary boss at Manchester, to pay me a living wage. Somehow it all happened and so it was agreed that after only joining the R.A.F. to fly in 1950, I could leave six and a half years later, having being trained at great expense to be a test pilot.

I left Boscombe with some trepidation. It was all very well to have decided on a career in industry but the R.A.F. was a very protective organisation, looking after its people. Industry was something very different and, though I did not know it at the time, about to lose the easy business with the MOD. Life was going to have to become very competitive to survive.

CHAPTER 4

A.V.Roe & Co., Ltd.

I joined A.V.Roe at Woodford in August 1956 after a very hectic but short flying career. Somehow it had all come about just as I had planned, when sitting in Wittering in 1949. I had learnt to fly, been trained as a test pilot and then been asked to join a firm to help develop a new aircraft. It was all rather unlikely, since I had nowhere to live and had lost the protective environment of the Royal Air Force with the Officers Mess. On the other hand, I had plans to get married in November.

In fact I had been flying for only six and a half years and my new colleagues seemed incredibly old and experienced. Roly Falk had hired me and his name was very well known, not only in the Aviation Industry but also by the large enthusiastic public that attended air shows. He was a brilliant pilot but, without wishing to be unkind, he was not a very good team leader and had not been to ETPS. At the time I joined, test flying was making the transition from the 'bescarffed' test pilot with his R.A.F. slang telling the Chief Designer what he needed to do to the aircraft, to the test pilot as an engineer, being just one member of the development team.

When Roly joined A.V.Roe, that great gentleman Jimmy Orrell was Chief Test Pilot and so Roly was given the title Superintendent of Flying. Jimmy had flown with Imperial Airways before the war and he had operated the Handley Page Hannibal across India; this in itself made me very envious because the Hannibal, with its four engines, two almost vertically above the other two, was always an aircraft I would have loved to have flown. But Jimmy was coming to the end of his test flying days when Roly was taken on to be the Vulcan development pilot. Clearly Roly had the necessary experience, which Jimmy lacked, of modern jet aircraft, having been on the prestigious Aeroflight at the Royal Aircraft Establishment at Farnborough. Roly was probably the ideal selection for Avro's at the time because he was a very outgoing salesman as well as a great exhibition pilot.

Development Vulcans and 707s

Without doubt Roly did a magnificent job for A.V.Roe, demonstrating the one third scale Avro 707 model Vulcans at Farnborough, followed by the prototype Vulcan. In 1958 when on an automatic landing programme, I was lucky enough to have the opportunity to fly one of the early 707As which Roly had demonstrated. I thought the flying qualities were desperate and, as far as I was concerned, it made his demonstrations even more impressive. Roly should really have been congratulated in not letting the adverse and demanding flying qualities of these aircraft at the time colour the future of the Vulcan. In fact, I have a theory that really good natural pilots don't see the problems for us mere mortals and, not surprisingly therefore, they are severely handicapped from becoming good development test pilots.

On 2nd August I flew my last flight in the RAF in a Valiant with Peter Baker, from Boscombe Down. We were doing ILS approaches at Wittering under automatic pilot control, which turned out to be an important help when I did the same job on the Vulcan some time later. Peter Baker had been on 12 Course and was on 'D' Squadron as the leading helicopter test pilot, having upset someone at Farnborough when the postings were being worked out; he was a really first class test pilot and our paths kept on crossing during our aviation careers. We kept in touch through the years when he went to Vickers to help in the Concorde development programme and then, finally and unexpectedly, he became Chief Test Pilot for the Civil Aviation Authority when Airbus poached two Chief Test Pilots in quick succession, Gordon Corps and then Nick Warner. Peter and I, in later life both became members of the Airworthiness Requirements Board, now unfortunately defunct as a result of European harmonisation.

On 8th August 1956 I made my first flight as a test pilot for A.V.Roe, flying the second prototype Vulcan VX 777 to extend the Vulcan flight envelope. Looking back, it was surprising that there was no formal check out with an Avro test pilot and that there had been no suggestion that I should have a qualified pilot in the right hand seat. The administration of the flying of military aircraft was controlled by the Ministry of Supply. There was an Air Commodore Flying in the Ministry in London with about ten people or so supervising the test flying in the Industry and laying down the rules, which were naturally very similar to flying in the Services with an authorisation book and a flying order book. We used to get inspected once a year which, at first, was a formality but after one or two accidents and incidents in the industry, the supervisory control was understandably increased. I'm not sure what view they would have taken if anything had gone wrong on my first flight at Woodford; certainly such lack of supervision would be unthinkable in the current closely regulated climate.

The procedure for my first test flight at Avro's was one I got to know very well in the years that followed. We had our pre-flight briefing in offices which had been built on to the side of the experimental hangar, on the south side of the airfield. In those days we did not always have qualified pilots in the right hand seat, the idea being that it would be better to have a flight test observer/engineer in the seat, who had the test plan with him, rather than have a pilot unfamiliar with the test program. I was very happy with this single pilot system but it was just as well none of us were ever incapacitated during a flight; the regulators in London would surely have blamed Avro's, notwithstanding that they knew how we were operating.

In the back of the aircraft we had an air electronics officer, AEO, to control the all important DC electrics on the Vulcan and who also acted as a navigator, using a hyperbolic navigation system left over from the War called Gee. The flying controls on the Vulcan were moved by individual electrically operated hydraulic motors with no manual reversion, so it was important to have someone in the back who knew how to deal with the electric generating system if anything went wrong.

We had another flight test observer in the back of the aircraft who looked after the instrumentation and kept an instrumentation log of the flight. At the time, all our test aircraft had upward of one hundred test instruments showing key measurements, fixed to a large panel, and a camera would take pictures of the panel as the flight progressed, routinely once a second and at 10 frames a second if the tests required it. There were event counters as well as a clock so that, after the flight, we could correlate the tests with the data. In addition, for certain tests we used a high speed Ultra Violet paper recorder which had key parameters such as control angles, wheel forces, speed and acceleration. These UV recorders were ideal for quick assessment of aerodynamic tests and were controlled by the rear flight test observer as required. All this instrumentation seems archaic by present standards but it produced results which were very effective.

For this, my first test flight at A.V.Roe, Stan Nicol, a very experienced flight test engineer, sat with me in the front, Ted Hartley was the observer in the back and Eric Burgess was the AEO. This flight followed the pattern of most flights at Woodford. After the briefing, we would wait for the aircraft to be declared serviceable, first by the Avro Flight Shed inspectors and then by the Aeronautical Inspection Department, AID, inspector, who represented the owner of the aircraft, in those days called the Ministry of Supply. All the military aircraft at Woodford belonged to the Government and they were operated under various development contracts. Only when we took an aircraft to Farnborough for the Society of British Aerospace Constructors Show did the aircraft become ours and then, of course, we would have to insure it.

We went downstairs from the pilots' offices which, unlike all the other offices, looked out across the airfield. We went into a rather utilitarian room full of metal lockers and got changed into fairly standard RAF flying clothing. The crew members in the back of the aircraft had to carry their parachutes out to the aircraft; the pilots' chutes were already fitted in the ejector seats. We walked across the tarmac to the white painted second prototype VX 777 and climbed in. As a result of my experience at Boscombe Down I had become quite adept at getting into the Vulcan, climbing first up the entrance ladder resting on the rear crew escape chute and then up the fixed ladder between the two pilots seats. It was all rather cramped but really it was a matter of practice. I had a habit of trying to do the routine things fairly quickly, like starting the engines, and I used to start the engines the moment I was strapped in; in fact there was a legend that I started the engines as I climbed up the ladder before strapping in but, as far as I remember, this was just a story to explain why some of the other pilots took so long to get the engines started. My excuse for trying to get the show on the road quickly was that the Olympus Mk 101 engines were very slow to start, with their relatively small starter motors, and, of course, there were four to get cranked up and patience was never my strong suit.

Charles Masefield, who joined the company some years later, tells the story that on his first flight with me he settled into the right hand seat expecting a briefing. Instead, he claims, there was a blur of hands and we were moving. He adds that once airborne I handed over the aircraft to him, got out a screwdriver and started removing the instrument panel. I find this story hard to believe and, certainly, I have no recollection of it. He may possibly be getting confused with flying with me in the 748 when, it is true, I used to open up the radio compartments and adjust some of the radios, where necessary.

Once the other crew members had caught up, we would go through the after starting checks and confirm that the instrumentation was working properly. The flying control positions were all shown on a special indicator which approximated to a view of the Vulcan from the rear; we could check that all the controls were working satisfactorily as we moved the stick. In spite of this, we still checked for movement in the correct sense with the ground crew, since in 1947 the firm had lost the then chief test pilot Bill Thorn and Roy Chadwick, the Chief Designer, in an Avro Tudor, as a result of the flying control wires being connected in the reverse sense during routine maintenance.

Vulcan Instrument Panel

On this first day I called the control tower, I had been allocated Avro 6 as a call sign, and got permission to taxi out. The ground crew unplugged the 112 Volt supply, removed the chocks and we were on our way. I turned right, taxied up the hill for a few yards and then turned right again down the short runway 36. Ken Cook, the Senior Air Traffic Control Officer, who had been on No. 1 ETPS Course, gave me permission to enter the main runway and I taxied down to the Poynton end. I turned round in the pan at the end and looked to the west on runway 26. Ken spoke to Manchester to get clearance for our take-off, since Woodford was in the Manchester controlled air space, and then we were on our way. The Woodford main runway was only 7,500 ft long, minuscule compared with Boscombe Down, but ample in length for the very powerful Vulcan, especially at the light weights that we were using. As we got airborne I selected the gear up and turned left on to 120° to head out to the east and out of controlled airspace. We had to maintain 3,500 ft. until clear of the airways and the Manchester Control Zone, unless Manchester gave us permission to climb early.

Once clear we started to climb to our first altitude of 35,000 ft and we called the local RAF radar to keep an eye on us. We reached our test altitude in only a few minutes and then we slowly worked through the test plan, turning on the cameras and recorders as required. Stan and Ted kept a log and I tried to carry out the desired manoeuvres as accurately as possible. After about an hour and a quarter we had finished our tests and I had managed to keep the aircraft to the east of Woodford, not too far away. In those days Woodford did not have any radar and we would get homed in by VHF radio, the AEO using Gee to monitor our progress. Manchester radar could see us and we positioned for a straight in approach. The Pennines were situated just to the east of Woodford, Kinder Scout being about 2,300 ft high, and so the safety height for the start of our approach was always 3,500 ft above mean sea level. We slowly reduced altitude as we approached the Woodford runway but we were fairly close to the ground all the way down. Finally, we crossed Poynton main street, the bungalows next to the airfield and then tried to touch down as soon as possible on the runway. It took me a little practice to get it right with the Vulcan and on this first day I tried too hard and we hit the ground rather firmly. I streamed the tail parachute and the flight was definitely over. Our standard procedure was to drop the parachute, if we used it, next to the fire engine and the ambulance which were always waiting at the traffic lights where the road round the airfield crossed the runway; it always seemed to me that their main function was to stop the traffic jumping the traffic lights, a very frequent occurrence. Once the tower had confirmed that the chute had cleared, I turned left and taxied up runway 36, left at the end and then down the ramp finishing between the two hangars where there was only just enough room for the Vulcan without the wing tips hitting the buildings.

We opened the entrance door and the safety equipment inspector, Derek Bowyer, climbed up to our ejection seats and made them safe by inserting the safety pins; Derek and his team soon got to know from experience that they had to be quick, since I had a tendency to leave the seats while they were still live if they were a bit slow. Looking back it seems a terrible thing to have done but wisdom and caution came with age and luckily we never inadvertently fired the seat. In later years I reformed completely and inserted the pins for both seats before I left the flight deck. We went into the changing room, dressed again and then had our debriefing. On this occasion I had not done any critical handling tests so no report was required. The flight test engineers had to wait for the camera film to be developed and then the film would be read by the film readers and the results transferred to tables and graphs.. All very slow by modern standards but very effective if rather labour intensive.

I flew in VX777 for three consecutive days which was slightly unusual. The problem with test flying at a firm is that most of the time is spent preparing the aircraft for tests, the actual flying does not take very long. We did some engine handling and checked how much fuel was unusable by emptying various tanks. The Vulcan had fourteen tanks, seven in each wing, and each tank had its own pump to feed the fuel . There was an automatic fuel proportioner system to feed from the tanks in turn so that the centre of gravity of the fuel, and therefore the aircraft, was kept pretty well constant. We could pump fuel between the front and back tanks to control the centre of gravity and we carried a slide rule to determine where the aircraft centre of gravity g was positioned at any one time. This was very important on the Vulcan since the aircraft was a delta and relatively limited in longitudinal pitching power and, therefore, control from the elevators. The fuel panel was cleverly located on a hinged panel between the two pilots.

I did not fly again for a week which was a long time for someone as impatient as myself. However, besides learning about the Vulcan at Woodford there was an enormous amount of work going on associated with the Supersonic Bomber. A.V.Roe's design office at the time, where all the work was being carried out, was in North Manchester at the Chadderton factory and it was here that all the large chunks of Avro aircraft were built. But Chadderton also housed the company headquarters as well as the design office. All the completed parts would be transported to Woodford and the main assembly sheds were on the north side of the airfield. When the aircraft had been built they would be towed across the runway to the two development sheds, from where we would carry out the flight tests.

The wind tunnels were at Woodford next to the Flight Sheds and a new supersonic blow down wind tunnel had just been completed to check the supersonic bomber design. A very large spherical chamber was pressurised over a period of about two to three hours and then all the air would be released through a small wind tunnel working section, where the air was at mach three plus for about ten seconds blowing over a model of an airplane, in this case the projected supersonic bomber. The tunnel worked well but the noise during the brief supersonic runs was insufferably loud and everything had to stop in the Flight Test offices. Lionel Leavey was the chief of the tunnels and his number two was an engineer I had known when we were both undergraduates at Cambridge, John Scott-Wilson. Our paths crossed again several times during our careers and he became Chairman of the Airworthiness Requirements Board when Peter Baker and I were members of the Board many years later.

The supersonic bomber was a challenging project. It was going to be made of titanium steel, fly at mach 3 and rely on TV Cameras for landing. Roly, Jimmy and I spent a lot of time looking at the flight deck design of the full scale aircraft, as well as at the projected scale models. We also looked at the latest aerodynamic data as it became available from Woodford and Chadderton. It was all very exhilarating to be associated with this work but I suppose I should have realised that the project was beyond the financial capability of the Country.

***

It was September 1956. Some weeks earlier A.V.Roe had just delivered the first production Vulcan Mk.1 to the Royal Air Force. Boscombe Down had given the aircraft an Initial Operational Clearance which meant that the aircraft could be used for flying training and not much else. In their wisdom the RAF had decided that they would make their first Vulcan operation a flight to Australia with Air Chief Marshal Sir Harry Broadhurst, C-in-C Bomber Command, as co-pilot. The aircraft captain was Sqn. Ldr. 'Podge' Howard who had been based with us at Woodford for over a year, learning all about the Vulcan and flying in the aircraft with the Avro test pilots. Apparently the round the world trip had gone very smoothly and the aircraft was due to arrive at London Airport in a glare of publicity. As chance would have it I was on my way down by train to Boscombe Down from London. The weather was appalling, pouring with rain, as the train travelled south of Heathrow on the way to Salisbury. At lunch time I was sitting in the crowded Officers Mess at Boscombe when we all heard the news over the radio. The returning Vulcan had crashed on its approach to the runway at Heathrow; some of the crew had been killed. It was a terrible moment for all of us, for the wives and families of the crew, for the Royal Air Force and for the Country as a whole. I can still hear the announcer reading the news bulletin.

Aircraft accidents only happen as a result of a collection of circumstances, some of them unforeseen, and all happening at the same time; the accident at Heathrow proved to be no exception. The aircraft was doing a Ground Controlled Approach to the runway, had come far too low and the main undercarriage legs had hit the ground just as Howard was taking overshoot action after he realised that he was not going to be able to land from the approach. The undercarriage legs swung back as the ground impact broke the 'drag' links which kept the landing gear in position and the legs rotated backwards hitting the rear underside of the wing. The geometry of the Vulcan was such that the gear hit the wing exactly where the control rods for all the flying controls were situated and this prevented the rods from moving. Consequently, as Howard tried to climb the aircraft away he lost the ability to control it. Both the pilots escaped using their ejector seats but the crew members in the rear cabin were all killed. As bad luck would have it there were not only three RAF regular crew members on the flight but also an Avro product support engineer, Freddie Bassett, who I knew well and who was engaged to the secretary of the experimental flight sheds manager.

There was of course an official Inquiry into such a spectacular accident conducted by a Mr Touche, as well as the normal RAF Court of Enquiry. The facts seemed to be that Howard was advised of the weather conditions at Heathrow, which were poor but did not sound impossible for landing; presumably he had decided to come down to a minimum altitude which would probably have been 200 feet and, from the weather passed to him, he must have thought he would have had a good chance to see the ground. The Vulcan had not been cleared by A&A.E.E. for ILS approaches and so Howard was carrying out an approach using runway approach radar, which was still available at the time though such civilian Ground Controlled Approach radars, GCAs as they were called, were withdrawn shortly afterwards as ILS became the standard civil runway approach aid. GCA in fact consisted of two radars, an azimuth radar to enable the controller to keep the aircraft accurately on the centre line and a vertical radar for monitoring the aircraft's approach path in the vertical plane and informing the pilot of any deviations from the ideal glide slope. The azimuth controller gave steering instructions to the pilot to keep the aircraft lined up with the runway and the controller also advised the pilot whether the aircraft was on the correct glide slope by reference to information provided by the 'tracker', the radar operator tracking the aircraft with the vertical radar. The Inquiry suggested that there seemed to be some doubt as to whether the tracker could actually see the aircraft on the radar due to the very heavy rain, and, therefore, whether the correct deviation of the aircraft from the glide slope was being passed by the GCA controller, but this of course should not have mattered, because the aircraft should not have gone below the approach weather minima.

Unfortunately for all concerned, the aircraft altimeters which gave the two pilots the height of the aircraft above the ground had two fundamental errors, which were not realised by the crew when the aircraft set forth on its world tour, since the aircraft had not been cleared for really bad weather approaches including ILS. Firstly, all purely mechanical altimeters as fitted to the Vulcan at the time would, inherently, have given erroneous information indication due to frictional lags; being a jet engined aircraft the plane was largely free of vibration, unlike a piston engined aircraft, so the reading of a mechanical altimeter would always have been significantly behind the true reading. In later years, this effect was reduced by putting vibrators on mechanical altimeters so that the lag effect was minimised but, at the time, the altimeters on the Vulcan did not have these vibrators and so the Vulcan altimeter would have over read the true height by about 50 ft due to frictional lag.

Secondly, and more significantly, in all aircraft an altimeter actually measures pressure, not height, but, nevertheless, it displays aircraft altitude according to a mathematical conversion formula. If the pressure that is measured is incorrect, then the displayed height will be incorrect. The problem is that all aircraft have to get the pressure from a static sensor situated on the fuselage of the aircraft itself and finding a suitable location which measures true outside pressure requires a lot of testing by the aircraft manufacturer, since a bad location will introduce errors in the indicated height, called position error. The Vulcan static pressure location on Howard's Vulcan not only had a significant position error but it was in the adverse sense so that, on the approach, the altimeter would have over read by about 120 ft. In total therefore Howard on the approach would have been about 170 ft closer to the ground than he would have expected.

Howard would have been under great pressure to land at Heathrow because of the publicity and the high powered welcoming committee. He almost certainly had decided to come down to 200 ft to have a look for the runway before initiating a missed approach procedure; many pilots, myself included, would have made just such a decision. On this occasion, however, the weather was much worse than Howard had been led to believe from the information passed to him and so, when he came near the ground, he would have been still in cloud. If he had decided to go down to 200 feet indicated on the altimeter then this height would in reality be at ground level taking into account all the errors. The vertical tracking radar would have lost the aircraft anyway if it had come so low and so Howard may not have realised he was undershooting. The view out of the Vulcan in rain on the approach was very poor and, unfortunately, Sir Harry Broadhurst, Howard's co-pilot was neither a qualified Vulcan pilot nor in current flying practice so Howard had no one to help him. Such is the way accidents happen and the allocation of blame is debatable. Sitting on the ground it is always easy to blame the crew but it must be questionable whether it had been sensible to despatch the aircraft for such a demanding exercise as a world tour when the RAF had no experience of operating the Vulcan.

We all felt a sense of personal loss for the people who had died, particularly as Freddie Bassett one of our support engineers was on board. We were very unhappy that the aircraft had entered service in such a terrible away. In addition we felt very sorry for Podge Howard who had been put in a very difficult position but, in fact, the

RAF took a very understanding view of the accident. Howard returned to Woodford in due course, understandably very shaken, and then carried on his career in the Royal Air Force as best he could.

***

I spent the next few months flying various development Vulcans, carrying out some of the enormous and very diverse tests that are required to fully certificate an aircraft, be it a civil or a military design. In addition I flew the new Shackleton Mk 3 helping Johnny Baker, the project pilot of the aircraft, with some of the testing including installing the Smiths Industries Mk.10 autopilot; the aircraft was just being cleared by Boscombe Down for squadron service. It was a pleasure to fly this latest mark of Shackleton with a nosewheel landing gear, after the struggles I had had fighting to get the earlier tail wheeled Shackleton Mk1s and Mk2s on the ground.

Shackleton Mk 3

During this period we had three pilots attached to the test pilots' office who were gaining experience of the various aircraft to which they were assigned and they provided a very useful source of co-pilots to augment the flight test observers. Firstly, Sqn. Ldr. Max Savage had replaced Podge Howard as the Bomber Command Liaison officer; he was with us for several years and fitted in well with the team. The other two pilots were employed to fly the aircraft carrying the short range Blue Steel air-to-ground missile being developed on the other side of the airfield to be carried under the V-Bombers. The full scale launching trials were to take place in Australia. In fact the two pilots were both ex-RAF, Tony Jones and Dave Haskett. In addition to these three there seemed to be a stream of visiting pilots authorised by the RAF to fly with us and it was always interesting to show visitors some of the unusual features of the Vulcan.

Vulcan Blue Steel

It was particularly useful to be able to take the design engineers flying and to demonstrate to them the problems that needed solving. These days it would not be permitted and it could be argued that there is now no need because of the excellence of the instrumentation and the availability of flight simulators. Bill Stableford was my favourite designer co-pilot; he was a very gifted mechanical and electrical engineer and designed not only the Vulcan's flying controls but also the autopilot installation. We worked very well as a team and I am sure his flying in the aircraft saved an enormous amount of wasted time, because he could see for himself some of the problems that we were experiencing.

My two most regular co-pilots from flight test were Jack Haddock and Ted Hartley. They were very patient and we got an enormous amount of work done. Neither of them could fly at all but, besides controlling the instrumentation, they operated the pressurisation switches in the air which were situated on the right hand side of the cockpit. If they were not with me and I had a particularly inexperienced co-pilot I operated these switches with my centre of gravity slide rule which was about 15 inches long and quite convenient for the task. On very rare occasions, such as going to the SBAC show or making a delivery to Boscombe Down, I actually flew the aircraft without a co-pilot at all, since the cockpit was so small and well designed that it was very easy to fly alone on the flight deck on a pure ferry in the UK.

Towards the end of 1956 the inevitable happened. Duncan Sandys, the Aviation Minister at the time, had a defence review and the Avro 730 project was cancelled. I was heartbroken; I had joined A.V.Roe specifically for the project and now the future was bleak. Still I suppose I was luckier than Jimmy Harrison; some years earlier he was going to fly the rocket Avro 720 when that aircraft was very nearly ready to fly, so cancelled projects had happened to him twice. I would have been even more upset but for the fact that my wedding was approaching with all the arrangements to be made and, luckily for all of us, Avro's had been authorised to develop the Vulcan Mk.2, a more powerful development of the Mk.1 with a longer range and greater altitude capability.

In fact I had plenty to keep me occupied. There were production and development tasks on the Vulcan Mk.1s, production and development of the Shackleton Mk. 3, there was a Valiant on the airfield used as a 'hack' for Blue Steel development supporting a Blue Steel Vulcan, and, finally, there was always the Company's communication aircraft, an Avro Anson 19 G-AGPG 'aggy paggy' as it was affectionately called. It was slow, viceless and very dependable; I flew many miles in it to Boscombe Down and back for all the numerous jobs and deliveries we had to do. In fact I flew a total of 200 hours during my first year at Avro's, which was not too bad bearing in mind that test flights were rarely more than an hour or so unless we were measuring high altitude cruising performance.

Measuring the high altitude performance of the Vulcan was one of the most time consuming jobs we had to do because each run took about ten to fifteen minutes and it took almost as long as that to stabilise the run before we could start measuring; on many occasions we had to abandon a run after spending a lot of time trying to get started. It never ceased to amaze Jimmy and myself how the effects of the Pennines 40,000 ft below us could upset a run. Basically, we needed to get a combination of power, temperature, altitude and aircraft weight so that we were climbing at about 30 ft per minute which meant that the aircraft weight divided by ambient pressure was constant, called in the technical vernacular W/p; this was the so called cruise climb. We would sometimes find ourselves at John O'Groats or miles across the North Sea; however we always tried to finish our runs over Lincoln ready for our let down to Woodford, though this was not always easy to do.

Cyril Bethwaite ran our Flight Test Department; he was a very experienced engineer and a good administrator. He liked to fly in all our test aircraft so that he could know what was going on. We worked together at Hatfield in later years when he was appointed Project Director on the Hawker Siddeley 146 and I was the 146's first project pilot. Cyril had come from Blackburn's at Brough. Like many really capable scientists and engineers he was an accomplished musician and was learning to play the clarinet, amongst other instruments. I always regretted my inability to play an instrument because I liked all kinds of music from jazz to the classics. I remember Cyril telling me how his clarinet instructor demonstrated to him how Acker Bilk, the well known and very popular performer at the time, was getting it wrong musically but not, I suspect, financially.

We never saw much of Roly Falk. He always seemed to be in London or at Chadderton planning some marketing scheme. He used to fly at Farnborough each year but very rarely flew for the rest of the year. How he managed it I could never discover. He was a natural pilot but he never really liked a very detailed job of work. He had not been trained as a test pilot but somehow he had got himself on Aeroflight at R.A.E. Farnborough when he was in the RAF. He had flown all sorts of aircraft including ex-Luftwaffe jet aeroplanes and consequently he had managed to convince Dobbie, Sir Roy Dobson, that he would be the ideal Chief Test Pilot to develop the Vulcan as a result of his jet experience.

Roly was always trying to sell himself to management and, by the time I arrived on the scene, Jimmy Orrell had been given the task of running the Blue Steel operation which solved the conflict of Roly, as Superintendent of Flying, and Jimmy as Chief Test Pilot. In fact as I have mentioned, Roly with all his quirks, some not too endearing, did a magnificent job selling the delta shape and the Vulcan to the RAF and to the Government. His flying at Farnborough with the model 707s followed by the prototype Vulcans was really superb and the flying formation of the models and the prototypes caught the imagination of the public. There were many stories of how he had to be helped strapping in to his aircraft at Farnborough after having a good lunch in the Avro Chalet and certainly these stories never lost anything in their telling; whether the stories were true or not, his demonstration flying was always immaculate.

The fact that Roly did not feel the need to fly regularly to keep in flying practice was perhaps best illustrated by one year in August when he suddenly decided he was going to do something he had never done before, which was to fly the Shackleton Mk.3. The particular flight he had chosen to fly was a delivery to Boscombe Down and I was going down as a passenger to be dropped off. We took-off with a poor forecast for Boscombe. Roly made one desultory attempt to land when we got there and then we returned to Woodford, much to my disgust. That was the end of Roly's Shackleton flying. We learnt later that he needed to renew his private pilot's licence and, since he did not have the necessary five hours flying in the last six months to apply for the renewal, he was forced to fly the Shackleton. Roly needed the licence since a valid civil licence was required to fly at Farnborough; this was because there was some strange quirk of the regulations which ordained that if we civil test pilots were to fly military aircraft we had to have a civil licence. Strangely, a private pilots licence would meet the regulations, even though it would have been more logical for us to have needed a commercial licence since we were flying 'for hire and reward' as the regulation specifies. Anyway, as I have indicated, the lack of recent flying did not matter to Roly and his flying at the SBAC show was as immaculate as ever.

Flight Testing to Win

John McDaniel, Cyril Bethwaite's deputy and eventual successor, used to say that Roly's main contribution to developing the Vulcan was recruiting Jimmy Harrison and myself, but Jimmy and I would never have had the chance to develop the Vulcan if Roly had not done such a magnificent selling job. He did not stay too long after I joined the firm and managed to get himself appointed a regional sales executive in Mexico. He was one of those larger than life extrovert test pilots who cannot exist to-day, because development flying is now a team effort and cannot depend on individual efforts. However, he was the first pilot who brought home to me the fact that working for a firm is really all about selling the aircraft or its equipment to the customer.

Jimmy Harrison was everything a test pilot should be. Unlike Roly, he had been through ETPS No. 8 Course, and he had had thorough engineering training as an apprentice in the R.A.F. Before joining Avro's, he had also been on Aeroflight and he was definitely a team member. He taught me the way test flying should be conducted, from the pre-flight discussion and briefing to the post flight de-briefing and the need for a fast well written flight report. I well remember one of his comments 'look for all your favourite phrases and cut them out!'. Jimmy became Chief Test Pilot when Roly finally retired a year or so after I joined Avro's. Roly's retirement had been probably quite a lot later than Jimmy would have wished because Roly's presence had inevitably hindered some of the development changes needed on the aircraft but Jimmy never mentioned the subject.

One of my first projects was tailoring the Vulcan Mk.1/Smiths Industries Mk.10 autopilot combination to work effectively. I found that the autopilot experienced all the difficulties flying the Vulcan which were encountered by the human pilot. In theory, it should have been straightforward for the autopilot to fly the aircraft at constant height on the cruise but, in fact, it tended to execute a long period phugoid oscillation, a roller coaster in modern parlance, with the altitude going up and down by two or three hundred feet. This was because on the cruise the mach trimmer, which was provided to give artificial longitudinal stability, would start to extend and interfere with the autopilot pitch control. Consequently, we had to make changes to the autopilot and to the flying controls to make the autopilot control

138

the aircraft satisfactorily. Increasing the autopilot elevator gearing tended to force the oscillation and we needed to adjust the pitch damping very carefully. The problem was compounded by the fact that the autopilot needed a lot of elevator to control the Vulcan but, in the malfunction case, this large amount of control, if unchecked, could break the aircraft. We had to develop a special protection system and then sell the solution to Boscombe Down.

Besides the need for the autopilot to control the aircraft at high mach number, it had to be able to steer the aircraft down the ILS approach and here we met another problem; the quality of the ILS glide slope radiation in those days was very poor and the autopilot would only work on the approach at certain airfields which had good linear beams. We learnt that the terrain at an airfield and the type of glide slope antenna were just as important as the choice of autopilot gain. Glide slope steering is always difficult with ILS beams, because the deviation from the centre line is an angular one and, since the radiating antenna is always at the touch down point, the aircraft is bound to go unstable near the ground as the physical width of the beam gets increasingly small; the trick was to arrange for the instability to take place below the height at which the pilot had to disconnect the autopilot because of ground proximity; for the Vulcan this was about 200 feet. Directionally, there was no real problem with ILS since the radiating cone was at the far end of the runway. We found, therefore, that we could always arrive lined up with the runway, but getting reliable glide slope steering down to an actual 200 ft above the ground was very demanding. In fact, we had to give the aircraft to Boscombe Down without an auto-ILS clearance while the Bomber Command airfields were being fitted with new glide slope antennae which gave decent glide slope propagation without the beam angular deflections being bent and distorted.

No sooner had we despatched the aircraft, XA 894, down to Boscombe Down for an autopilot clearance than we started to prepare for Vulcan Mk.2 automatic landings. Up to that time, all the automatic landing work had been carried out by the Blind Landing Experimental Unit, BLEU, first at Martlesham Heath and then at R.A.E. at Bedford. However, all the aircraft they had used were propeller driven. Nevertheless, it was almost certainly true to say that at that time, with all the equipment still analogue, the UK led the world in this development work. The Vulcan was the first aircraft to be certificated for automatic landings outside the control of BLEU and, not surprisingly, BLEU were somewhat apprehensive about how we would manage; it was rather like a mother releasing a child into the outside world.

Very sensibly, it had been decided that the automatic landing system on the Vulcan Mk.2 should be cleared in stages and that the automatic throttle system should be flown first on a Vulcan Mk.1 together with the new integrated flight system that had been specified for the Vulcan Mk.2. Vulcan XA899 had been allocated for the task and, on the last day of October 1957, we made our first flight in the aircraft; I was accompanied by Derek Bentley in the right hand seat who was the flight test engineer responsible for the automatic landing programme. The throttles seemed to work quite well, though the switching system which had been installed at the request of BLEU to enable the pilot to operate the system, was indescribably difficult to use. We made one or two flights adjusting the optimum gearings. One Saturday morning, when I had taken a day off, Jimmy Harrison flew the aircraft in turbulent weather conditions and reported that the system was almost out of control. It soon became clear that BLEU in their wisdom had decided that the automatic throttle could be made to work by moving the throttles in response to speed error alone. This approach had apparently worked on their piston engined aircraft but was useless for the Vulcan. The problem was that the throttles had to move quite a lot to respond to speed error but this large movement was no use if the conditions were turbulent due to the slow engine response. The throttles became hyperactive and the speed would oscillate wildly around the target speed.. The only way to get the system to work was to use much smaller throttle movements and sense movement in pitch so that if the aircraft pitched nose-up for example, the throttles would move approximately the correct amount to keep the speed constant before the speed started to drop.

BLEU took great exception to being told by us that their design just would not work, but the Smiths Industries design engineers saw immediately the force of our argument and got permission from the Ministry of Supply to redesign their auto-throttle computer to admit pitch as well as speed error into the computation.
140

We flew five months later with their new design and the new auto-throttle switching arrangements and we had no further trouble with the system. I have mentioned this incident to show how easy it is for acknowledged experts to get things completely wrong. As a result of this and many similar incidents, my approach was always to question everything and never to assume that everything I was being told by experts was necessarily correct.

The new flight system we had on XA899 was the Smiths Industries Military Flight System, a development from the Civil Flight System that Smiths Industries had sold to British European Airways for use on their Comets and Vanguards. The idea behind these new integrated systems was to make it much easier for the pilot to fly the aircraft and follow the necessary flight profiles by just looking at two instruments, the artificial horizon and the compass; it was one of the first examples of integration of flight information to make the pilot's task easier. Unfortunately, Smiths Industries had not followed the lead of the United States instrument manufacturers. Their competitors, Sperry, Bendix and Collins had all designed their compasses so that the compass card rotated as the aircraft turned; the pilot had only to look at the top of the card to see which way the aircraft was heading; this of course was the same system as the basic magnetic compass card.

Smiths Industries for some reason decided to do it a different way. The compass information was on a moving needle and the pilot had to keep moving the card; it was no longer instinctive for the pilot to find out which way the aircraft was pointing by looking at the compass card. It seems incredible now but somehow Smiths Industries had managed to sell the system to BEA. Jimmy and I hated it and complained loudly to everyone we could get to listen but of course the contract had been signed and nothing could be done. I asked Captain Majendie, a famous ex British Overseas Airline Captain and then the managing director of the Smiths Industries factory at Cheltenham, why the compass was designed with a moving pointer and he said that this made the compass more reliable. Of course he had to find some excuse to justify the design but the facts were that it was no more reliable, probably less, than moving card designs and most pilots hated it. I have always taken the view that a pilot, whoever he works for, should always insist on what he believes to be right and I have always felt that Majendie let the piloting fraternity down in agreeing to the Smiths Industries engineering design. His job had been to sell the system to the customer, which he had done with great success, but it proved to be a pyrrhic victory for Smiths. The compass design, combined with the design of the artificial horizon which also had its problems, ensured that Smiths Industries would never again sell a flight system to a major airline.

Interestingly, the Smiths Flight System demonstrated once again the adaptability of the human being. Pilots needed a lot of training to use the Smiths system but once they had flown with it for some time they started to extol its praises; the fact that it was not basically instinctive, and required much more concentration to use, did not dampen their enthusiasm. British European Airways and British Overseas Airways pilots who flew the system on their aircraft made no complaints at all as far we knew.

Whilst we hated the compass of the Military Flight System we did not succeed in changing it at all. However, we hit a fundamental design problem on the artificial horizon. The design concept was that if the pilot kept the horizon bar over the glide slope deviation pointer the aircraft would fly smoothly down the glide slope. This was clearly satisfactory for some aircraft but not for all; in the case of the Vulcan, the aircraft would go unstable before it had reached its 200 ft. minimum height. No provision had been made to alter the effective gain between the horizon and the glide slope pointer and, in fact, it was very difficult to make a change since by definition the glide slope pointer should always show the angular deviation. Majendie reacted very strongly to my criticism but I was not about to back down. Eventually he came up to Woodford and flew in the right hand seat of XA899 so that I could show him the problem and he could fly some approaches himself. At the de-briefing after the flight he effectively admitted there was a problem by saying it was not necessary for the pilot to follow the glide slope pointer slavishly all the way down the approach. I was horrified since his attitude was quite unacceptable operationally.

I had got to know the design engineers at Cheltenham quite well by this time and I suppose they had got to know me. They had accepted the design changes to the auto-throttle and they now started scheming how to fix the problem of getting satisfactory glide slope steering. John Gorham was the Project Manager and John Hollington, the lead engineer for the system, provided the intellectual horse power. Gorham flew with me in the front of the aircraft and John in the back and between them they sorted out the necessary changes. The system was never really satisfactory but it worked and, luckily, the Vulcan Mk.2 when it came along was less demanding than the Vulcan Mk.1. John Gorham eventually left Smiths Industries to work for Lockheed on the L1011 installing the latest Collins flight systems into the aircraft; he never came home but started his own consultancy on the West Coast and I used to meet him when I was in Los Angeles on business. John Hollington became Chief Engineer at Cheltenham at about the time I left Woodford to join the Smiths Industries Aerospace Board as Technical Operations Director and we worked together, very effectively, for another fifteen years.

The UK Government procurement arrangements were not really satisfactory at that time. The three Services had to use the Ministry of Supply to place contracts with Industry and the Ministry was not project orientated so that, for example, the radio and radar equipment reported to one head civil servant at the same level as the aircraft procurement. There was no total system approach. The Ministry was responsible for supplying satisfactory equipment to the aircraft manufacturer and, of course, if the equipment did not work the aircraft manufacturer had to be paid for the work involved incorporating the changes. Consequently, the costs of any project always seemed to rise unexpectedly. For example, the Ministry had to pay Smiths Industries and A.V.Roe for all the work correcting the auto-landing development problems we had on XA 899 and that was really a very minor example.

The procurement system was finally changed only after the Nimrod Airborne Early Warning programme failed to work, but the writing had been on the wall for years. I remember Gilbert Whitehead, the Chief Engineer at the time, pleading with the Ministry to have one person responsible for the Nimrod AEW but to no avail.

Flight Testing to Win

I suppose people were just too jealous of their own positions and, of course, there was no way that GEC would agree to report to A.V.Roe on the project. Nowadays, the aircraft manufacturer is responsible for the whole project, usually on a fixed price basis, and it works well; it seems amazing that different Governments kept the Ministry of Supply organisation unchanged for so long. It is true that the Government kept on changing the name of the Department but unfortunately not much else happened.

The Vulcan Mk.2 had a number of major engineering and aerodynamic changes compared with the Mk.1 and as many of these system changes as possible were being evaluated on the Mk.1 in preparation for the first production Mk. 2 aircraft. For example, the Mk 2 was to have a 200V constant frequency 400 cycle AC system with four alternators which, conceptually, was much better than the heavy and unreliable 112V DC system of the Mk.1 but it was going to take a lot of development. Vulcan XA 893 was the Mk.1 aircraft scheduled to develop the electrical system for the Mk.2, and was fitted with a hybrid electrical system, half DC and half AC and the AC was rectified to supply power for the Mk.1 electrics. The aircraft also had a Ram Air Turbine to provide emergency power to the electric power controls in case of failure, though this was only to get the aircraft down from high altitude; an auxiliary power unit, APU, was added to get the aircraft back on the ground.

I did a lot of the flying on this aircraft and it was like a lot of test flying, deadly dull. The AEO spent his whole time switching the alternators on and off, paralleling and switching their output to a large electrical load in the bomb bay which we called the toast rack. Margaret and I went on holiday to Spain that summer and on the way back through Barcelona I chanced to a pick up a copy of the Daily Telegraph. I was amazed to read that Jimmy Harrison, by then Chief Test Pilot of A.V.Roe, had had to bail out of my Vulcan 893 over Lincolnshire due to an electrical failure. When I got back he told me that, somehow, all power had been lost and he knew immediately that he only had a few minutes on the aircraft batteries before he would lose all control. Jimmy did a superb job getting all the crew members safely out of the back of the aircraft and then he and Ted Hartley ejected from the front. Ted loved it since he was a member of the Territorial Army and used to go parachuting for fun. I was very relieved that all this had happened to Jim when he flew my aircraft and not to me. I hoped I would have done as well but I was not sure. There but for the grace of God....

Besides a new electrical system and a new flight system, the Mk.2 was being fitted with much more powerful engines than the Mk.1. The chosen engine was the Olympus Mk.200 starting at 17,000 lb. thrust compared with the Olympus Mk.100 which started with 11,000 lb. thrust. Tommy Frost, who had left B Squadron to become Chief Test Pilot for Armstrong Siddeley at Bitteswell, had not yet started the Rolls Royce flight Test Centre at Filton and so Rolls Royce did not have a test bed for developing the Olympus. We did all their Olympus development at Woodford and I had already done a lot of test work on the Olympus 102 and 104 which were fitted to later production Vulcan Mk.1s. Vulcan XA891 had been allocated as the test bed for the first Olympus Mk.200s and all four Olympus 100 engines had been changed to 200s at the Avro modification centre at Langar near Nottingham. On 20th June 1958 I went over to Langar to collect the aircraft accompanied by Dicky Proudlove who was the flight test engineer in charge of engine development. The engines only had 16,000 lb. thrust initially, but the aircraft was light, and we leapt into the air like a front line interceptor fighter. I pulled the aircraft up into a very steep left hand climbing turn and then did a wing over so that we could fly low over the hangars and the crew who had done all the work. We returned to Woodford feeling very exhilarated.

Engine development was always required to get the right optimisation between performance and handling; in addition, a lot of measurements of the engine blade stresses and strain gauging were required to ensure that the blades were not suffering undue stress or resonance. The Olympus tended to surge if the throttles were advanced too quickly, making a spectacular bang at low level and flaming out at high level. The necessary adjustments to prevent this happening were made on an incredibly complicated analogue fuel control unit, which had innumerable capsules, metering jacks and sensor pipes coming from the engine. Nowadays, digital engine controls make things simple; in those days it was almost a black art to get the engine to run reliably. We spent hours at altitude trying to surge the engines, initially with great ease, and when this happened the companion engine would invariably flame out at the same time because of the common air intake. It needed a very quick reaction from the pilot to get an immediate relight on the two engines using the igniter buttons on the top of the throttles; a failure to get both engines to relight meant losing tens of thousands of feet in order to get the recalcitrant engines to start again. Low level it was easier to sort things out though I do remember going down to Filton one day and flying over the Chief Engineer's office making a double engine surge to emphasise the point that more development work was needed.

Early in 1958 we had been discussing in the pilots office whether the Vulcan could emulate the USAF B47 bomber and carry out 'toss bombing'; the idea was that the safest way to launch an atom bomb was to pull the aircraft up into a loop, release the bomb on the way up, and then do a half roll at the top of the loop so that the aircraft finished up going the opposite way and several thousand feet higher than when the manoeuvre had started. The classic name for this aerobatic was a roll off the top, whilst the Americans called it an immelman. The flight test engineers did lots of calculation and, in particular, John Gilder our performance expert was convinced that all would be well. One day Jimmy Harrison decided to do a roll off the top and it worked exactly as Gilder had predicted. I followed Jimmy's example the following day in XA 894. We started at 330 kt. and 5,000 ft., opened the throttles fully and pulled the stick back until we had 3 g normal acceleration. As the horizon reappeared upside down and the speed dropped, the pull force was relaxed and when the speed was about 170 kt. or less, a half roll was carried out using plenty of rudder to try to keep the sideslip down. It was a great thrill the first time and we soon got used to doing rolls off the top getting more expert as time went on.

***

Author and Jimmy Harrison at Farnborough

1958 was an important year for A.V.Roe as we were getting the first production Vulcan Mk.2 XH533 and we had entered the aircraft for the SBAC flying display at Farnborough. We had also entered XA891 so that we could demonstrate the new engines and this was going to give me my first opportunity to fly at Farnborough. Jimmy and I discussed at length what our demonstrations should be, bearing in mind that we only had six minutes for both aircraft. I decided that with XA891 I would like to do two rolls off the top, one from take-off immediately followed by another one whilst Jim would do a normal horizontal display, albeit with some rolls. In reality, I would have liked to have started my take-off from the far end of the Farnborough runway as I knew this would make the first roll off the top much more spectacular because it would be more readily visible to the crowd but Jimmy was not too keen and it would certainly have caused difficulties for the Farnborough controllers.

Vulcan Mk 2 XH558
The only Vulcan still flightworthy

I spent the month of August practising for Farnborough. I decided that 270 kt. would be adequate to commence the pull up manoeuvre and that we would use a take-off weight of 105,000 lb., giving 5,000 lb. of fuel available for each engine. I started the half roll at 150 kt. and the total gain in height was about 3,000 ft. I immediately throttled right back and dived as steeply as I could so that I was able to start another roll off the top opposite the control tower albeit rather higher than I really wanted at about 1000 ft. I then turned downwind for landing as Jimmy made his first run. My total time from take-off to landing was three minutes and fifteen seconds.

Finally the great day arrived and on 31st August we left for Farnborough. The firm always had to borrow the aircraft from the Ministry of Supply and then insure them for the show. I had a flight test observer, Ted Hartley, in the right hand seat. We had fitted an accelerometer on the flight deck which for this week was going to be our primary flight instrument.

I flew down to Farnborough with a great sense of excitement. Instead of watching passively the exploits of the famous, I was going to have a chance of flying at the Show myself. As we approached the area, the airfield radar got us to join up with a photographic Handley Page Hastings which had had the parachute door removed. We formated as the photographers lent out into the airstream taking pictures and I followed the hand signals moving in, out, up and down. Finally they were satisfied and we left to join the Farnborough circuit.

Looking down we could see the acres of white tents and the flags streaming in the breeze. It was a great moment as we touched down; I held the Vulcan's nose right up in the air for as long as possible and then cleared the runway. We had booked a slot so that we could practise our demonstration and, after some time, we were given permission to start. The practice was watched by the flying control committee chaired by Pat Hanafin, Group Captain Flying at Farnborough, from the top of the Control Tower. I am not sure when the arrangement of checking all the displays was started, but certainly the terrible accident to John Derry some years earlier in the de Haviland 110 when the aircraft went into the crowd had formalised the workings of the committee.

Jim took off first in the Vulcan Mk2 VX777 and then I lined up XA891. I opened the throttles, held the aircraft on the brakes until the power was so great that the aircraft started to slide and then lifted my feet off the brake buttons on the rudder levers so that the aircraft leapt forward. Ted called rotate at 120 kts. and I lifted the aircraft just clear of the ground. I selected the landing gear up and pushed as hard as I could as the aircraft accelerated, pressing the electric trim switch fully forward the whole time. As the end of the runway disappeared from view Ted called 'pull up' and I pulled back until we had 3 g.. I looked up as far as I could through the windscreen, which was not very much and Ted kept on calling the g as we climbed into the sky. I tried to keep the g constant as the speed dropped and then at what I judged to be the right moment as the upside down horizon came into view, I stopped pulling the stick back, applied full aileron and also rudder to ensure that the aircraft rolled. Aileron by itself on the Vulcan at slow speeds generated a lot of yaw and not much roll; yaw in the correct sense made the aircraft roll and hence we always used a lot of rudder as well as aileron at slow speeds.

To my great relief as the ground came into view our wings were level and we could see the airfield where we expected it to be and I dived as steeply as I dared with the throttles closed. As we came opposite the chalets and exhibition halls I did another roll off the top starting at about 800 ft. At the top of the second roll off the top I turned left downwind for landing and as I touched down, Jimmy Harrison flew by doing a roll in front of the exhibition tents.

Landing the Vulcan was always very satisfying to a pilot because it was quite a challenge to do it right. The view was poor and speed control was difficult since the final approach speed, that we liked to use for slow landings, was unstable. The pilot always wanted to have the touchdown speed as slow as possible to reduce the need for wheel braking; if the speed was right it was possible to pull the stick back and raise the nose of the aircraft after touch down which caused a great increase in drag and avoided the need to use the tail parachute. In fact at Woodford on a good day with the wind from the South it was possible to turn left onto the short runway with the nose still in the air, just. The landing speed margin was quite small either way; if the speed was too fast the aircraft had a significant ground effect, particularly on the Vulcan Mk.2, which made it glide seemingly forever down the runway, whilst if the speed was too slow the aircraft would head rapidly into the undergrowth, accompanied by a great thump if it was not close enough to the ground.

One of the givens at Farnborough is that the spectators cannot see an aircraft that is turning left for landing, the normal way on a large aircraft because the pilot is sitting on the left. Consequently, I should have done a right hand circuit, notwithstanding it would have been difficult to see the runway turning finals; it took me a lot longer than it should have done during my many years flying at Farnborough to learn that it was necessary to turn right for landing if anybody was to see the landing.

I landed uneventfully after my practice, taxied to my appointed spot and got out feeling pleased with myself. We took our overalls off and by then my car had been driven down from Woodford. I drove off to the Queens Hotel where we were staying, conveniently situated about 500 yards from the nearest airfield gate and the Empire Test Pilots School. Even better it was this gate that was used for entering the exhibition area.

Traditionally, the A.V.Roe test pilots had always stayed at the Queens Hotel for the SBAC show organised by Philip Kitson, our public relations officer. It was an ideal location for the test flying fraternity of the time; our evening entertainment during the week was spent between the Queens bar and the Empire Test Pilots School bar. It may have been immature but we revelled in it, talking about all the news and meeting all our friends. The only thing we regretted at the time was that there was not a TV camera in the ETPS bar so we could tell in the Queens who was in ETPS. Alas a few years later everything changed for the worse, when the School was moved to Boscombe Down and we lost our focal point after the flying was over. But in 1958 nobody foresaw what would happen and we all had a great time.

The next day was press day and our first demonstration. After breakfast I crossed the road, looked at the A.V.Roe stand and had coffee in the firm's chalet overlooking the main runway. A little later I returned to the Hotel, picked up the car and drove over to the Control Tower car park and went into the pilots tent for the first time for briefing. Pat Hanafin was a very experienced test pilot, though I don't believe he had attended ETPS. More importantly, he had a great rapport with all the pilots; he knew what it was like to fly at Farnborough, he understood the desire of all the pilots to demonstrate their aircraft to the best of their ability and the pressure that the pilots were under. He introduced himself and his team, explained the rules, such as the display line which the pilots were not allowed to cross and the minimum heights. As a result of the Derry accident in the de Haviland 110 some years earlier, no turns were allowed towards the crowd so the aircraft had to be lined up with the runway or pointing away from the crowd as the aircraft went in front of the crowd. This was very restrictive and the rule was relaxed in later years; however it meant that in the first few years I flew at

151

Farnborough it was impossible to keep the aircraft in front of the crowd for very long because of the 'no turning' rule.

After briefing in the pilots' tent we had lunch and re-checked the programme. In plenty of time we drove to our aircraft, got dressed and strapped in. We carried our the check lists and then, at the behest of the tower, slowly taxied towards the start of the runway; the adrenalin started to flow as, for the first time, I looked head on at the tents, the flags and the people, an unforgettable moment. We were given permission to line up and finally the great moment arrived and I was flying in the SBAC show.

All went as planned and as practised and three minutes and fifteen seconds later we were landing again. I felt very pleased with myself and probably let it show in the bar that night. The gilt was taken off the ginger bread slightly because our great rivals, Handley Page, had got their first Victor Mk2 at the show and they too were demonstrating toss bombing, but of course they did not do two in a row as we did.

The following day the trade papers at the show were full of the aerobatics that Jimmy, Johnny Allam in the Victor and myself had carried out the day before. I decided that I would have lunch in the A.V.Roe chalet rather than the pilots' tent in order to bask in the congratulations of the sales team and the senior managers of the Company. After the briefing I drove over to the chalet and after some pleasantries with the people I knew I sat down to lunch, fairly early so that I could be back in time for my allocated slot in the show. Jimmy Kay, our managing director appeared and when he spotted me he rushed over. I had no doubt on the subject; he clearly was going to congratulate me. I remember his words so clearly to this day "Please hurry up, we need your table for lunch".

Looking back, it was probably the best thing he could have said. I don't think it was deliberate. He probably had not been in the chalet on the Sunday for the press day. Later on in my career, I learnt that the seating arrangements at lunch were the one critical thing for companies exhibiting at the SBAC show; the flying display was definitely secondary and was there merely to attract the customers, not to convince them. My ego was definitely dented, which I am sure was good for me. What was important at the time, though I did not realise it until years later, was that I failed to notice, when I was in the chalet, what in fact the watchers could actually see. I did not appreciate the obvious point that a demonstration must aim to present the aircraft for as long as possible in front of the Company chalet. I should have realised that the A.V.Roe chalet was not at right angles to the runway and it was impossible to see the first part of the runway. The other point I did not grasp at the time was that people in the chalet seldom watched the aircraft for long, certainly not while they were having lunch.

I returned to the other side of the airfield to fly and the week progressed steadily. One day it was raining, which was always a challenge to a Vulcan pilot. The windscreen wipers were worse than useless and the view became even worse. In fact, I used to land by lining up the aircraft with the runway and then looking out of the side window. A given touch down speed required a certain height of eye above the ground so the technique was to get the speed correct for the flare with the throttles closed and then keep pulling the stick back to hold the flight deck at constant height; then, as the aircraft slowed down, the wheels dropped onto the runway, hopefully with a satisfying rumble. Of course this technique only worked if the flare speed was right; too slow and there was a horrible bang, hopefully on the runway; too fast and the aircraft seemed to skate forever to the far end of the runway.

At Farnborough, the runway touch-down area was marked clearly in the world-wide approved manner, some way up from the start of the runway. However, in order to enable the pilots to have the maximum take-off distance available, there was a taxi-track which led behind the control tower, round a bend and then joined the runway some two or three hundred yards before the touchdown point. This narrow extension of the runway was called the bottleneck but it was widened to the full runway width about three hundred feet before the permitted landing zone; the bottleneck could not be used for landing because of the proximity of the houses on the main road in Farnborough town.

On this rainy day during the show I adopted my normal landing technique, aiming for the start of the runway, short of the permitted landing markings. I stopped the two outboard engines just before touch down as I usually did when I was demonstrating the Vulcan, to cut down the idling thrust of the engines and thus reduce the amount of braking required. I made an incredibly smooth landing; wet weather always smoothed out landings, probably because the wheels spun up to speed more slowly due to the slip of the wet surface. I hardly needed any braking at all to clear the runway; we never used the parachute unless there was an emergency of some sort.

In the bar that evening someone chided me for landing in the grass. I did not know what they were talking about but early the following morning I drove out to the runway to discover that there were clear tracks of eight wheels, corresponding to the spacing of the left Vulcan undercarriage bogey, on the grass just to the side of the narrow bottleneck. The tracks were about twelve feet long before the wider part of the runway commenced. An hour or so later I met Pat Hanafin by chance in one of the exhibition halls and I immediately apologised for my mistake. He said that there was no problem and that was the last I heard of the incident; in later years the happening would have been made a cause célèbre at the pilots' briefing, probably quite correctly since the Vulcan must have been very low as we crossed the Farnborough main road before landing.

In retrospect, I realise that my desire to touchdown early on the runway was probably due to the way Jimmy Harrison used to demonstrate the aircraft and we had an unofficial competition to see who could touch down first. Jimmy should have realised years earlier that touching down early satisfied only the pilot's ego since we were quite invisible to the watchers in the Chalet. Unfortunately, on this occasion, I was not quite in the middle of the narrow bottle neck so my short landing did not count!

After the flying each day we used to go over to the chalet and have a drink. One day in the middle of the week the public relations officer of Hawkers, David Bainbridge, said that one of the secretaries wished to fly in the Vulcan during the show. This started the rot and I think we flew several passengers in the back of the aircraft during the week. It must have been much worse than a trip in a roller coaster. The intended passenger would be briefed in the morning by Eric Burgess, our engineer who controlled the electrics in the rear of the aircraft. Only the pilots had ejector seats; the three people in the back faced rearwards; they had parachutes but near the ground they would have had absolutely no chance of getting out of the emergency escape chute. There was no view outside in the back except for the bomb aimers window underneath the pilots and it was hard to imagine a more claustrophobic environment. But they loved it. They seemed thrilled with the experience; definitely something to talk about. I was reminded of my favourite Latin tag "haec olim meminisse juvabit" --- one day it will be pleasant to remember these things.

Margaret, my wife, came down at the end of the week and, not to be outdone, also flew in the back. The week finished with two public days on the Saturday and Sunday which were very well attended. In later years I tried to get hold of pictures, stills or movies, of our flying but for some reason there were none available. There was one, taken by Flight magazine I think, of XA 891 vertical at the far end of the runway with a spectator by the runway with his hands over his ears but alas I cannot find it!

After the show was over it was the tradition then for the President of the SBAC to give a champagne cocktail party for the pilots who had taken part in the Show. Jimmy and I took our wives along and as far as I remember we went in Jimmy's car to the middle of the airfield where the President's tent was located. I kept imagining that the champagne was going to run out and I was definitely not in very good shape when we returned to the Queens; the only thing I can remember is carrying Margaret into the hotel, which was the first and last time it ever happened.

I have always been an early starter in the morning and so the following day, despite the previous night's excesses, I drove to the aircraft, with Margaret, to fly back to Woodford. We had a minimum crew, myself, Margaret in the right hand seat and Eric Burgess in the back. I had checked the weather which was not very good at Woodford and getting worse, so we got airborne without delay. I needed to use my slide rule to get the aircraft pressurised. On the way home I rolled the Vulcan because Margaret said she had never been in a roll in a Vulcan and, after a radar let down, we landed at Woodford.

Jimmy Harrison was never an early starter and, unfortunately for Jimmy, Maureen, not to be outdone by Margaret, had insisted on also going back in the right hand seat. It was several hours later before Jimmy got airborne and he was flying XH533, which was equipped with our bête noire, the Smiths Military Flight System.

Jimmy was a superb aerodynamic test pilot, but not an expert on aircraft systems. The development work on this instrument system had been my responsibility and Jimmy had not flown XA 899 very much. Not surprisingly, Jimmy did not like the system but normally it did not matter when he was test flying because he had Max Savage in the right hand seat who could keep the flight system under control by leaning over and adjusting Jimmy's compass.

By the time Jimmy reached the Manchester area the weather was deteriorating fast. Woodford was in the Manchester Control Area and Manchester radar positioned the Vulcan for the Woodford radar to control the approach. Woodford radar was not particularly exact though the controllers always did a superb job bringing the aircraft down so that they could line up with the runway, but there was no vertical radar advisories of height. It took Jimmy three attempts to get in and I don't know to this day how he did it. We were all convinced that he and Maureen were going to have to land at Manchester or at a Bomber Command airfield and that Maureen would have to emerge onto the tarmac. That day was the first and last day that wives flew in the front of the Vulcan, or in the back for that matter.

Margaret asked me in the evening after we got home whether having her on board the aircraft made any difference to my flying. I, perhaps unwisely, told her the truth that, as far as I was concerned, when I flew an aircraft I was only concerned to fly it as well as I possibly could and land safely, regardless of the passengers. I believe that this is true of all pilots and I am always amused when I hear the argument advanced by airline pilots that flying large aircraft with so many passengers is such a great responsibility that they need to be paid extra money. In my experience, the larger the aircraft, the easier they are to fly and, incidentally, the more help the pilots get from the systems within the aircraft and from the dispatchers on the ground. I am sure that were I a senior airline pilot I would advocate the same arguments as the airline pilots but, in reality, I believe that a pilot is not influenced by any other factors but the need to get the aircraft back on the ground safely, having met the operational requirements.

Incidentally, test pilots in the UK Aircraft Industry did not have a Union. We got paid much less than airline pilots, unlike the French test pilots who not only got a lot more than their airline pilots, but paid no income tax. Most people who did not know the situation thought we got danger money but nothing was further from the truth. The facts were that the UK Industry had lots of people who wanted to be test pilots and the firms operated a market economy. In France the job was considered dangerous and comparisons were made with steeplejacks. Moreover, I think the French firms valued their pilots more than UK firms.

Flying at Farnborough for the first time had been a marvellous experience for me . However, aerobatics in the Vulcan soon came to an end. We had delivered the very first Vulcan prototype, XV770, to Rolls Royce fitted with the latest Conway engines which were to go in the Victor Mk 2. My great friend from the RAF in Germany, Keith Sturt, was doing most of the flying. One day Keith was flying the aircraft at the Syerston air display and the aircraft broke up and crashed during a straight run past the crowd. There was an amateur movie sequence of the break-up and the experts said that Keith had been exceeding the maximum permitted speed. I was not so sure. We knew that the Rolls Royce crews had been rolling and half looping the aircraft. Keith was not a reckless pilot. What Rolls Royce maintenance engineers did not know was that the engineers at Woodford always used to inspect the Vulcan nose ribs when we were doing aerobatics even though this inspection was not a regular one described and listed in the maintenance manual. The space was very small and Woodford had a special man who could do the job. Damage was often found to the nose ribs which had to be repaired, especially if the pilot had pulled a little too much g. I don't believe that the Rolls Royce engineers had been routinely checking the nose ribs and it is my belief that the aircraft was probably damaged before Keith took-off that day.

We got a letter a few days after the accident from the Ministry of Supply saying in effect that enough was enough and, as far as I know, we never did any aerobatics again in the Vulcan. Perhaps it was just as well, as our debate in the pilots office had not been restricted to rolls off the top. Gilder had calculated that we should be able to do loops as well. However, the loop was a much more serious proposition since, during the last part of the manoeuvre, the aircraft would be pointing straight down at the ground and only by pulling g could the aircraft be recovered back to level flight but, unlike a fighter aircraft, the Vulcan only had a maximum of 3 g available; if the aircraft was too close to the ground when it was vertical it would either break up through the pilot pulling too much g or it would hit the ground. I always remembered the terrible saying that Dicky Martin, ex Chief Test Pilot of Glosters, had taught us — 'you could always tell how good the display pilot was by the angle at which he hit the ground.'

There was another problem about looping the Vulcan. The view out of the aircraft was nothing short of appalling; we had problems enough trying to keep straight doing a roll off the top. If we were to do a loop we would not know, until too late, whether we had kept the wings level and, if the wings were not level, then we would be carrying out a rolling pull-out which was even more demanding on the aircraft structure than a symmetrical application of g. It was with some secret relief that we heard that we were forbidden to do any more aerobatics and no longer had to agonise on whether to carry out our first loop.

***

Coming back to Woodford after the heady experience of flying at Farnborough was rather a depressing experience, but only for a moment or two. There was work to be done. We had only just received the first real Vulcan Mk.2 in time for the SBAC show and there were many corners of the flight envelope to be explored before we could offer the aircraft to A&AEE for a full CA release. I spent a lot of time carrying out engine development flying in XA 891, not that the engine was bad but the analogue fuel control unit needed a lot of tuning.

In October, I managed to get my first flight in a Victor Mk.1 courtesy of Graham Moreau at Boscombe Down. It was an interesting experience to fly a competitor's aircraft, built to the same specification as the Vulcan. The aerodynamic design was much more conservative, though it had a high tailplane which meant that under some conditions if the aircraft stalled there was no way of recovering except perhaps by streaming the tail parachute as a last resort; the elevators were completely useless in a stall being immersed in stagnant air from the wings. However, the Victor had a much better cabin layout than the Vulcan; the crew were behind and slightly above the pilots and so the crew could all see each other which encouraged a feeling of togetherness. The provisions for rear crew escape, or the lack of such provisions, were exactly the same as the Vulcan, but the Vulcan crew were definitely better off, providing the nose landing gear was up, since they could drop out of the escape chute while the Victor crew had to go out sideways with the wing and the engine intakes right behind the door.

The three V Bombers

The pilots' view over the nose was slightly better than the Vulcan, particularly as the aircraft was not so nose-up on the approach. Flying the approach was also easier since the aircraft had speed stability and much less concentration was required to keep the desired speed. However, the touch-down speed was at least 10 knots higher than the Vulcan and there was no aerodynamic drag, so there was no way of stopping without streaming the tail chute. As is usual in these circumstances, the Victor pilots liked the Victor and the Vulcan pilots thought that the Vulcan could do no wrong. Later on I did a lot of flying in the Victor Mk.2 but I always preferred the Vulcan, not because my firm built it but because, in the end, the thing that really mattered in any aircraft was how easy it was to get back on the ground safely and be able to stop. As far as I was concerned the Vulcan scored hands down.

Of course I was still flying the Valiant on the Blue Steel programme from the other side of the airfield so it was interesting to be able to compare all three V bombers. The Valiant was very pedestrian but very easy to fly, though the artificial control forces from the air filled dustbins that provided the feel were very high.

That autumn I felt that I was not being sufficiently stretched mentally or doing enough flying to be kept busy. My wife, who was teaching all day, and I signed on for an external economics degree course at Manchester University. For me it was very different from the precise sciences I was used to and I liked the fact that there could be a difference of opinions on a subject. Sadly my school, which taught me mathematics superbly, had had no time to teach me the humanities. Unfortunately, I was only able to do one year but the thing I remember best from the course was not the economics, but the philosophy that our tutor Stephen Baddeley propounded with enormous enthusiasm. Not that the other tutors did not do a good job teaching economics, it was just that economics did not lift the spirit in the same way as philosophy.

The reason why I did not finish the course and had to give up economics was because Avro's had decided to re-enter the civil marketplace and manufacture an airliner again, which as far as I was concerned was good news. It was to be called the Avro748. All Avro's designs, whether they ever saw the light of day and left the final assembly sheds or not, were given a design number; the Vulcan was 698, the 707s were just that, the supersonic bomber was allotted 730 and the models 731, and the new airliner was given the number 748, by chance just one more than the Boeing 747. However, unlike the 747 this aircraft was to be a small, twin engined turboprop aircraft using two Rolls Royce Dart engines and carrying 48 passengers. The marketing concept justifying the decision was that there were still thousands of old twin piston engined Douglas DC3s, Dakotas, flying around the world, flying into appalling airfields, without the ability to fly on one engine in the event of failure. A.V.Roe decided therefore that there was a gap in the market for the 748, certificated to the latest civil safety requirements, which could operate safely into these difficult airfields under all conditions with a really short take-off and landing capability and actually replace the DC3s. I was delighted as I now had something to which I could look forward and for which I needed to prepare.

***

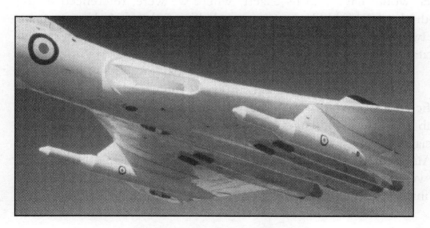

Vulcan Mk2 with Skybolts

In fact the Vulcan development was still proceeding fast with a major new programme. The UK had decided that the Vulcan should carry the United States air launched ballistic missile, the Skybolt, being developed by the Douglas Aircraft Company in Santa Monica, California. Two Skybolts would be carried, one under each wing; each

161

Skybolt weighing 15,000 lb. In order for the Vulcan Mk.2 to be able to do this the wing of the aircraft had to be strengthened considerably; the design work was carried out and modified airplanes emerged from the production line. The powers that be decided that it was necessary for an unmodified Vulcan to go to Edwards Air Force Base in the Mojave desert to have certain trials carried out and Vulcan XA535 was the aircraft chosen.

I immediately volunteered to take the Vulcan to Edwards. Trips like that were very rare for industry test pilots and the trip would be not only my first overseas flight but also my first visit to the USA. We planned the flight meticulously, particularly as the aircraft had very little navigation equipment. I was determined to do the trip in one day since the airline Boeing 707s were flying routinely from London to Los Angeles and, to my mind, it would have emphasised how little fuel the Vulcan really carried if we had had to night stop on the way. Dicky Martin came with me and we flew to Goose Bay in Canada to refuel. The second leg to Edwards against a headwind was a much more critical leg, particularly as we did not carry a TACAN receiver, which would have told us exactly where we were, referenced to the hundreds of TACAN beacons situated all over the USA. However, we had two RAF navigators in the rear of the aircraft and we even carried a sextant.

We flew at 50,000ft well above all the airliners so that the air traffic controllers let us do what we liked and we were able to cruise climb for optimum range; this sort of flying had been one of my specialities when I was in the RAF and I remember writing an article in 'Air Clues', the Royal Air Force magazine introducing the concept. We were able to put precept into practice, all went well and we finally got into contact with the Edwards radar six hours after leaving Goose Bay.

Flying over California and landing at Edwards Air Force Base was a dream come true as far as I was concerned. It had always been my ambition to do test flying in the USA where all the advanced flying was taking place and I had even written to Boeing in Seattle to try to get a job, but to no avail. In fact I also had tried to get on to the space programme in response to an advert in Aviation Week but the reply pointed out that only US born citizens were being considered.

In England we were used to flying over the green countryside and distinguishing the airfields from other features; in California we had to get used to looking over the desert and distinguishing airfields from various shades of brown. The lake bed by Edwards seemed vast as we let down to land and saw the enormous runway running straight on into the sand. We taxied in to the ramp and were met by Fitz Fulton who had come to Woodford a few month earlier on a briefing visit; Fitz later became a very distinguished test pilot for NASA. In fact many of the pilots we met there, later had distinguished aviation careers either in the services or in industry.

Vulcan 2 and B52 at Edwards

That evening, after our arrival, we went into Lancaster with our resident Skybolt representative, Harold Newton, based near the Douglas plant in Santa Monica, and ate in his favourite Mexican restaurant. Dicky and I kept dropping off to sleep since, by our UK clock, it was 4am in the morning and we had been flying for 14 hours. The proprietor claimed never to forget a face and even offered a free meal to anyone who had come back a second time for a meal and who he had failed to recognise. Dicky at about dessert time, woke up and exhibited a pyromaniac tendency by trying to set fire to the paper Mexican ornaments suspended from the ceiling, a very unwise thing to do bearing in mind the ultra dry atmosphere of the desert. The whole incident was very immature but I suppose we were feeling quite unjustifiably pleased with ourselves at the time. Harold told us later that when he returned for another meal he was hoping that he was going to get a free meal until the owner suddenly appeared and turned him out of the place just as he was starting to eat.

The following morning I had to taxi the aircraft to the spot in the desert where the radio equipment evaluation was to take place. Unfortunately I had ignored my basic rule of never trusting the experts and my local co-pilot, who claimed he knew the exact location of where we were to go, got completely lost and I was forced to taxi over some hard packed rocks to reach the site; this proved to be a very costly few yards as a completely fresh set of tyres had to be sent out from England for our return flight. Dicky and I then drove down to the Georgian hotel in Santa Monica where we stayed for a day or so, paying a duty visit to Disney World at Anaheim.

Author and B47

After Dicky returned to England I went back to the desert and did some flying in some USAF aircraft; I managed to get my hands on the B47 which was becoming quite a rarity; I flew with Jack Allevie who had been on No.12 at ETPS and so understood British English. It was a fantastic flight; the view through the clear large canopy seemed limitless and I was able to carry out several landings on the lake bed. I also flew the B52 with Fitz and the F100 with Bob White, getting my first experience of supersonic level flight. Before leaving, Fitz took me to a meeting of the burgeoning Society of Experimental Test Pilots and I enrolled, probably the first UK member. I was pleased to have the opportunity at the time and in later years they made me a Fellow of the Society, which made me very proud. Whenever I had the chance I would attend their annual symposium at the Beverley Hills Hilton in September; the technical standards of the papers were very variable but it was wonderful to have the opportunity to meet so many new contacts and old friends.

Author and B52

Besides flying in the B52 we managed to do a photographic sortie with a Vulcan formating on a B52 and I believe this was quite a popular postcard on the Base for some time. Ossie Hawkins, who had joined our team at Avro's, and I flew the Vulcan back from Edwards a month or so later, again without an overnight break. We landed at dawn, not at Woodford, where the weather was below limits, but at Manchester next door making an ILS approach. I suspect this was illegal and that we should have landed at some Bomber Command airfield but we wanted to get home to bed. The incident would have gone unnoticed except for the fact that Dicky, who went over to reposition the aircraft when the weather cleared, apparently blew a lot of tarmac away as he taxied out for take-off.

RAF Engineers changing wheel at Gan

In fact 1961 was a good year for ferrying aircraft around the world. In December we had to take the Blue Steel development Vulcan to Edinburgh field in Australia. Johnny Baker who left Woodford to become the Chief Avro Blue Steel pilot in Australia was my co-pilot. We had to use RAF bases and we chose to go via El Adem in North Africa, Aden, Gan in the Maldive Islands, Changi in Singapore and then direct to our destination. We had no supporting aircraft or tail parachutes but I insisted on taking a spare pair of wheels. We stopped for our first night in Aden but had to park on a generally unused part of the apron because of a visit by some member of the Royal Family. The following day we left for Gan and landed in a downpour; as usual I kept the nose of the aircraft in the air after touchdown as long as I could but was horrified when I lowered the nose wheels and started to brake, well below the theoretical

166

aquaplaning speed, that nothing happened as we skidded along the tarmac. We did stop just before the end but it was an unnerving few seconds.

The following morning we discovered we had a puncture from a nail we had picked up in Aden; my pair of wheels came into their own but the problem was how to jack the aircraft without the right gear. The RAF crew in Gan were magnificent; they made a 3ft wooden ramp just wide enough for a pair of Vulcan wheels and then they towed the aircraft up the ramp so that half the eight wheel bogie on one side of the aircraft was in the air. They had put a very small batten at the end of the ramp which was just as well since once the Vulcan on the tow started to go up the ramp, the wheels took the whole wooden ramp along with them; without the batten the aircraft would have dropped off the end of the ramp like a stone and might have been damaged badly. Once stationary again the crew soon changed the damaged set of wheels. Luckily, I had had the foresight to bring my snorkel and flippers with me and so was able to have an extra day swimming inside the coral reef, five yards from my room in the mess, looking at the most amazing and colourful fish in the world. I still feel to-day that I was incredibly lucky; at the time Hans Haas had a TV show full of shots of swimming underwater, also in the Indian Ocean, from his three masted yacht Xarifa, but I was sure that his fish were as nothing compared with mine.

The following day we flew to Changi in Singapore, still an RAF base at the time but now the world famous international airport. We prepared for the final leg the following day. The airfield was still quite short, 2000 yards I believe, but I had worked out that it was just possible, first thing in the morning when the temperature was cool, for the aircraft to take-off at full fuel load. We got up well before dawn and took off while it was still dark; the end of the runway seemed to come up very quickly but we just made it and arrived at Edinburgh Field near Adelaide six hours and forty minutes later; unfortunately the great continental interior was obscured all the way by a red dust cloud. Before returning home I managed to go to Melbourne and visit the Royal Australian Air Force test establishment where I met up with Vince Hill from my ETPS course and Milt Cottee who flew the Valiant flight when the main spar cracked

167

through a fatigue failure. The thing I remember about the visit was arriving at the London hotel in Melbourne at 5 o'clock in the evening which, in those days, was the universal Australian closing time; the space on the very wide steps leading up to the entrance was completely taken by the local male population exuding bonhomie and I was a bit nervous forcing my way up into the hotel.

In due course we got our first production Vulcan Mk.2, XJ784, with 21,000 lb. engines and rapid engine starting so that we could start all four engines at the same time and have them idling in about 40 seconds ready for take-off; this capability was to meet an operational scramble requirement when the other side had launched their missiles or were flying towards the UK. Jimmy was by this time getting involved with the first 748 so I looked after XJ784. Rolls Royce at Filton had by now got a flying test bed and had cleared the engine handling, or so they said. In fact the engines surged the way all new Olympus engines had always surged and the development team from Bristol had to visit us, look at the records and develop the engine just as they had always done.

I was looking forward to taking XJ784 to Farnborough in 1962, being towed to the side of the runway and, when the control tower fired a green very light, I was going to start all the engines and get airborne in less than a minute with 84,000 lb. thrust and an aircraft weight of about 105,000 lb. However things did not work out. Jimmy Kay our managing director, who had taken over from Dobbie when Dobbie went to head Hawker Siddeley in London, had to leave due to a Board Room row involving Harry Dobson, works manager and Dobbie's son. Air Chief Marshal Sir Harry Broadhurst, 'Broady', whose career had not been impaired by his rapid exit from the Vulcan at Heathrow, had just retired and was appointed to take over from Jimmy Kay. The RAF had only agreed to his rapid appointment to Hawker Siddeley, Manchester Division, because they wanted to get some of the Vulcan programmes back on schedule; Sir Harry took the view that we could not afford the time to have XJ784 at Farnborough; it would slow up engine development. Despite my pleading he would not change his mind.

Luckily Vulcan XH533 had re-emerged from the experimental flight hangar equipped for the automatic landing development, so that I had some interesting flying to do instead of fuming over not being allowed to fly XJ784 at Farnborough. The aircraft had the latest automatic throttle changes, which we had developed on Vulcan Mk.1 XA899, a radio altimeter which was new to the Vulcan and the Leader Cable Receiver. Everything functioned well and we were soon able to let the autopilot control take the aircraft down the glide slope, turn left from the localiser onto the runway centre line when the Leader Cable signal was picked up and then flare according to the design control law based on the height output from the radio altimeter. In fact things went so well that I flew Ray Bray, an R.A.F. Bedford test pilot, in the right hand seat to demonstrate our rapid progress. Apparently, in flying Ray I had inadvertently transgressed some rule which said that we should not carry out an automatic touch-down until Bedford said that it was all right for us so to do. The following week at Farnborough I discovered that an interfering auto-landing technician at Bedford had reported me to Director Flying but luckily common sense prevailed and we heard nothing more at Woodford.

I flew with Jimmy Harrison in the new Avro 748 at Farnborough. Even though the speeds were a lot less than the Vulcan, the demonstration which Jimmy did was very exacting, in order to get the best out of the aircraft in the time available. As usual, there was very little fuel on board and the aircraft was virtually empty except for Jim and myself; we occasionally carried a passenger who we wanted to spoil in the jump seat. The highlight of the flight was the landing since we needed to show the incredibly short runway distance required by the aircraft; potential customers had to be made to believe that the aircraft really could replace the Dakota. In order to get maximum braking it was necessary to get the wheels on the ground as soon as possible and then select propeller ground fine pitch at the same time as stamping on the brake pedals. Occasionally, we got it wrong and put the brakes on before the wheels were on the ground which was extremely embarrassing as there was no anti-skid protection on the wheels until they had spun up to speed; premature braking resulted in scrubbing the tyres, normally causing the tyres to deflate completely.

Flight Testing to Win

Demonstrating the Avro 748 at Farnborough, or anywhere else for that matter, was much more important than demonstrating the Vulcan. With the Vulcan we had a captive customer and, in reality, we were just showing off the aircraft itself, demonstrating the firm's prowess and of course drawing the crowd. With the Avro 748 we had real competition and we needed to persuade potential customers that our aircraft was the one for them. Right from the first flight, we all knew that our job as test pilots was not just to get the aircraft certificated; we had to sell it for the good of the firm and ourselves.

My next few months were spent developing the automatic landing system, carrying out crew training with the Aerolineas Argentinas pilots, who had arrived to collect their first 748 aircraft, and doing the development work on the Skybolt aircraft, XH537. At that time, without the help of simulators, fine tuning an aircraft to get repeatable automatic landings under all weather conditions was very time consuming and the Vulcan was no exception. Many landings had to be made, varying the large number of autopilot gearings and the various switching heights for the leader cable and the radio altimeter. Directionally we had no real difficulties; our problem was to make sure that the aircraft landed firmly, that it did not float down the runway but that it touched down in the designated area, allowing plenty of room for stopping. If we came in slowly the aircraft would thump on the ground in windy conditions and if we came in too fast it would float right down the runway. I finally realised that it was necessary to vary the normal approach speed for weight by a factor which varied with the headwind component of the actual wind. Once we adopted that solution we had no further problems and the longitudinal dispersion, that is the range of touch down positions, was satisfactory. However, it took us some time and several hundred landings to reach our final settings, just in time, in fact, to coincide with the RAF deciding that the V Force did not need automatic landing capability after all. I did not mind too much; I had learnt a lot which was to prove very useful in later certifications and in my subsequent career with Smiths Industries.

What was so sad about all the work that was done in the United Kingdom on automatic landing was that the UK never really benefited. The Trident was certificated with its triplicated analogue system and scores of boxes and the system worked very well for

British European Airways. However, because the aircraft was not bought by another overseas airline in large quantities, certainly not one that cared about automatic landings, no more equipment was sold. By the time the equipment was fitted as standard, autopilots had gone digital and neither Smiths Industries nor GEC provided airline autopilots equipped for auto-landings. Smiths Industries did have a chance later with the Airbus programme when they were leading the autopilot work, but when the UK withdrew from the Airbus project, the French firm SFENA took over the lead and the chance was lost. In fact, airlines were ambivalent for many years about automatic landings because of the cost of keeping the crews trained, but modern flight simulators have rectified this situation.

***

The Vulcan was always a very interesting aircraft aerodynamically. Its 'high speed' performance above .9M was atrocious and its low speed handling on the approach was not particularly good either. I always used to think that at really low speeds with the stick fully back, the aircraft was fairly innocuous but there was one accident at Boscombe Down with Ossie Hawkins which resulted in the rear crew members being killed. We never really understood what had happened but we believed that Ossie was demonstrating the low speed handling to his Boscombe co-pilot. It may be that Ossie allowed excessive sideslip to build up with the stick fully back so that the aircraft went into a spin. Ossie could not recover the situation which was made worse by the windscreens fogging up for some reason so the pilots could not see out. The two pilots used their ejector seats but it was not possible for the Boscombe Down Royal Air Force navigators in the back of the aircraft to bale out. Certainly in all the thousands of hours I did on the Vulcan, I had no idea that this situation was possible and, I suspect, we were all a lot more careful when we did slow speed flying after the accident. Jimmy Harrison very nearly lost his job because, as usual, the flying regulations and the authorising procedures were not followed to the letter but that is often the way with accidents.

The Skybolt programme was an important one and I was delighted when we were able to fly the Skybolts on the Vulcan for the first time; the missiles weighed 15,000 lb. each on an empty aircraft weight of 100,000 lb. so the aircraft was much heavier than usual. On the day of the first flight with two missiles attached we had, as bad luck would have it, a very senior Air Marshal from the Ministry of Defence visiting Woodford with Broady in attendance. We got airborne on our very carefully planned flight but the undercarriage had barely retracted when I got a message from the control tower to fly past the Woodford Club House to show off the Skybolts. I must admit that I did not take kindly to the instruction but submitted to the order with bad grace; Sir Harry was wise enough to know that if I did not like the handling of the aircraft I would have refused to come and my reluctance was really due to the fact that we had worked out a test plan which we were now going to have to change. Anyway I did a couple of low very noisy runs and then we left to measure the effects of the missiles on the basic Vulcan.

Interestingly, the only really noticeable aerodynamic effect of the missiles on the Vulcan was during landing. The Vulcan always had a pronounced ground effect if the speed was a bit faster than it should have been but, with Skybolts on, the ground effect was incredible and I was forced to push the aircraft very firmly onto the ground and use the tail parachute; I suppose the effect was predictable because the missiles were so close to the ground and during landing the air was trapped underneath the very large wing with the Skybolts acting as fences, so that the air had nowhere to go.

The first flight with only one Skybolt was also interesting. We had a very careful pre-flight briefing from John Scott Wilson, who by then was Chief Aerodynamicist, which concluded that the effect of having a single missile would barely be noticeable from an asymmetric viewpoint, which proved to be absolutely true. However nobody realised, including me, until five seconds into the take-off, that the inertial effect of only having one missile would be very large indeed during accelerations. As I released the brakes the aircraft apparently swung towards the missile and I needed what seemed like full nosewheel steering and a lot of brake to keep it straight. I pulled the aircraft into the air with a large slug of rudder against the missile wondering what was going to happen next, but the moment I reduced power and started to climb at constant speed every thing seemed back to normal. I mention this incident because it shows that, even with the

172

most erudite scientists and engineers, mistakes can occur but fortunately these mistakes are now very rare. A flight simulator would have shown the effect immediately.

Summing up the Vulcan, it was a lovely aircraft to fly in many ways. A large airplane with a fighter control column and almost fighter responses. However, it is amazing that an aircraft with such a poor view and very demanding low speed handling could have been so universally accepted by the Bomber Command crews. Luckily, it was only used once in wartime, against Argentina; with the help of all the flight refuelling resources of the Royal Air Force, one aircraft dropped a few 1,000 lb. bombs on the runway at Port Stanley in the Falklands

Flight Testing to Win

CHAPTER 5

El Avro and other aircraft

Avro 748 Series 2 at Santos Dumont, Rio de Janeiro

The launch of the Avro 748 in 1959 was a very significant turning point for me, as well as for A.V.Roe. There were still thousands of Douglas DC3s flying around the world, into appalling airfields because the aircraft were available, cheap and there was no replacement aircraft that could do the job to modern safety standards. A.V.Roe's decision that there was a gap in the market for the 748 was operationally accurate, but I wonder now whether they had forgotten, or chosen to ignore, the fact that the countries that needed the aircraft the most, generally speaking, did not have any money. In the event Avro's made quite a few 748s but not their fortune out of the aircraft. The 748, or 'El Avro' as it was affectionately called, became well known all over South America. Unfortunately, Hawker Siddeley unfeelingly made A.V.Roe and Co. Ltd. call itself the Manchester division of Hawker Siddeley, forgetting or perhaps not caring that 'El Hawker Siddeley' not only did not have the same ring in Spanish as El

Avro but that it was also unpronounceable to the Spanish and Portuguese speaking people of South America. On the same theme of lack of market awareness, we were allowed some years later to have a brand new demonstration 748 aircraft and we had the opportunity to have it registered G-AVRO; however nobody was brave enough to authorise us to use this registration. It was, in my view, a wonderful sales opportunity wasted because junior aspiring corporate executives were afraid to question their superiors. It really hurt me every time I saw Britannia's Boeing 737 G-AVRO flying into Manchester.

Armstrong Whitworth Argosy

I realised straightaway that flying a civil aircraft would give me an opportunity to get away from the constraints and purposes of military flying. I had become envious of civilian test pilots and their ability to fly around the world and, in truth, I did not really relish what we were trying to achieve with the Vulcan, namely carrying atomic bombs into deepest Russia. Coincidentally, the Hawker Siddeley Group which owned A.V.Roe had just had another reorganisation so that the Armstrong Whitworth division at Bitteswell had become unified with us. We were in fact taking over their operation, closing Bitteswell in due course, and thus getting the benefit of economies of scale, using a phrase my economics teacher had just taught me. Our new name, the first of many in the next few years, was to be Avro

Whitworth, and we now became responsible for the Argosy, a twin boom transport aircraft with civil as well as military applications.

I was asked by Cyril Bethwaite, whose flight test empire had suddenly increased, to help with the stalling programme on the civil variant which was giving some problems. This gave me my first taste of meeting the British Civil Airworthiness Requirements, BCARs, and I realised that this document was infinitely more formal than the military Av.P 970 requirements, for the obvious reason that a lot of commercial money depended on the ability of the aircraft to meet the rules. BCARs were broadly speaking similar to the requirements of other countries which had their own certificating authority. Every country in which the HS748 operated would have to be satisfied that the aircraft complied with their own certification rules as well as the UK rules..

The Avro 748 decision was a turning point in my career and though I did a lot more military flying on different types of aircraft as the years went by, my heart was set on eventually concentrating just on civil aircraft. Consequently, pilot licensing became an issue since I was not prepared to fly the 748 on a private pilot's licence. I did not wish to be looked down upon by the airline pilots with their Airline Transport Pilots Licences, ATPLs as they were called. Furthermore, I wanted to be able to fly the aircraft for hire and reward. Consequently, I decided that I needed to acquire an ATPL.

The syllabus of an Airline Transport Pilots Licence covered a lot of ground including a considerable amount of theoretical work on radio and astro-navigation systems. The received wisdom was that a lot of studying was required and it was probably best to attend a full time course. I elected to try to pass the exams by doing a correspondence course and Jimmy Harrison kindly agreed that the firm would pay. I signed on for the course with a firm called Avigation and booked the examination at the same time, allowing about six weeks for the studying. The paperwork arrived and the postman had a very hard time delivering the material; in fact I think it came in two very large parcels. The concept of the course was that the student would do a section from a particular subject, fill in the answers at the back, send it off for marking and then learn from the mistakes when the marked papers eventually were returned. It seemed to me that months would go by before the course would be finished and I was far too impatient for that. Luckily, Avigation were very helpful when they discovered that I had already booked the exam and parted with money; they informed me that I would need yet another large packet, the official answers to the questions if I was to have any chance of passing the exam, and a few days later the postman had to make another difficult delivery of very big envelopes.

Life came to a stop at our house in Woodford. Margaret was magnificent and excused me from all work except studying and about a month after I started I went up to London for the two day exam. There was a third day, a week or so later, when I had to have an oral examination on the stars; I was not too concerned over my performance on the written examinations but I did not do particularly well answering questions on the stars since all I knew were the Great Bear and the Pole Star, even though I had done some homework on some of the other famous constellations. I suppose I felt that there was not much chance of having to use an astro-sextant in the years ahead. Anyway, my lack of knowledge of the Universe did not seem to matter and my hard work paid off. Margaret and I were both delighted when the post arrived one day and I learnt that I had passed first time, with some rather spectacularly high looking marks. The penalty for all this work was giving up my economics studies which, in hindsight, was a great shame. My philosophy tutor told me sadly that I had quite a good brain going to waste!

Passing the exam did not unfortunately enable me to get a licence. To start with I was very short of the necessary flying hours. The regulations said that I had to have a certain number of hours navigating from one airfield to another. I also needed a lot more hours flying at night. The examinations requirements for a Senior Commercial Pilots Licence and for an ALTP were the same but the flying hour requirements were less and so I decided I had better get an SCL first. I solved the night flying requirement by getting permission to fly a Shackleton from Boscombe Down to Gibraltar on a navigation exercise one night. I marked my log books, sent them to the Civil Aviation Authority and so got my Senior Commercial Licence. In due course I was able to exchange the licence for an ALTP as my hours built up; the problem basically was that civil

178

regulations, very understandably, only recognised flying hours even though flying hours, per se, meant absolutely nothing. A military test pilot is lucky if he does 250 hours a year, an airline pilot probably does at least 600 hours a year, but the military test pilot will have flown the aircraft in charge and will actually be flying the aircraft all the time. An airline pilot will have the autopilot in most of the time and have gained very little extra flying experience. This fact was rapidly demonstrated on the 748 programme itself since once the 748 started flying our flying hours built up dramatically as we flew all over the world; of course, most of that flying was done by the autopilot whilst we navigated the aircraft. The only real 748 flying was test flying or demonstrating the aircraft to potential customers, the latter flying being often much more demanding and particularly important. There was no point in having a perfectly certificated aircraft if no one wanted to buy it and we had to satisfy the potential customers that the aircraft could do what we said it could.

1959 was a very quiet year except for the preparation that was taking place for the 748. The project was started without any customers and it was with a great sense of relief that the sales team managed to get Aerolineas Argentinas to sign for nine aircraft with an option for three more. We had a celebration dinner in the Midland Hotel in the centre of Manchester with the team from Aerolineas. As luck would have it, I never managed to get to Argentina, though I went to many parts of the world including many countries in South America with the 748, demonstrating the aircraft, training flight crews, operating it and delivering it.

I remember being very frustrated that year and I started looking around for other jobs. By the time the year finished I had flown less than 200 hours and it was not all test flying. I found it very demoralising. There was very little that was new. We had our first Vulcan equipped for flight refuelling and I spent some time at Boscombe Down looking at a tanker aircraft trying to push the Vulcan probe into a drogue. We did a bit of flying in a Blue Steel Vulcan which had appeared and was being prepared for delivery to Australia. Jimmy Harrison kindly let me share the flying with him during the SBAC show where we demonstrated the Vulcan Mk.2 again. We were still very constrained in what we could do because of the rule preventing turning towards the crowd. The effect of this was that all turns had to be done at either end out of sight and though we were working like maniacs turning the aircraft, the watchers in the chalets must have wondered where we had got to. If we flew past at 300 kt. or so we had to turn right through 90° and then immediately do a 270° to get the aircraft pointing back towards the airfield; we were only allowed to pull 2.5 g so that it all took a long time. We were still doing a left hand circuit for landing out of sight of the crowd so in reality we wasted most of the six minutes we had available for our display. Still, as usual, for us it was a wonderful week meeting our friends and seeing what was new.

Immediately after the Show the Lear Instrument Company demonstrated a Beechcraft fitted with their latest flight system; it was the first proper flight system I had flown and it was a delight after the Vulcan system. It was the start of my education into the optimum method of displaying and integrating information to the pilot and it proved invaluable to me in later years.

In November I had to take my first civil instrument rating test for my Senior Commercial Licence and it was necessary to go to the Civil Aviation Flying Unit at Stansted to be examined flying a Dove, by one of their qualified examiners. My preparation for the test was extensive since I was unfamiliar with civil procedures and flying the airways. We still had only our Anson as our communication aircraft so I was unable to get any practice in a Dove but I did manage to do a little flying in a simulator. I was very, very nervous driving down to Stansted; stories abounded on the number of people who had failed their initial instrument ratings. I met my examiner, Mr Carroll and after the briefing we went out to the aircraft.

The test was imagined to be conducted in icing conditions so the drill was to walk round the Dove looking at the various holes and crevices for ice and removing it on the way. There was a story about Cliff Rogers, a test pilot for Rolls Royce, who, on being asked by the examiner whether that was all he was going to do as they finished their circuit, panicked and walked round the aircraft twice more. Cliff was also the pilot who, on hearing some candidate on the airway making some dreadful mistake on procedure talking to the airway controller, chipped in on the airways frequency "Poor b****, he's failed". Stories of instrument rating tests by CAFU were legion and in those days we all knew the registration letters of their Doves by heart, hearing them being used frequently by the candidates calling the air traffic controllers on the airways.

After starting the engines and taxiing out, I saw that we had an engine rpm drop on one of the engines that was, strictly speaking, outside the permitted limit when I was testing the magnetos individually with the engine at full power during the pre-takeoff check. The examiner was clearly quite used to this problem but the difficulty was how to let the candidate know that he would not be failed if the mag. drop was accepted, since in practice the Gypsy Queen engine with its inverted cylinders was very prone to these drops, which disappeared after a few minutes flying. He let me know that in his judgement it would be all right to continue and so we launched forth into the air. The flying was all procedural, estimating the times up and down the airway, talking to air traffic, and continually removing the imaginary ice, in conversations with the examiner. After what seemed an age, though in fact the whole flight only lasted 50 minutes, we entered a holding pattern. I had spent an inordinate amount of time calculating, using the forecast wind, how long I needed to fly the outbound leg and the parallel leg coming back so that the holding pattern would take exactly 4 minutes. Luckily the wind must have been somewhere near the forecast because, to my great relief, I saw the radio compass needle start to rotate, showing we were overhead, a very long two seconds after the appointed time.

The final part of this psychological battle was the ILS approach and luckily I had some experience in making these approaches. Like the Valiant, there was no sophisticated flight system in the aircraft, just a horizon, a compass with a moving card, and an ILS indicator with the two needles, localiser and glide slope. This meant that the pilot had to mentally adjust for the range of the aircraft from the airfield, in order to judge what heading and pitch correction was needed for a given deflection of the needles, to keep the airplane on the localiser and glide slope centre lines. Luckily the Dove flew relatively slowly on the approach so it was possible to keep the needles roughly in the middle until the Decision Height when a missed approach procedure had to be carried out. I informed the controller that I was carrying out a missed approach, which must have been no surprise to him since that was the way every Instrument Rating Test finished. When we got back on the ground we had our debriefing and to my relief I was told that I had passed. The initial test was always the main hurdle at the time since CAFU would only delegate renewal tests to approved examiners, they reserved the initial tests for themselves. In fact I went to Stansted to renew my instrument rating for several more years until we had our own examiner, but it was the first visit I remember.

Jimmy meanwhile had carried out his first flight on the new aircraft and the Avro 748 development programme was on its way. I flew the aircraft with Jimmy in July and in command with Colin Allen as co-pilot two weeks later. We had recruited Colin, who had been a pilot with Vickers at Wisley some year or so previously flying the Viscount, to carry out crew training with the airlines. When he left Vickers he had joined Decca on the record side but decided that he wanted to return to flying. As we had no experience of training airline pilots Colin's experience was very necessary.

Testing the 748 had a very different tempo from military test flying. Hawker Siddeley was spending their own money developing the aircraft, instead of getting every bill paid by the Government with a handsome mark-up. We needed to get the aircraft meeting the requirements as quickly as possible, as well as ensuring that it had the performance we had promised in the contract. The performance we had to demonstrate was divided into two parts; there was the cruise performance which did not affect the safety of flight but mattered to the customer and there was the certificated performance that was supervised by the Air Registration Board, as the certification authority was called at the time, the Safety Regulation Group of the Civil Aviation Authority as it became later. The performance the ARB was primarily interested in was the runway, the single engined climb and the all engines operating performance. This performance was related to the agreed handling speeds, such as V_{mcg}, the minimum control speed on the ground with an engine failed, and V_2, the take-off safety speed with an engine failed.

We found that, whereas we could demonstrate the take-off and landing performance promised by our aerodynamicists quite easily, we always had the greatest difficulty meeting the engine out climb performance. We rapidly learnt about the Rolls Royce Dart Engine and all its idiosyncrasies. The engine was in its heyday on the Vickers Viscount and it had plenty of power for that four engined aircraft. The situation was very different for us; unless we could meet the promised single engined climb performance, the aircraft would be completely uneconomic for an airline operator. We accused Rolls Royce of not giving us enough power and they denied this accusation. We tried different engines on the aircraft and some were better than others, not surprisingly. We managed to get an acceptable performance in the end but only after we had discovered that the engine power, which was determined by adding water methanol to the engine in hot climates to keep the indicated torque pressure constant, varied enormously with engine oil temperature. We suspected that Rolls Royce knew this all the time since they were continually bringing out modifications which tried to remove this sensitivity, giving the engine less power but increasing it's overhaul life. On our part, we either contested the modifications or insisted on higher torque pressure numbers and, therefore, compensating power.

Meigs Field

The cruising performance of the 748 was not sparkling and certainly not as good as our main competitor, the Fokker F27, which had the same engines. That aircraft had been in production for some years and a lot of aircraft had been sold to operators all over the world. Furthermore, we could not fly as high as the F27, but there was absolutely no doubt that the 748 runway performance was considerably better than the F27. On a typical route structure with limiting airfields our sales engineers could demonstrate that our aircraft was economically superior because of the ability to take off with a greater payload. Unfortunately, the fundamental problem was that the airlines that had limiting runways and still operated DC3s were generally broke. The majority of the financially solvent small airlines in the Western World had good airfields and the F27 was fine for their operation. In the whole of the USA, for example, where the F27 had done particularly well, only Meigs field on Lake Michigan, then the downtown Chicago airfield, had a runway which needed the 748 rather than the F27. Interestingly, even that airfield has now been taken out of service, apparently on the grounds of it being a security risk to the skyscrapers close-by.

Vulcan landing at Farnborough

Farnborough came round yet again and this time Jimmy was demonstrating the Avro 748 G-APZV for the first time. I had Vulcan XH534 to myself and to be honest I don't think I did anything much different from our normal routine; Ossie Hawkins flew with me for the first few days and Graham Moreau, a test pilot friend from Boscombe joined me on the public days. I had become quite adept at landing the Vulcan Mk.2 very slowly by then and Jimmy remarked to me some time later that Ossie was a bit surprised one day when we were coming in quite slowly, to see my right hand reach down, not to apply more power as he was expecting, but to cut off the fuel to the two outer engines. It must have been all right because we did not make any more marks on the grass nor were we told off the following morning at briefing for touching down before the touch-down markers. Most people did not realise how high off the ground the pilot's eye was as the Vulcan Mk.2 got into ground effect with maximum lift from the wing, all eight elevons fully back.

My test flying was now a mixture of civil and military flying. Whenever I had the opportunity I flew the Avro 748 G-APZV, usually on performance testing. I didn't normally like being a co-pilot but I used to fly with Jimmy when we were doing runway performance. Since our strong selling point was being able to operate from short runways, we wanted to squeeze the last inch out of the aircraft's performance. We had to establish the minimum control speed on the ground, V_{mcg}, which was a very demanding test; the engine was stopped at the critical speed and the propeller feathered. It was then necessary to accelerate and climb away, without exceeding a lateral deviation of 30 feet, to the take-off safety speed. If we got the speed too low then we would deviate excessively; judgement was then required as to whether it was possible to carry on and get airborne or whether the take-off should be abandoned. Luckily we never damaged ourselves or the aircraft doing these tests.

I well remember John Carrodus of the ARB coming up to Woodford one day to check the handling of the latest 748 with uprated engines. He had a couple of goes trying to meet the V_{mcg} speed we claimed but failed and then asked me to demonstrate it. We changed seats, he cut the engine at the prescribed moment and then burst out laughing when he saw me applying the ailerons, rudder and elevator, all instantaneously to full travel but within the rules; this procedure prevented the aircraft from leaving the runway prematurely and keeping within the prescribed 30ft deviation. We changed seats and he had no further problem. The point of the story here is that it is necessary to take advantage of every facet of a regulation if the performance is to be achieved.

The problem with the 748 was that there was only just enough rudder to meet the handling requirements, while the pedal forces required to apply full rudder were only just within the limit of 180lb. In a way this was a tribute to the designers of the 748 since if there had been too much fin or rudder the performance would have been adversely affected and the aircraft would have been less competitive against the F.27. However, for us it was a problem since we had to demonstrate that the aircraft did meet the requirements to the ARB's satisfaction and, of course, we then had to train the customers' crews on single engined flying.

Nowadays the problems of asymmetric flying are almost completely hidden from the pilot since modern aircraft have fully powered rudders, probably fly by wire, and the pilot does not have to push very hard to apply full rudder. However, the basic problem of controlling a twin engined aircraft on one engine has not gone away as the tragic accident to Airbus's chief test pilot, Nick Warner, while testing an A330 at Toulouse reminded us all.

Single engined take-offs for performance measurement was very important and we devised a fast analysis procedure, so that we could tell whether each take-off met the expected target. This arrangement saved us hours of flying and many days in the flight test programme. Measured landings were always exciting since, even though we had both engines running, the performance rules meant, in effect, that you had to crash the aircraft onto the ground and apply full braking, hopefully without bursting the tyres. We understood from Colin that Vickers had badly damaged one of their test aircraft trying to get the optimum performance; fortunately none us ever broke any of our aircraft, though we all had a good try. The 748 was not beautiful, but it was strong.

We had started to get more orders for the 748 and we were forever giving brief demonstrations at Woodford to potential customers. It was always a challenge deciding how much flying to let the evaluating pilot do. Jimmy told me that one day at Farnborough when he was forced to fly after the show with candidates lined up by the marketing department, he invited the airline visitor to make the approach. There was a language problem and Jimmy was convinced that modesty forbade the visitor from taking the controls. Anyway Jimmy insisted with apparently somewhat mixed results only to discover on the way back to the chalet that his visitor was the airline's chief engineer! This incident confirmed our view that some of the visitors produced by the marketing department at Farnborough were not always worth flying; the marketeers felt they had to use the aircraft after the show to demonstrate how hard they were working.

Most pilots like to be put into the left hand seat and do all the flying and, if this can be done, then usually the visiting pilot will be delighted and start telling the rest of the airline how marvellous the aircraft is. The problem we always had was judging whether the visiting pilot was any good. We usually tried to get some advice from the salesman who had brought the potential customer over to be flown. The problem was accentuated by the fact that the nosewheel steering control on the 748 was only on the left hand side and it was difficult to get used to because there was a dead area when the tiller was central; if the pilot was poor we had to try and control the aircraft on the ground using the brakes, which was most uncomfortable for all concerned. Generally, the more senior the pilot the worse he was and, unfortunately, the more important he was. Luckily pilots did not buy aircraft, the financiers did, but it was always nice to have the company pilots keen.

I had hoped to do more and more of the certification test flying on the 748 but Jimmy Harrison was very able and, understandably, very keen to do nearly all of the work. On most aircraft and the 748 was no exception, some of the critical handling tests only just met the required handling standard; this is as it should be since if the handling is made too good the performance may suffer and, of course, the customer is buying performance, not handling qualities. In fact, it may be a matter of opinion whether an aircraft does meet the requirements of a particular handling test and Jimmy did not want too many views. He had the responsibility of certificating the aircraft and was only getting it modified if he felt it was necessary to be able to get a Certificate of Airworthiness for the type. He could not afford to have dissenting views from people who did not know the aircraft as well as he did, since, naturally the firm only wanted to do essential modifications. Equally, getting the best performance out of an aircraft, particularly on the runway, is not easy and on the 748 Jimmy was doing most of the flying and getting very good results; he did not want a lot of poor results from pilots who were still learning to fly the aircraft.

748 Flight Deck with Capt. Ben Narciso, Philippine Airlines and Bob Stubbs, Operations Manager

The Avro 748 only sold to customers because of its short airfield performance so that, as I have mentioned, we had to get the very best measured take-offs and landings that we could. Jimmy Harrison had set a fantastically high standard when he certificated the Avro 748 Series 1 and we who followed him always had the greatest difficulty making the later improved Avro 748 variants actually have better performance than Jimmy had achieved. Furthermore, there was always a lot of measurements to be made on the new variants since the airfield performance of an aircraft may not be extrapolated from sea level and the temperature conditions in England to, for example, Colombia at 8,000 ft altitude and temperatures well above the International ground level standard of 15°C. We always had to go overseas and make new measurements, every time we needed to get higher and hotter conditions than we had had before and getting the required performance was no sinecure.

We found one wonderful spot for high altitude and hot weather trials, Asmara then in northern Ethiopia and now the capital of Eritrea. It was near the equator and 7,500ft high so the actual temperature at Asmara at any moment was actually the variation from the International Standard Atmosphere, ISA, since it is assumed that the atmosphere cools by 2°C per 1,000 ft.. It was very pleasant to be cool on the equator with the temperature at 15°, knowing that we were meeting our required test conditions of ISA+15.

A few miles away was Massawa, at sea level on the Red Sea where we could test the aircraft on the ground at a very high ambient temperature, to try to ensure that the engine compartment would not overheat under the most adverse operating conditions for which the aircraft had been cleared. Asmara was beautiful, abundant with bougainvillaea, jacaranda, mimosa, hibiscus, oleander and other wonderful flowers, together with wonderful people and excellent hospitality; I felt very fortunate at the time just to be there and it was a terrible day for Asmara when civil war broke out in Ethiopia.

Another enjoyable piece of performance test flying was when we tried to sell the Avro 748 to Bolivia. La Paz, the capital, was at 12,000ft and the airfield was above the town at 13,000 ft. We had only cleared the 748 for operation up to 9,000 ft. at Quito in Ecuador and we were not allowed to extrapolate our performance up to the altitude of La Paz. Harry Fisher and I had to fly an aircraft across the Atlantic and then down the Western seaboard of South America in order to carry out the tests. The ferry was exciting because there was civil unrest in Peru and we had to land at Lima before the curfew was imposed. We just made the hotel in time and heard the firing all night. In the morning we set out again and climbed to the south until we were high enough to cross the Andes at 21,000 feet. The weather was kind and we managed to find a crossing point so that the mountains were not too close underneath. We descended towards La Paz and we put our oxygen masks on as we depressurised the aircraft for landing.

The next few days we carried out engine cut take-offs and single engined landings under the supervision of Bill Horsley of ARB on the 13,000ft high airfield. We also flew up and down Lake Titicaca on one engine, measuring climb performance. Every evening we drove down the escarpment to the town, one thousand feet below, feeling we had a done a good days work. Funnily enough none of us seemed to suffer from lack of oxygen and the shortness of breath that we had expected at that altitude. We even had time to go boating on the lake and see the very numerous local Indian population with their legendary capes and llamas. Again we knew were all very fortunate to have had such an opportunity to see other parts of world as a result of test flying; it certainly was not what I had expected to be doing when I first went to ETPS at Farnborough. In retrospect, we were particularly lucky as we were able to see these places before the advent of mass tourism

Certification measurements were always done on tarmac runways but the airfields the airlines used were rough and very often stony. We had to develop take-off and landing techniques to ensure that the 748 could operate from these strips. Luckily we had an early chance to refine our procedures when the Royal Air Force wanted to buy a military version of the 748 and they made us operate from a rough strip at Martlesham Heath to demonstrate that the aircraft could do what we said it could.. The actual demonstration that we did is described in the next chapter but the techniques we developed at Martlesham for flying from rough airfields proved invaluable in the many years we demonstrated the 748. In particular, one of our earliest customers was a UK airline called Skyways which specialised in carrying passengers from a grass airfield called Lympne, near Hythe in Kent, to Beauvais in France. The airline was owned by Eric Rylands and possibly his bank.

The Skyways operation was not easy because of the soft nature of the grass and the technique we had used at Martlesham was ideal when the field got boggy as it often did. I had decided by now that I needed to use my newly acquired Airline Pilots Licence to get experience carrying fare paying passengers and flying out of Lympne was the perfect opportunity. I got Jimmy's and A.V.Roe's agreement that I could fly with Skyways and I started spending my week-ends driving down to Kent and then going backwards and forwards to

Beauvais carrying holiday makers. The flying was very demanding because of the poor surface of the airfield but it was very good training for me. How no one had an accident I shall never know. When the going got really soft we use to operate from Gatwick; Lydd next door would have been more sensible but I think there was a financial problem, like non-payment of the landing fees, which prevented this happening. I enjoyed the experience and the extra money that I earned. I helped Skyways for two consecutive Easters 1964 and '65; I think they stopped operating fairly soon after that but I learnt a lot about flying from bad airfields, as well as flying with an airline which had difficulties making ends meet.

***

During my years at Woodford I flew regularly at the SBAC Show at Farnborough and at the Paris Show at Le Bourget. Flying at an air display needs a lot of planning to get the best return for the very considerably investment the firms make entering their aircraft into the flying display. I flew three types of aircraft at Farnborough during my time as a test pilot; we started with the Vulcan, then the Avro 748 and, finally, the Nimrod. They all required different treatment to try to demonstrate the aircraft's performance.

The Vulcan was the most exhilarating of the three aircraft to demonstrate. We cut the fuel to the bone and in later years we had something like 80,000 lb. of total thrust with a take-off weight of 115,000 lb., a good power/weight ratio for a fighter at the time, let alone a bomber. When I first flew at Farnborough we were still governed by the rules imposed after the accident to John Derry. The one that made our demonstrations difficult was that no turns could be made turning towards the crowd. This meant that in a normal horizontal demonstration the aircraft had to turn at either end of the runway and complete the turn before flying past the crowd. We were normally allowed five to six minutes but most of that time was spent turning the aircraft round. All we could do was take-off, turn round, fly back at maybe 350 mph, turn round again, let the speed drop and do a slow run and maybe one more run and turn back on finals. We would, of course, have liked to repeat our rolls off the top but there was no way that the powers that be in the corridors of Whitehall would permit it, probably because they were nervous that the R.A.F. Squadron pilots would try to emulate us without proper training; the operational need for the manoeuvre had long gone away.

For us working on the flight deck it was very hard work indeed. We had an appalling view, we were limited in how much angle of bank and acceleration we could apply and we were working hard struggling to turn the aircraft round at each end of the runway. Furthermore, the view from the Vulcan was so bad that even with a left hand circuit we had to turn the aircraft round for landing without being able to see where we were aiming. We learnt to recognise all sorts of buildings as we pirouetted round and somehow we always managed to finish up landing near the beginning of the runway at the right speed. We were our own severest critics.

When we had finished flying we usually felt that we had done a good days work, though always wondering how we could have improved the show. I remember that we had the greatest difficulty at the beginning of the week in completing the demonstration we had planned in the permitted time; by the end of the week we seemed to have lots of time in hand. However, I do not believe that we got the optimum demonstration out of the aircraft. We needed to keep the time spent doing turns as short as possible and to do this we should have flown at a lower speed. Certainly I tended to be too fast so that my turns took too long. The other mistake I made when flying the Vulcan was the touch down point. I tried to land as soon as possible and the location of the chalets were such that the spectators could not see the aircraft until it was well down the runway; the chalet line was not parallel to the runway but looked to the left. The people in the chalets, who paid our salaries and their prospective customers, were positioned so that they could only see the runway intersection well down the runway.

As I have remarked earlier it would have been a better spectacle if I had landed the Vulcan as slowly as I did but much further down so that the very slow touch down could be seen. Again another improvement might have been to do a right hand circuit so that the aircraft was in view all the time since, when turning finals, we were allowed to turn towards the crowd. However, if the view from the left was bad, there was absolutely no view to the right from the left hand seat so it would have meant either flying the aircraft from the right hand seat or letting the pilot in the right hand seat do the right hand turn until the runway came into view. Though I did realise the advantage of doing this, I chickened out because it would have been all too easy for the right hand pilot to have misjudged the turn so that we would have been unable to land. On a conventional aircraft with a better view and better ability to control the speed, a right hand circuit would have been not unreasonable but we did not do it on the Vulcan. I am sure the spectators enjoyed watching the Vulcan fly with its praying mantis shape and the deafening roar from its engines but in retrospect I believe we could have done our demonstrations much better. As has been said many times, hindsight is a very exact science.

The Avro 748 was an entirely different challenge. There was no spectacle to excite the viewers; the important thing here was to keep the aircraft in view. For the 748 however, turns could be done very quickly because the speeds were so slow. The aircraft was sold because it had a very good performance from short airfields. Consequently, we would fly the aircraft at as light a weight as possible, haul it shuddering into the air, do our fast and slow runs and finish up with a very short landing.

In those days the wheels were prevented from skidding if the pilot applied too much brake by the Dunlop Maxaret brake valve but, unfortunately, as I have mentioned, this valve only worked once the wheels were spinning. Woe betide the pilot who, in his eagerness to stop the aircraft as quickly as possible, landed with his feet on the brakes; the tyres would be scrubbed and in bad cases they would burst. I must plead guilty to doing this twice, on both occasions demonstrating single engine landings when we had, unknowingly, touched down on one side only. The first time was at Farnborough and the second occasion was at Paris where I had to take the aircraft onto the grass to avoid blocking the runway and stopping the show. Very embarrassing!

One year, it was decided to demonstrate our short field performance by flying on a grass strip parallel to the runway. We loaded the passengers in full view of the crowd and then took off, flew past the crowd and finally landed back on the grass. I did not like the idea then and I still think it was a bad thing to have done. Air Shows attract accidents because the pilots are pushing their aircraft to the limit, be it a fighter aircraft or a slow transport aircraft like the Avro 748 and we might have had a catastrophic accident through trying too hard. The firm's management always claimed that it did not put the pilots under any pressure, but the pressure on the pilots from the marketing staff was always very high and these lunch time watchers were always the most critical.

Towards the end of my time flying at Farnborough we were finally allowed to turn towards the crowd. For the 748 this was ideal since it meant that we could keep the aircraft in full view of the spectators all the time finishing with a right hand circuit, the pilot in the right hand seat either turning the aircraft on finals or talking the pilot in the left hand seat round the final turn.

Nimrod

The last aircraft I flew at Farnborough was the Nimrod. There was not much you could do with an aircraft that flew very slowly and was, basically, as old as the world's first passenger carrying jet aircraft, the Comet, from which it was derived. Luckily, by then I had finally realised what the spectators could see and what they couldn't. I would take-off and keep turning the aircraft round right in front of the chalet until it was time to land. We had our flaps down most of the time and someone in the aircraft would spend the whole time calling out the acceleration and the height; the first to avoid bending the aircraft and the second to avoid upsetting the flying control committee by getting too low. We finished with a right hand circuit because, on the Nimrod, the view was excellent from the flight deck, though we very nearly got it wrong on one occasion due to the wind. It was with Charles Masefield, I think, and we got too close to the runway before turning finals; Charles took the controls for the turn and when I was able to see the runway it was clear that we were going to cross the centre line. I just managed to touch down without having to request an overshoot. There was a photograph of the Nimrod in the following week's Flight magazine, showing the aircraft with an excessive amount of bank just about to touch down; it looked a fine action shot and I wish I could find it.

There is one aspect of flying at a show which is important for a slow aircraft and that is the wind. If there is no wind then there is no problem, but on a windy day the pilot has to consider the effect of the wind very carefully. All the time the aircraft is flying it is being carried downwind, but the pilot has to keep the aircraft in the correct position for his demonstration referenced to the display line. If the wind is blowing from the crowd then when the aircraft completes half a turn away from the display line it will be further from the crowd by the wind speed multiplied by the time spent turning. If the pilot then carries on turning back to the display line so that the aircraft will have done a complete turn, it will be displaced from the display line by the wind speed times the total time for the turn. In other words the aircraft will be in the wrong place, too far from the crowd and not on the display line. Of course the pilot could slacken off the turn in order to reach the display line but this would waste valuable time; the only solution was to try to turn much more tightly at first, then only a small relaxation of the angle of bank would be required to regain the display line at the end of the turn.

The reverse problem, which could be more serious, was when there was an 'on crowd' wind. In this case, if the pilot is too enthusiastic for the first half of the turn the aircraft will be too close to the display line when the second half of the turn is carried out. This is the really dangerous situation because the pilot knows that the flying control committee is watching and filming the display; he may pull too much 'g' to stop crossing the line and damage the aircraft or even possibly cause an accident. The pilot therefore has to be very careful, with an on crowd wind, that the first part of a turn away from the crowd is relaxed so that the bank can be increased within limits on the second half.

The turns described above are just examples of the effect of wind; the pilot has to allow for wind the whole time, for example making a tight turn onto finals as I mentioned earlier flying the Nimrod. I was very lucky not to have to go round again and come back after the show on that occasion.

As I have indicated, the discipline during the years for controlling air displays has understandably increased. The display line has been moved further from the crowd and the minimum height for fly pasts and turns has been increased. The whole show is videotaped and all pilots have to be checked in a practice display before they are allowed into the show. Nevertheless, however strict the rules and discipline, accidents are always more likely to occur at air shows than anywhere else, since the aircraft will always be much nearer the limit of their flight envelopes and, at the same time, they will be close to the ground.

Flying at Farnborough, or at any air show, is very exhilarating and pilots always try to do the very best they can. Towards the end of my flying I felt the pressure more and more just before take-off but, once the aircraft started to roll, any apprehension always disappeared. I regard myself as very lucky to have had the opportunity to fly in so many air shows but I am I sure that I did the right thing to stop when I did, approaching fifty. We all get old differently, but I am convinced that even though the tendency is for test pilots to fly to ever increasing retirement ages, physical deterioration, unfortunately, will always win against experience. It may be alright for an airline pilot with a younger first officer to fly until sixty five years of age but it cannot be right for a test pilot doing critical manoeuvres. This is a sensitive subject amongst the piloting fraternity but, in my experience, attitudes as well as eyesight and hearing don't improve with age.

***

During the time when I was particularly frustrated with not enough action, I looked around the UK industry and, of course, was very jealous seeing that the British Aircraft Corporation was building the Concorde, teamed with Aerospatiale. The UK Government would have stopped the project many times over, because of the vast expense, but the nice thing about an international project, if one is involved, is that though they are almost impossible to start, once started they are almost impossible to stop. The French, of course, believe in technology as a worthwhile end in itself with great benefits to be obtained for France; in the UK we are much more short term in our approach. Luckily, the Concorde was born and has been a marvellous example of Europe's technical skills if not of its financial acumen. It seems incredible that the Concorde has finished flying and nothing has replaced it. Of course economically the reasons are clear. Subsonic aircraft will always be cheaper than supersonic aircraft, both to develop and to operate and the supersonic boom mitigates against overland operation, so that there are very few commercial routes available to airlines. A supersonic aircraft is just not an economical proposition if true costs, development as well as running costs, are taken into account. In addition people today are much less tolerant of noise and pollution. Unfortunately, Concorde was very noisy from the engines and also from the overflight supersonic double bang but noise problems are almost certainly soluble. It may be just possible, sometime in the future, that the need for raw speed for certain people or organisations might justify another commercial supersonic aircraft to be built but in my view it is unlikely, bearing in mind the dwindling resource of fossil fuels.

I was very envious of the Concorde test pilots and one day I learnt that Brian Trubshaw, the BAC chief test pilot, might have a vacancy. We met secretly over dinner in some flesh pot in the south of England. I have no head for alcohol and Brian was an excellent host. He offered me a job but I decided that it would not be sensible to make the move since I could never have been Chief Test Pilot, only number two to Brian. However, I did manage some time later to achieve my ambition of flying the aircraft thanks to the generosity of Jock Cochrane, then Brian's deputy.

Concorde testing took place from an old RAF base at Fairford and the aircraft for my flight, G-AXDN, was being prepared for cold weather trials at Moses Lake in Washington State. Jock had one more flight to do before leaving for the USA and he invited me to come along. I drove down through the night, had breakfast at a hotel near by and then went to Fairford. We had the pre-flight briefing and then climbed for miles up to the flight deck, even higher than the Vulcan. I sat in the right hand seat and surveyed the instruments, quite modern at the time but archaic by present standards. There were only two new instruments to show the pilot that he was not in a Vulcan; there was the aircraft skin temperature to alert the pilot if he was going too fast and the aircraft might melt or at the very least distort, maximum 127°C. The other key instrument was the combined centre of gravity/maximum speed indicator, because the Concorde could only go supersonic if the centre of gravity was in the right place and, therefore, the control surfaces at the back would be effective enough to fly the aircraft. This instrument made it very easy for the pilot to check whether the flight engineer had indeed transferred the fuel before going supersonic.

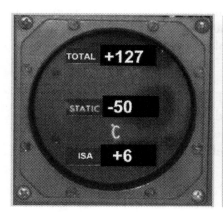 

Skin Temperature   **Machmeter**

I taxied out following John's instructions to allow for the fact that we were sitting miles in front of the landing gear, quite disconcerting when making a tight turn. We managed to get to the runway without going off the narrow perimeter track and completed the normal vital actions. Air Traffic gave us our clearance and off we went. I was, of course, used to handling four small throttles on the Vulcan so the flight deck did not feel too strange. The view was not particularly great because of the visor, but then I was used to that as well. I let the brakes off as the power came on and we hurtled down the runway. I pulled the rams horn wheel back, rotated the aircraft the agreed amount on the pitch attitude display and we leapt into the air. The nose was rotated, the visor was raised and looking forward it was similar to being in a Vulcan. However, inside the flight deck there was no contest in Vulcan comparisons; there was plenty of room, no parachutes and coffee was being served. We climbed up to 50,000 ft. in the Bay of Biscay as we went supersonic, a non-event thanks to the skills of the aircraft designers. John let me try some of the system malfunctions that the designers had allowed for, which were, of course, innocuous since an aircraft must always be capable of being flown by the airline's worst pilot. In fact, I have always been much more worried about the malfunctions that the designers have not allowed for, but that is another subject.

Concorde G-AXDN

It was a memorable and uneventful flight and as usual it was the landing that I was looking forward to. I followed all the instructions, the visor was lowered, the nose was lowered and we started down the approach. The flight engineer called out the altitude and, at the right moment, I pulled the stick back and closed the throttles. I applied my normal landing technique of choosing a height of eye and pulling the stick back to maintain the eye height so that the undercarriage approached the ground. Whatever I did seemed to work but I began to get very scared because nothing seemed to have happened; in reality we had touched down so smoothly that I for one had not realised we were on the ground. Of course, I would have known we must have been down if I had looked at the airspeed indicator since it was way below flying speed. I opened the throttles again, rotated the aircraft and went round for another landing. I should have stopped while I was ahead but being big headed I decided to try landing without the benefit of the automatic throttles; the Concorde was very speed unstable on the approach, much worse than the Vulcan, so it was an important thing to experience. It was much harder work on the second approach and the landing was not so smooth but luckily uneventful. John took over and did the last landing demonstrating the very short landing capability of the aircraft if one does not have to worry about who is paying for the wear and tear on the wheels and brakes.

It was a great experience and one I shall always treasure. I flew as a passenger in the Concorde quite a few times to the USA and back and it was a wonderful aircraft, unfortunately only for a privileged few. However, it did show, perhaps for the first time, to our brothers in the USA that Europe can produce great feats of engineering. Brian, John, Peter Baker and the rest of the test pilots in the UK and France can look back on the aircraft with pride.

A few years later I was asked to write an account of my Concorde flight for inclusion in a small art exhibition featuring the loss of memorable objects. I have included it at the end of this chapter.

***

I became Chief Test Pilot in 1970 when Jimmy retired and took over Product Support from Bill Sturrock; Bill went out to Venezuela as Senior Marketing Executive, Central America, and we carried out several customer demonstrations together. My first job as CTP was to organise the ferry of Victor Mk.2s from Radlett to

Woodford to be converted into air-to-air refuelling tankers when Handley Page finally had to stop operating because of financial problems. We had always had a love/hate relationship with Handley Page because not only did they compete with us with the Victor but they also had produced the twin engined Dart Herald, though not with much success. By the time Handley Page finished 'Hazel', nobody ever knew Hazeleden's real first name, had retired and Johnny Allam had taken over. Johnny helped us enormously, organising the ferry of all the aircraft from Radlett, just north of London, to Woodford. They were parked on the airfield for many months before they were converted into tankers for the RAF. It was bad luck for Handley Page but good news for us at Avro's.

We were quite busy at the time since we had the Avro 748 to support world-wide, the Nimrod Mk.2 programme was running, the Vulcan and Shackleton programmes were still struggling on and the Victor was just starting. I had to recruit some pilots, Tony Hawkes, a Harrier pilot from Hawkers at Dunsfold, Charles Masefield when Beagles went bust and later, Robbie Robinson from 'B' Squadron at Boscombe. We also managed to upgrade two flight test observers, Kevin Moorhouse and Dave Pearson, to become commercial pilots.

Soon after I took over from Jimmy, Hawker Siddeley decided that they would build a new airliner at Hatfield called the HS146. At the time Hatfield was running out of Trident work since, though the three engined aircraft was judged to be the right solution at the time for smallish airlines, it was Boeing, unfettered by the lack of vision of British European Airways, who got the size and specification right, selling the Boeing 727 in large numbers all over the world. Of course, lack of work at a factory is not a very good reason for starting a project and it was particularly bad in this case since there was no suitable engine for the 146. Consequently, the decision was taken to use an unproven helicopter engine, called the Avco Lycoming 502, as the power plant and to fit four of them instead of two larger engines.

Cyril Bethwaite was promoted to be the 146 project director based at Hatfield and the powers that be, encouraged I suspect by Cyril, appointed me as project pilot. This was a slightly difficult situation since John Cunningham was very much Chief Test Pilot of

Hatfield, a household name with a very distinguished war and peacetime record. However, he was nearing retirement and he clearly would not be in charge by the time the first 146 flew. He was very good about things and I started spending a lot of my time flying backwards and forward to Hatfield in the Dove, having lengthy discussions about the flight deck and the projected handling of the aircraft with the Hatfield design team.

The HS146 had the distinction of being the first aircraft that was designed to the new European Joint Airworthiness Regulations. These regulations were started to try to unify the standards not only within Europe but also across the Atlantic with the FAA. At the time the Joint Airworthiness Authority was concerned purely with aircraft design standards but, eventually, it became the European authority for most aviation safety matters.

It was a good time to be designing a new aircraft since simulators were now available and in fact we learnt many valuable lessons experimenting in the simulator. The aircraft was awkward to control in roll and we were continually tuning up the design of the aileron and roll spoilers, getting the right relationship between aileron deflection and spoiler deflection. On the flight deck we started to lay out all the controls and designing the windscreens. It was then that we realised the real problem with the 146 concept. The aircraft was to have four engines and the regulations for designing aircraft with four engines are much more demanding than for a twin engined aircraft, since the operator is allowed to operate in more hazardous conditions, like flying fare paying passengers over the Ocean or into very hilly terrain. What it meant to us, trying to design the aircraft, was that every system we looked at started to become complicated. In fact, one of the reasons I had been chosen to be the project pilot was that I knew about relatively small aircraft operating in difficult conditions and I knew how important it was to keep things simple; what you don't fit to an aircraft can't go wrong. It was very sad to see the complicated operating problems being built into the aircraft systems.

To give one example of how the 146 was penalised, in the 748 each wing was full of fuel with one outlet in each wing feeding the associated engine. There was, of course, provision for cross-feeding but this was an emergency condition not normally required. In the 146 this solution was not allowed; there had to be four outlets, one for each engine so each wing had to be divided into two wing tanks with provisions for internal cross-feeding in emergency as well as across the aircraft. The same sort of considerations applied to every system we touched, hydraulic, electric, de-icing etc. We had to be able to cope with a double engine failure and keep on flying. Because I was getting so involved with Hatfield I had decided to take the Trident technical examination so that I could get the Trident on my pilot's licence. For the same reason I also took and passed the technical examination for the twin-engined business jet, the HS125; both these aircraft were designed by the Hatfield team, and both aircraft seemed, in my book, to be unnecessarily complicated. It rapidly became very clear to me that the 146 was going to be in the best Hatfield 'lets keep it elegantly complicated' tradition.

I had one fringe benefit from getting the Trident on my licence. I managed to arrange the delivery with Ron Clear, a Hatfield test pilot, of a new aircraft to Canton, as it was then, in China. We were moving house at the time and I had strict instructions to be back in time. The only thing I remember about the trip was that we had to refuel in India on the way and the fuel company would not accept credit cards. Ron held the 'ferry float' but this was not enough to pay for the fuel but luckily I had come reasonably well provided with my own personal US dollars for doing some shopping in Hong Kong; with this money we were able to proceed.

On arrival in Canton the system was that the ferry crew were taken to the hotel and then there was a banquet in the evening. I made it clear that, though I could stay for the banquet, I would have to leave for Hong Kong first thing in the morning. It was a splendid evening and I have had one night in China. The following morning I was taken to a very luxurious train which could only go to the Hong Kong border at that time. We had to walk across a wooden contraption which looked liked the 'Bridge on the River Kwai' and wait in a steaming hot crowded room for the next local train. The train duly arrived and stopped about ten times in the New Territories before suddenly entering on the last stop or two into the thriving modern city of Hong Kong. At the train terminal I found my way into a rather poorly furnished room and to my amazement there were my bags from the train. I was back in time to help Margaret with the move.

HS146 many years later

Laying out the flight deck of the 146 started to develop from what should have been a very simple task into a nightmare, because we had to leave room for four of everything and cater for the emergency cases. John Wilson, a very experienced test pilot turned flight deck design engineer, was my colleague and mentor at Hatfield and we spent many hours trying to find the best way through the jungle. John was a very deep and lateral thinker, always full of new ideas and, later, we spent some years together sitting on the Society of Automotive Engineers S7 Flight Deck Committee when I was working for Smiths Industries.

Of course we had to choose avionic equipment for the 146 and the critical items for the flight deck were the autopilot and the instruments which, by the '70s, were getting very complicated mechanically as all the necessary information was being integrated on to just two instruments, the Attitude and Heading displays. Instrument displays did not go electronic for another ten years so the computation was still analogue. The main contenders to supply the instruments for the 146 were Sperry at Phoenix, Collins at Grand Rapids and Smiths Industries at Cheltenham, England. John and I were agreed that Smiths could not provide the instruments even though, by then, they had seen the error of their ways and made the compass card rotate. I took the opportunity to do a tour round the USA and visited Avco, Sperry, Collins and the SETP annual convention in Los Angeles. It was very instructive and I returned convinced that we should purchase the complete package from Sperry, who could then be responsible for the integration of the autopilot with the instruments so that they would have common switching and control laws.

Smiths Industries however wanted very much to sell their autopilot to Hawker Siddeley and Roy Sisson, their managing director and later a great friend, mounted a superb marketing campaign at Hatfield and at Kingston, Hawker Siddleley's aerospace headquarters at the time, to get the contract. John and I were slowly worn down and the decision was finally made in Smiths favour with a celebratory dinner with wives at the Savoy. It was a real lesson on how marketing should be done, combining technical thrust, commercial terms, flying the national flag, calling in the free lunches and all the years of association in the SBAC. John and I both knew in our hearts it was the wrong decision and in later years Sperry, later Honeywell, took over the whole flight deck from Smiths. Not that the Smiths autopilot was bad, it was just that the Sperry system was better, was sold in much greater quantities and the airlines knew and wanted Sperry equipment; the truth was that few airlines at the time had heard of Smiths Industries.

In 1974 the British Aerospace industry was nationalised and Vickers joined in with Hawker Siddeley. Sir Arnold Hall refused to put any more money into the HS146 and the project was stopped. I was very disappointed since it was very stimulating to be working on a new aircraft with new ideas and standards. In 1976 the programme restarted with instructions from British Aerospace management, as the firm had become, not to change the design work that had already been done. This was an impossible mandate to give a design team, particularly with regards to equipment, since technology had made all sorts of new solutions available. When an aircraft design is started it reflects the technology available at the moment of inception, in exactly the same way as a new computer can only have to-day's components. Upgrading an aircraft design in later years is always difficult and expensive and, in many ways, it is probably better to start again as, for example, did Boeing when they decided to manufacture the Boeing 777; in computer terms it is always possible to upgrade the microprocessor engine, but there are lots of other components that will then have to be changed and it is always difficult to know what changes are worthwhile. I always felt the 146 suffered not only from having four engines when it should have had only two, but also from the fact that it was designed five years before the project actually started.

After the 146 work stopped I returned to Woodford once more to the 748 and the military aircraft. The Nimrod AEW aircraft project had appeared, in competition with the Boeing AWACS, though it was clear right from the outset that the divided management between GEC and Hawker Siddeley did not bode well for the programme. The problem was that there was no prime contractor and the Government procurement system did nothing to sort this problem out. I remember trying to get a sensible aircraft intercommunication system installed but since the system chosen came from GEC, we were not allowed to make suggestions. After many, many millions of pounds were wasted, the RAF got its way and purchased the Boeing AWACS.

Nimrod AEW

I was getting towards the end of my time at Woodford. I had noticed that old test pilots get fixed in their ways and become very inflexible. I had not forgiven myself some years back for not carrying out a demonstration in Chile when Charles Masefield and I flew out to take a 748 borrowed from LAN Chile to a particularly unattractive venue near Cape Horn with a very steep hill of indefinite height at one end of the runway. The airfield looked very dangerous and the weather was not much better but, had I been younger, might I have done the demonstration? I would probably have assumed blindly that if the DC3 could do it, so could the 748, though the problem was exacerbated by the fact that the airfield only had petrol and not turbine fuel. I heard that Smiths Industries had just made their operational adviser redundant but they also realised that they had to boost their resource of modern operational experience. I think John Wilson tipped me off about Smith's problem and I wrote to Roy Sisson offering my services. It took a few months but it was clear to me that though by then the 146 had restarted, the opportunity for me at British Aerospace had gone and I decided that a seat on the Smiths Industries Aerospace Board was the right solution at my advanced test flying age; in this way I ended my first career and started my second and never regretted it for one moment.

I had done flying and I never look back. Margaret is a genuine historian; I am not, though I accept that there are a lot of valuable lessons to be learnt from history. Hugh Pope, one of my bosses at Smiths Industries some years later, always said people don't change, and though I didn't agree with him at the time, I believe he was right. I always like to look forward to new objectives and I hope I always will. Anyway, rightly or wrongly, I decided to leave British Aerospace and start a new career. The family felt the knock-on effects since they all had to move south. Margaret gave up a high powered job in education and our son had to go away to boarding school; luckily our daughter was going to University so changing house did not matter so much for her. My only regret was leaving our super house in a lovely village with a wonderful pub, the Admiral Rodney; perhaps my real mistake was not letting Margaret carry on working. I could have looked after the house and had lunch every day in the Admiral Rodney, but somehow that wasn't in my character!

Addendum to Chapter 5

Flying the Concorde

Extract from Exhibition Memoire Collective, March 2005

Concorde Exhibit Frédérique Decombe

Like so much in life the flight in the Concorde happened because we did a deal. I let the Concorde test pilot fly an Avro Vulcan, a subsonic delta bomber and he let me, a Vulcan test pilot, fly the supersonic delta Concorde. Incredibly, the great day arrived and it was like a dream come true, the aircraft was there, beautiful, gleaming white on the tarmac, waiting to go.

Entering the Concorde for the first time was an amazing thrill, turning left on to the flight deck, not right as a passenger, knowing I was going to fly the airplane.

We started the engines and I felt enormous pride as I taxied out. It was all mine. I looked at the runway stretching into the distance and then I moved the four small levers fully forward. The engines roared as the four afterburners came on and the aircraft leapt forward, the airspeed increasing incredibly quickly. The critical speeds came and went, V_1, so that we could not stop, V_r and I pulled the control wheel to rotate the aircraft, and V_2 and we were safely airborne. With the aircraft nose high in the sky to stop the speed increasing, the drooping nose was raised, the undercarriage was retracted and the afterburners were turned off. We were airborne like any other aircraft, except we were in the Concorde.

In no time we were at 30,000ft and the afterburners were switched on again. The aircraft went supersonic but there was hardly a tremor. Soon we were at twice the speed of sound over the Bay of

Biscay drinking coffee and talking normally to one another. It was like magic and only the instruments told us we were at Mach 2 and at 50,000ft height.

Our tests were routine and there was time for me to fly the aircraft with some of the safety features removed to see if it was safe to fly. It was not difficult, but then an airliner has to be capable of being flown by an airline's worst pilot. We ate our lunch on the way home, in style, on a tray.

I turned downwind for landing. The long nose was drooped and I could see the runway. As we approached the ground the engineer called out our height and I pulled the stick back to prevent the aircraft hitting the ground. The speed dropped but I felt nothing. For a moment I panicked but in reality we were on the ground and I had felt nothing because the runway was so smooth. I opened the throttles up and went round again trying to control the speed without the help of the automatic throttles, needed to fly this unstable aircraft. This time we all knew we had landed; maybe I should have stopped after the first landing.

I walked back to my car as if I was still in the air. An ambition realised. Will there ever be another Concorde? Unlikely, because however efficient a supersonic aircraft can be made, the subsonic aircraft will always be more efficient and cheaper to develop. In the years ahead people will look back and say how was it that there was ever a Concorde? All it had was speed, but then that is what aviation is all about.

Flight Testing to Win

CHAPTER 6

Selling the 748

The Avro 748 was a challenging aircraft to sell. There was no doubt that the airlines operating the DC3 needed a modern aircraft replacement with the latest safety standards, but the airlines were always short of money. In addition, the airfields on which the DC3 operated were invariably rough and short so that there was always considerable doubt by the airline whether the 748 could actually operate on these strips without being damaged. Consequently, Hawker Siddeley always had to mount a two pronged attack to win the customer; firstly finance had to be arranged and secondly, the customer had to be convinced that the 748 could really do the job.

The situation was compounded by the fact that the 748 had a competitor, the Fokker F27, which used the same Dart engines as the 748 but had a high wing configuration. The F27 flew faster than the 748 and slightly higher but its short field performance was not as good. Avro's, and indeed most airlines, did not believe Fokker's claim that their aircraft, because of it's lower drag in flight, could do just as well as ours when operating from a short rough strip, even though it did not have such a good short field performance.

The pilots were not of course the final decision makers when an airline chose which aircraft to have, assuming that the finance had been arranged, but it was important that they were convinced that the 748 could do the job for their airline and operate on the airline's routes. Consequently, we were continually being asked to take 748s on demonstration tours to the countries of the airlines concerned and convince the potential customer that there was not a problem. Generally the demonstrations were quite short, a day or so flying from their worst strips, but sometimes we had to operate with fare paying passengers substituting for a DC3 for weeks at a time. This involved registering the 748 demonstration aircraft in the country concerned and, in addition, since we always had to have one of our pilots on board as captain, our licenses had to be validated for the country concerned. This latter point was always a problem since only I and Dicky Martin had Airline Transport Pilot Licenses; the other pilots had private pilot licenses which, for some obscure reason, were all that the UK deemed necessary to be test pilots, notwithstanding that we were flying for hire and reward.

The first of these long demonstrations was in 1966 in Brazil when Varig wanted to be sure that they could safely retire their DC3s and equip with 748s. I remember it very well since this was a new type of demonstration for all of us. I had flown the aircraft out from England just before Christmas with the two Varig pilots, Chaves and Leonel, and two A.V.Roe engineers, Frank Lord and Keith Openshaw. Our route was across the North Atlantic via Reykjavik, Frobisher Bay, Goose Bay, Washington DC, Nassau, Antigua, Georgetown, Belem, Brasilia and Sao Paulo. It had taken us four days to reach Belem at the mouth of the Amazon; the heady days of the Opera house in Manaus and the flourishing rubber trade in Belem had long since gone, thanks to the rubber plant being smuggled by Henry Wickham to England and then Malaysia. The town was at tropical heat, very high humidity, thundery and most uncomfortable. Insects were everywhere as we unloaded the aircraft in the steaming dark night, discovering as we did so that for some inexplicable reason there was no clearance for us to proceed to our destination. Our objective was to prove to Varig that our aircraft could truly replace the DC3 which they used in large numbers; the stakes were high for Hawker Siddeley since there was the possibility of a large order; I was very sad to leave home as it was going to be the first Christmas we had missed as a family together.

We were driven to our hotel and I went up to my room which was only kept cool by the continual roar of an air conditioner let into the wall. I was so tired I dropped to sleep immediately in spite of the noise; there was clearly no hurry to get up in the morning since without our clearance we were not permitted to take-off. Somebody hammered on my door at about 8am and we learnt that we had finally got our clearance to proceed. We took off from the steamy heat heading South for Brasilia 1,000 miles away. As we clambered up into the sky we watched the jungle drift by below. After four hours, clearings started to appear and, finally, we could see the modern architecture of Brazil's reluctant capital and the contrasting favellas with the temporary shacks where the workers existed, at the four corners of the town. A quick refuel and we were off to Sao Paulo.

Two and a half hours later we were over a concrete jungle and relatively modern factories, a complete contrast to Brasilia.

Captain Westarp, the senior Varig pilot in charge of the evaluation, greeted us and we went into the operations room to discuss the Varig evaluation plan. Our first problem was that it was necessary to carry a wireless operator in Brazil with a morse key, since it was the only way that the aircraft could keep in touch with the operations room and learn about the weather at destination airports. I had expected that Brazil would have cloudless blue skies at all times but we soon learnt that nothing was further from the truth. As the morning fog cleared enormous thunderstorms invariably appeared and we had to try to pick our way through the storms with our weather radar to our insignificant destinations. We had to rely on receiving scrappy bits of paper from our wireless operator telling us what to expect at our next port of call.

The other problem that we had was that the rules very sensibly said that aircraft flying into the interior had to have two radio beacon receivers to cater for single failures and our demonstration aircraft had only one. Varig should have told us of this requirement since there was no way we could have found it out by consulting UK documentation. We telephoned our base at Woodford straightaway, but it took several days for the equipment to arrive and even longer for the kit to be fitted.

We had a splendid Christmas Dinner as guests of Varig in their base at Porto Allegre. Varig was a co-operative owned by the employees, originally German in extraction, and this was their annual business meeting. The head of the airline, Ruben Berta, went round all the tables talking to all the people, seemingly knowing them all. He chatted to us on the way by. I will always remember him as a true leader of men in the days before the accountants took over running airlines. With the Christmas holidays over we flew back to Sao Paulo to meet up with the radio equipment which had finally arrived from England.

Corcovado

Varig was a professional airline and so, very sensibly, they had insisted that we operated first from their worst airfields to ensure that the aircraft was capable of substituting for their DC3s before we carried any fare paying passengers on the rough airstrips. However, they started the 748 flying the air bridge from Sao Paulo to Santos Dumont, the downtown airport of Rio de Janiero, probably so the aircraft could be seen, perhaps to allow us to get used to the local conditions and for the Varig operations staff, accompanying the aircraft, to learn how to despatch the flights with the correct take-off weight for the runway length and ambient temperature. It certainly was a wonderfully scenic trip flying down the coast, round the Corcovado overlooking Rio and then landing in the middle of the Town.

Foz Iguaçu

After the air bridge we started to fly on some rough strips which allowed us the opportunity to fly over the magnificent Iguaçu Falls on the borders of Brazil, Uruguay and Argentina. These flights confirmed my view that one of the advantages of being in charge of one's own aircraft was the ability to overfly and examine these wonderful natural beauties of nature and take unusual photographs.

Fuel drums at Bom Jesus du Lapa

215

Handling the fuel pump

Since the strips we were visiting only had aviation petrol for the DC3s the airline had positioned 40 gallon barrels of aviation turbine fuel at our planned refuelling stops together with drums of water methanol. To facilitate quick refuelling we carried a refuelling pump around in the freight hold.

Over Wing Refuelling

Our first flight substituting for a DC3 and carrying fare paying passengers was from Belo Horizonte along the Sao Francisco river, with eight stops finishing in Bahia at Salvador on the Atlantic Coast. We had wanted to position the aircraft at Belo Horizonte the night before but we had not finished fitting the second radio beacon receiver and, as so often happened, when the aircraft was ready the weather was not. We went to the airport restaurant in Sao Paulo and had some of the very strong sweet coffee, for which the country is renowned, waiting for the weather to clear. Waiting is always difficult and we debated what we could do. The Sao Francisco route was a very popular one with the Varig pilots since it meant a night stop in Salvador, but the difficulty was that it was not possible to fly into any of the intermediate airfields on the way in the dark. Clearly, if we could not get started by about midday we had no chance of getting through to the coast unless we overflew some of the stops. After a time we gave up trying to second guess the despatchers and got reading material out of our navigation bags. Frank Lord, our engineer, went to check the aircraft.

Every half hour the weather for airports all over Brazil was sent to the operations centre at Sao Paulo and then retransmitted to all the airfield teleprinters. We checked the reports and at 10.30 the weather started to clear. The weather at Rio, as our diversion, was also clear so the seven strong Varig evaluation team plus Frank and myself got into the aircraft and Chaves flew it to Belo Horizonte. There was some delay, since there were other aircraft ahead of us all having to make radio beacon instrument let-downs; we saw the ground at about 500 ft and the runway a few seconds later.

We got to the ramp at 12.30 to find that despite the lateness of the day the flight had not been cancelled, notwithstanding that we could not get to our end destination before it got dark. We had a full DC3 load plus the evaluation team, about 32 people in all. I went with Leonel to flight operations to discuss matters with the despatcher. He had been talking to Captain Westarp in the main Varig flight operations centre in Sao Paulo and Westarp's instructions were very clear "Keep going until it gets dark. Stop wherever you are. Carry on again in the morning."

Rio Sao Francisco

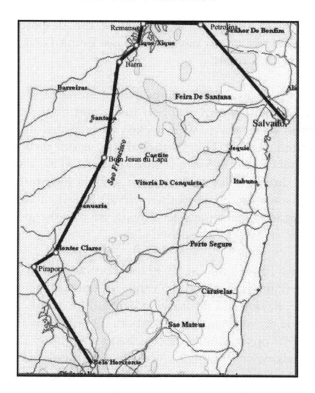

Belo Horizonte to Salvador

Leonel taxied out and we took off for the Sao Francisco river. Once we left Belo Horizonte we were far away from civilisation. There was no means of communication with the ground except with an HF set operated by our Varig operator using a key; he spent the whole time transmitting to Sao Paulo and receiving the latest weather. There were the normal thunderstorms building up but the route seemed reasonable.

Pirapora

We flew down the Sao Francisco competing with the paddle steamers that were also doing the route. We went to Pirapora, Montes Clares and Bom Jesus de Lapa. At each stop we left the rough strip and taxied to a hut which served as the passenger terminal; we were greeted by the local population, their children, their dogs, cattle and chickens; the livestock sheltering under the aircraft's wing to keep out of the stifling heat. We added the fuel out of the drums that had been prepositioned, using the pump and then added water methanol to the tanks located in the wing fillets on top of the wing at the fuselage join, to boost the engines in the tropic temperature. At each stop the despatcher worked out our take-off weight and we checked it against the Flight Manual.

Welcoming Committee

The freight was loaded by the perspiring porters, the passengers clambered aboard and we got permission to start the engine using our internal batteries; the propeller turned very slowly at first, then quickened imperceptibly as we opened the fuel high pressure cock. The igniters lit the fuel and the propeller accelerated faster; the jet pipe temperature rose rapidly heading for the limit and then, just at the critical moment, the temperature steadied and the engine rpm stabilised. It was time to start the other engine.

We left Bom Jesus de Lapa as the heat of the day started to subside. The Varig pilots said that we would not enjoy night stopping at Barra, our next port of call, and somehow we just made Xique Xique as it got dark. The Varig open baggage truck came out to greet us; we all clambered aboard, passengers as well as crew, the bags were loaded next to us, and we were taken to the local hotel, a hut divided into two for the men and women. We had a wonderful shower from a bucket and a very adequate meal. Exhausted we slept on straw mattresses until dawn when we were all woken up. Passengers and crew made their way back to the aircraft and we carried on towards Bahia stopping at Remanso, Petrolina and finally Salvador. I had hoped that Varig would have sent an aircraft out from Salvador to meet us but not a bit of it; this was to be a real test.

When we got to Salvador there was no respite from the heat and the demands of flying fare paying passengers from the short unprepared airfields. We watched the big jets flying over our heads from Rio to the flesh pots in the USA and Europe, making their contrails in the sky. Somehow the world had got it wrong; we were working our backsides off, uncomfortable, getting poorly paid while our less qualified colleagues sat in luxury connecting and disconnecting the autopilots.

We returned slowly to Belo Horizonte retracing our steps, whilst the nosewheel steering started to malfunction making taxiing very uncomfortable. We got there just as it was getting dark and then flew back empty to Sao Paulo. We had made eleven landings that day starting at dawn and finishing at about eight o'clock at night. We debriefed the following day to Westarp and I remarked that the 748 evaluation had to be a test, not of the men, but of the machine.

For the next month we flew everywhere in Brazil except up the Amazon to Manaus. We saw more of the country than most Brazilians see in a lifetime. A wonderful country and I was lucky enough to return two years later with my family to help train the new pilots on the aircraft they had ordered. However, our return to England was marred by the unexpected. We left Sao Paulo and retraced our steps to Belem and Antigua. In order to save time we decided to cut the corner and land at Bermuda, where the airfield was operated by the US Navy as part of the second world war 'lease lend' agreement. To our horror our landing permit request had been altered without informing us; it had only been validated to the renewal date of our annual insurance and not for twelve months as we had requested. The US authorities were as difficult as possible, making us re-apply to the Pentagon for permission to proceed and they would not let us leave until we had the clearance in our hand. I had to fly to Washington to get the permit and, when we finally taxied out to leave, we were made to stop and show the permit to some officious person on the base. We felt that with allies like that, who needed enemies. I took time out when I got back to write to the Office of the President of the United States pointing out that that wasn't the best way to deal with friends. I didn't get a reply but then I didn't expect one!

***

Another demonstration I remember well was in Columbia but it started badly in Panama, training the local airline, COPA, on their first aircraft. I had become overconfident. Crew training seemed routine compared with test flying, or display flying at Farnborough or even demonstrating the 748 to potential customers. We were at 1,000 feet on the final approach into Tocumen airport, there was a storm ahead but it did not look too severe. My trainee pilot, Captain Cowes the Chief Pilot, said we should stop the approach and wait for the storm to clear; I consulted the weather radar where the storm did not seem too bad and I decided to ignore his advice thinking it would be good experience for him. Suddenly we were immersed in torrential rain with severe buffeting and it was clear that landing was out of the question. I initiated a missed approach and got completely disoriented; I knew that we must climb to avoid the neighbouring hills but I could not decide on the correct heading to level out.

After what seemed a lifetime but was probably only a few minutes, the Avro 748 came out of the side of the storm at about 10,000 feet and peace was restored. I informed air traffic of the situation and, eventually, when the storm cleared we were able to land. My pride had suffered an enormous blow and I could hardly look the experienced Panamanian pilot in the face. Even now, many years later, I feel ashamed of the way I handled the situation. Like many pilots before me who have made mistakes, I was lucky to be alive.

When we entered the operations room there was a call from our marketing operation in Manchester, which luckily made me forget my recent stupidity. They wanted to demonstrate an Avro 748 to the Colombian Air Force and asked me to try to borrow the brand new 748 which I had just delivered to COPA. Since the aircraft was the first of the new fleet and scheduled services were not due for another six weeks it seemed possible to use the aircraft but, not surprisingly, I was only able to get the airline to agree to the loan after Hawker Siddeley had agreed to make some significant financial concessions on the price of spares. In addition, COPA wanted Captain Cowes to go with the aircraft.

As has been remarked, the Avro 748 was an aircraft with an excellent short field performance, but it was not the fastest aircraft in the world. Nevertheless it enabled airlines to replace their 40 year old Dakota aircraft with equipment which met the latest safety standards. However, it was not quite as simple as that because certification measurements are mainly concerned with take-off and landings and these are always carried out on tarmac surfaces. Short airstrips in the Third World were invariably earth, stone or grass, so that the acceleration and braking performance could vary enormously depending on the weather and the condition of the surface. It was not surprising therefore that potential new purchasers of the aircraft always wanted to take the demonstration aircraft to their worst airfields, to see if the Avro 748 could really do all the things we claimed. On our part we had become pretty experienced in making these demonstration flights to poor airfields, since they were vital if a sale was to be made.

My immediate problem for this demonstration was how to crew the aircraft. I knew I would have to have a Panamanian captain as co-pilot but I did not feel able to carry out the demanding flying involving critical take-off and landings and 'outback' navigation without some help. Bob Dixon-Stubbs in our office at Woodford was our operations manager cum navigator cum private pilot and had an immense experience of flying into the interior of third world countries. I asked him to join me in Panama for the operation and, as usual, he was a tower of strength.

The four of us, Bob, Cowes, our support engineer and myself, left Panama early in the morning and set course for Colombia. As was usual on these occasions we carried a 'get you home' pack of critical flight spares, the main items being wheels, brakes and the tools and jacks for changing them. We climbed steadily to 15,000ft and then entered Colombian airspace.

Bogota was 8,000ft above sea level and surrounded by mountains which bore the scars of incautious airborne travellers caught out by the thunder clouds that invariably cloaked the hills. We let down into the valley keeping strictly to the published procedures and eventually saw the town with the airfield close by. We landed uneventfully on the very long runway, the length being needed to give

223

time for the jet airliners to reach their take-off speeds in the rarefied atmosphere.

We were met by Ken Egerton, the 748 sales manager, Juan McAllister our local and very distinguished looking agent and Bill Sturrock, still the Product Support Manager at Woodford but shortly to become the Regional Sales Manager for the area. We went to the Hilton hotel downtown and had our first preliminary meeting in the bar. The demonstration needed meticulous planning since the Air Force wanted us to go straightaway to its most critical airfield, Leguizamo, while for our part, we wanted to keep the aircraft's weight as light as it could be when we got there so that we would be as far away as possible from the maximum landing and take-off weights permitted for the airfield. We also had to deal with the imponderable vicissitudes of the weather. We had to determine how much fuel to carry to complete the course with adequate reserves, how much water methanol to carry to ensure the engines had enough for the boosted take-offs on the route, how many spares to carry to have a reasonable chance of getting home and, last but not least, we had to guess how many passengers would turn up on the day for the trip.

The issue of passenger numbers was always a difficult matter when planning a demonstration flight. I well remember one occasion with Charles Masefield as my co-pilot in Djakarta when we had been assured that only a handful of people would be on the demonstration. Because it was a long round trip, we therefore decided to take fuel for the whole journey rather than waste time refuelling at some unlikely and inefficient spot. The morning arrived and our demonstration flight had clearly been oversold; all the airline management seemed to have turned out and the plane was full. The maximum take-off weight for the aircraft was 45,000lb and, with the fuel we had loaded, we were up to about 48,000lb and counting. Charles and I were in complete agreement as to the correct course of action, defuel the aircraft before proceeding and take on fuel en route; but we were also in complete agreement that what we needed to do, if we were not to impair the sale, was to take-off without any delay. On the very slow climb out of Djakarta, as we illegally exceeded our maximum take-off weight and at the same time extended the flight envelope of the 748, we discussed how long it would have taken to defuel the aircraft and by how much we were eating into the design safety margins. Still we felt our breaking of the rules was not as bad as the Captain of a 748 in Antigua who had so many passengers that he had them standing in the freight compartment like a London transport tube train. "What else could I do?" he explained "we could not leave them behind."

For this particular trip Juan assured us that only about twelve Air Force personnel would come on the trip and he decided that besides the sales team he would ask his secretary, a very attractive ex-Avianca stewardess, to serve the refreshments, a vital ingredient for any demonstration and normally consisting of alcohol in some form with some sandwiches at the very minimum; the chief salesman always made the crucial decision on what sustenance was required to match the importance of the passengers.

The route planned by the air force included a variety of difficult airfields starting with the worst in the south of the country on one of the head waters of the Amazon on the boundary of Peru and Ecuador. Leguizamo was a 3,000ft strip of grass growing through pierced steel planking, a favourite military way of laying down an airfield in a hurry. The surface is fine on day one, when the airfield is opened for business, but once the grass starts growing through, the coefficient of friction for braking when it is wet approximates to a very fast skating rink. We charged our salesman therefore to find every reason to tell the customer that we should do the route round the other way so we could land at as low a weight as possible. However, the customer, probably because he was pretty smart, decided that Leguizamo was to be our first port of call.

Bob and I went round to the Civil Aviation Authority as was our wont to check all the airfield and navigation facilities, since experience had taught us never to trust the local aviators. I remember the final words of advice from the man in the office "Never go to Leguizamo if it has been raining and the runway is still wet". Suitably boosted in confidence we went to the meteorological office to check the weather and we were reassured that the rain, which had been falling in the south for the last 48 hours, would probably just have stopped and that all should be set fair for our trip in the morning. Bob and I looked at one another, wondering what the weather was really going to be like and how slippery the strip was going to be.

225

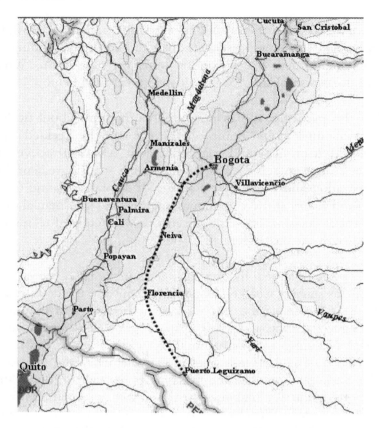

Colombian Andes and Puerto Leguizamo

The route was down a valley in the Andes but towards the end it was possible to turn left, overfly a navigation radio beacon and then do our final let-down using the beacon at Leguizamo. We had four airfields to visit with a total distance of about 750 miles and we calculated the fuel again and again to decide on our minimum reserve at Bogota. We knew that the pilots would wish to fly the airplane doing some take-offs and landings and each take-off used a considerable amount of methanol because of the high temperatures. We allowed therefore for some extra methanol and fuel above the minimum required for the basic demonstration to cater for the pilot flying. We kept to a full set of wheels since one never knew what the future held with regard to runway surface, punctures and who might land with his feet on the brakes, a sure way of ruining irretrievably a set of tyres if not the wheels themselves.

226

We assembled at dawn. The weather did not seem too bad and they said the rain had stopped at Leguizamo. Everyone seemed happy and relaxed for a day's trip that kept them away from their offices or other unpleasant commitments. Only Bob and I knew the difficulty of what had to be done with a wet slippery runway, but we had to look supremely confident and as if we did not have a care in the world. The key decision maker was a pleasant, ebullient, overweight Colonel who clearly, for that morning at least, was the greatest of friends with Ken and Juan. He decided to sit in the right hand seat and give us the benefit of his advice to ensure we arrived at our destination safely.

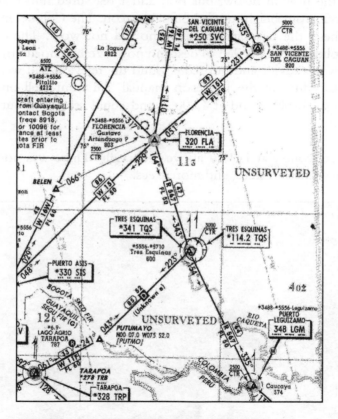

Radio route to Puerto Leguizamo

We taxied out and climbed west into a rain sodden, grey and cloudy sky, notwithstanding we were near the equator. We turned left down a valley in the Andes as soon as we could and occasionally we could see the menacing mountains on either side climbing into the clouds. The Colonel, ever helpful, told us we could cut the corner and that we did not have to keep in the middle of the airway. We thanked him for his advice but did not budge. The locals became accustomed to the terrain and many, unfortunately for them, became too casual.

After about two hundred miles we were able to turn left and leave the Andes behind us and fly over the plains and forests below. We approached the penultimate radio beacon and at this point the Colonel became agitated. We needed to start the let down immediately to fly over the beacon below, but Bob and I reassured him that we were conserving our height until the final beacon. The Colonel in this case knew best; the beacon at Leguizamo did not work. The cloud cover was solid and we needed to descend now. We had no alternative but to follow his advice and hurriedly found the relevant bad weather let down procedure in the Jeppeson manual. All went well on our descent and we broke cloud at 1,800 ft and could see for about five miles ahead.

We set course at 1,500ft above the jungle. There was nothing to help us navigate but trees, and more trees.

Colombian Jungle

I engaged the autopilot and set Bob's heading for Leguizamo, 100 miles away, with infinite care hoping against hope that the check of the compass at Panama had been an accurate one. The cloud base started to lower and we were forced to reduce altitude. It started to drizzle and the visibility dropped to two miles; we were down to 900 ft. After thirty minutes I slowed the aircraft down and hoped for the best; the Colonel went quiet as we had to drop down to 600ft above the trees. Suddenly through the murk I saw a change in the dark green landscape and then a clearing appeared with a few buildings and a landing strip next to a large river. I slowed right down and lowered approach flap whilst I circled the strip below 500ft to size up the situation. I suppose the right course of action would have been to depart for the next airfield but, as always, we were caught by circumstances. To avoid landing would be a fail and the contract could well go elsewhere. I remember a very senior director of Hawker Siddeley saying how his pilots were never under any pressure and the decisions were always up to the Captain; he clearly had no idea what it was like to be Captain in these circumstances.

We headed downwind towards Peru. I had to let down to 400ft to keep the ground in sight and I suddenly realised as we crossed the river into Peru that the jungle had a good 100 ft altitude in its own right. We banked left between the clouds and the trees, put the landing gear down and, continuing the descending turn, selected full flap. Still turning to keep the field in sight we cleared the trees as we crossed the river and I had to dive bomb the other bank 300 yards away to try to get down to the start of the landing strip. I rolled the wings level just before we touched and fortunately touched down not too far from the beginning of the grass strip. The airfield was like a mound so that once you were past half way there was no help from the slope. I put the propellers immediately into ground fine pitch, which gave the normal drag braking effect and then applied the brakes; nothing much seemed to happen as we slid and slithered up the strip. The end of the strip came in sight approaching far to quickly for my taste but somehow we managed to stop with a few feet to spare. I turned the aircraft through 180 degrees, no mean feat bearing in mind the width of the runway, and taxied to the parking area just off the strip. Bob and I said nothing. All in the day's work. We tried to make it look as if it was quite normal to land on fields like Leguizamo.

We sat still and slowly unbuckled our straps. The Colonel seemed delighted and rushed back to talk his people.

Porto Leguizamo

If we had been nervous, so had the passengers. They had apparently prepared themselves to meet their maker in the manner recommended by the Catholic Church, but seemed relieved that their preparations had not been required. As far as I can remember they did not kiss the soil but they seemed really pleased to be standing on it. There was an Officer's Mess close-by and we were driven in open trucks to this hutted luxury. It was 9.30 in the morning but clearly in the circumstances not too early for refreshment in the guise of whisky, gin, beer or whatever. Somewhere, I have a picture of Bill and Ken standing next to the aircraft in the rain on the steel planking looking dazed but I am not sure whether the picture was taken before or after the visit to the mess. However, I do remember hearing Bill say it was the first time he had ever flown in an aircraft with one wing in the clouds and the other in the trees.

The passengers slowly relaxed and prepared for the next leg to Tres Equinas 80 miles to the north. We taxied delicately on the sodden surface to the end away from the river and took-off clearing the other end with a yard or so to spare. We crossed the river into Peru, just getting over the towering trees, so close we could see the branches in every detail, wet and glistening as we peered into the gloom below the leaves, the trees slowly sliding close by underneath. We turned, keeping low, and headed North; the weather improved as the heat of the day started to make itself felt in the low level tropical atmosphere. We were slowly able to climb and started to feel slightly more comfortable as the jungle began to get smaller.

748 Landing on Stones

Tres Equinas was a different proposition to Leguizamo. The airfield was 3,500 ft long but the problem here was that the surface was stony. Stones were always worrying for any aircraft during landing or take-off since some inevitably followed the laws of Gaussian distribution and occasionally hit critical parts of the aircraft, like the propellers. In the 748 we had learnt the hard way from experience, so that the bottom of the aircraft was now always covered with fibre glass in the sensitive areas, as were the flaps in order to prevent damage. Our recommended operational procedures were designed to minimise stone damage, but random stone damage was always a worry. Unlike Ken Edgerton's predecessor, who after one stony landing immediately drew the customer's attention to the lack of damage, we never looked at the aircraft after a landing but left the

231

company engineer to inspect the plane after all customers had left and then whisper in our ears if there was a problem.

Typical stony airfield

In fact, we had no problem landing at Tres Equinas and the braking was quite good. Once again we parked the aircraft and went to the mess and once again liquid refreshment was the order of the day. When we all reassembled I taxied out for take-off. The problem at Tres Equinas was that there was a hill just in line with the runway which had to be cleared, even on one engine. We took off uneventfully, but I was glad we had two engines.

The next leg was another 30 minutes and the passengers were well looked after by the stewardess. We landed at San Vincente; the pattern had been clearly set and the team trooped off to the Mess. We stopped here for lunch and then left for Villovicencia, a long paved runway close to Bogota but 7000 ft lower down in the jungle. It took us 50 minutes and the pilots suddenly realised that they had not flown the aircraft. They started working out who had had the least to drink and, therefore, who should do the flying; luckily just as they had established who was going to be the fortunate man, the stewardess, very well trained and still immaculate, announced that they had all had far too much to drink and none of them was going anywhere near the controls.

We climbed up out of Villovicencia to clear the mountains and did a visual let down to Bogota, the weather having now cleared. My last memories of the demonstration were Ken, Juan and the Colonel swaying on the tarmac and Juan incautiously asking them to go home with him, apparently much to the disapproval of Mrs McAllister. Still we sold six aircraft to the Air Force so I suppose it was all worth while.

***

It was 1967. We were on the other side of the World. Philippine Airlines were considering replacing both their F 27s and DC3s with the one aircraft type, the Avro 748, which would be able to service all their domestic airports. However the airline wanted a three month demonstration by a 748 working all their routes with fare paying passengers before they felt certain our aircraft could do the job and would sign the contract. Dicky Martin and myself were doing the demonstration with three Philippine airline captains, Ben Narciso, Guerzen and Castro.

We were in the middle of the three months demonstration when I suddenly got the news over dinner that there had been an accident at an airfield called Malaybalay in the Southern Philippines. Our 748 was needed to fly down very early the following morning to take the accident investigators to the accident site. We had been planning a day off and do some aircraft maintenance but that obviously would have to be shelved. Clearly something had gone badly wrong in the Southern Philippines which necessitated using the Avro 748.

We took off at 3.30 in the morning. I had not had much sleep even though I was in bed soon after nine o'clock. My mind was trying to understand what had happened from the little information they had given me over the phone. I knew an accident to an F27 had occurred but not much else. This puzzled us since, as far as we knew, it did not have the performance to operate from that airfield.

Flight Testing to Win

The alarm had gone off at two o'clock and I had taken a shower in the old fashioned bathroom, with the insects scattering as I turned on the light. In 1967 the rash of modern international hotels at Makati and elsewhere had not been built and in Manila the choice for us had been between the Manila, where our competitors the Fokker representatives always stayed, and our hotel, the Hotel Filipinas. It had not been too bad at first since our two young children could use the pool but when this started to go dark green, life became difficult.

It was hot and sticky as I got dressed, with only the hotel's rudimentary air conditioning system, but I tried to keep cool as I put on my uniform, blue trousers and white short-sleeved shirt. Once dressed there was not much else to do; all the necessary equipment and information was in my standard black leather bag with its top opening flap to allow easy access to all its contents when on the flight deck. I said good-bye to my wife and took the ancient elevator down to the lobby.

Frank Lord, our Company engineer, was waiting for me and we went out into the street. The heat was oppressive, even in the middle of the night, and the humidity seemed like 110%. The flying insects swarmed around the lights at the front of the hotel and their dead bodies were everywhere. The car was waiting for us and we drove down a deserted Roxas Boulevard. It was so late at night that the street was no longer full of Jeepneys taking passengers around the numerous night clubs on the strip. The burnt-out shell of the latest club arson could be seen as we turned left at the bottom of the street and proceeded towards the domestic airport.

Even though it was in the middle of the night there was plenty of activity in the domestic terminal, which was used solely for internal flights. Unlike the International terminal, there had been no obvious attempt to modernise the buildings which were really a conglomeration of huts. Frank went out to the aircraft and I pushed my way through the throng to the operations room. Ben Narciso, one of the three Filipino captains who were qualified on the Avro 748, was already there and we discussed the weather to the South. Our first stop, Mactan near Cebu, was not a critical airfield being a 10,000 ft strip of concrete which the United States Air Force used as an air

234

base; we were landing there to pick up key personnel from the southern region of Philippine Airlines.

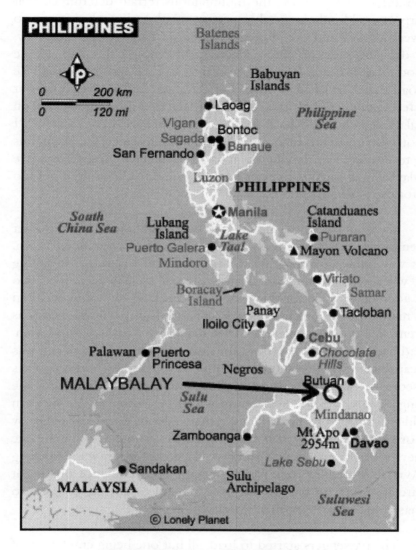

Philippines and Malaybalay

Our destination, Malaybalay 400 miles to the South, on the side of a Volcano, was an entirely different story; it was a difficult airfield for any aircraft, short and surrounded by mountains. The Avro 748 could only land if the landing weight was reduced well below its

235

maximum permitted landing weight and, equally, the take-off weight was restricted due to the short airfield length and the high ambient temperatures. Furthermore, the mountainous terrain determined that the airport could only be used in perfect weather since there were no bad weather aids and the approach was up a narrow valley. Luckily, there did not seem to be a special problem for this trip as the monsoon was not due for another month and we confirmed that the fuel load that I had had to work out the night before, based on our expected passenger load, looked to be satisfactory to reach Mactan, on to Malaybalay and then back to Cagayan where we were to refuel. I did not wish to waste time refuelling at Mactan since the night was going to be quite short enough as it was and the team needed to arrive at Malaybalay at dawn to get out to the site and back before it got too dark for us to take-off.

We went out to the aircraft and once again the heat hit us after the temporary relief of the noisy air-conditioned operations room. Frank was there checking that the spares I had requested, including some wheels, had been loaded into the rear freight hold. The two flight attendants, male for this trip, were checking the cabin and Ben and I made our way through the narrow aisle, lifting our flight bags as we went. We got into our seats; I let Ben fly the first leg to Mactan. He had been flying the Avro 748 for nearly two months now and was very capable and very enthusiastic about the airplane. The Philippines had scores of little airfields and needed modern aircraft to take the passengers safely from these stone and grass strips to the modern airfields with paved surfaces. The alternative to air travel was either by boat or rough roads through the mountains or both and the surface journeys took days instead of minutes. Hawker Siddeley was providing the Avro 748 to the airline for three months to convince them that the aircraft could do the job they needed and to encourage them to purchase the Avro748 for their internal network.

The passengers started to load, all but one being employees of Philippine Airlines; they looked grim and already weary from the short night's sleep. There was no conversation and we requested start-up clearance from the tower the moment the steward confirmed that the twelve passengers were strapped in. Air Traffic Control gave us our clearance almost immediately and we taxied out. There was no wind and we requested runway 16 to save time so that we could climb straight ahead to our destination. The tower agreed to this since there were no other conflicting movements and Ben taxied onto the runway; I turned off the air conditioning fan to conserve engine power and we took-off. At 130 mph Ben pulled back on the control column, rotated the aircraft and we slowly climbed away from Manila.

The 748 was a very uncomfortable aircraft in the heat of the tropics. British engineers living in England had never seemed to grasp the need to keep passengers cool and the problem was compounded by the fact that the air conditioning took a significant amount of power out of the engines, power that was desperately needed to get the aircraft to climb. The aircraft used two Rolls Royce Dart engines driving Dowty four bladed propellers and there was precious little power to spare if there was an engine failure. The moment we were safely airborne I selected the pressurisation and settled down to the long wait for the cabin temperature to drop.

The lights of Manila took a long time to disappear behind us as the aircraft made altitude. It is probably true of most aircraft that they take between 35 and 40 minutes to reach cruising altitude and the 748 was no exception. In the tropics, the performance of the 748 was hardly sparkling but in due course we levelled off at 17,000ft. The aircraft started to accelerate so that, eventually, we settled down at about 250 miles per hour and the extra speed of the air over the heat exchangers started to pull the cabin temperature down.

Our flight to Mactan was scheduled to last two hours and I had taken more care than I chose to admit the previous evening to determine how much fuel to carry. The problem was that Malaybalay was a grass strip, only 3000ft long, on the side of the volcano. It had a significant gradient and the problem was compounded by the closeness of the hills. We had already operated with fare paying passengers out of the strip, but only after carrying out route proving with the airline, simulating engine failure at the maximum permitted weight. At the time, only the old Dakota aircraft flew into the field and the airline wanted to get rid of them. The airfield was particularly critical for take-off because the mountainous terrain forced the pilot to take-off uphill and land downhill. This meant that for landing the aircraft had to brake heavily to stop on grass, a surface which is notoriously slippery, particularly when wet.

For take-off the aircraft had to motor up the slope to reach flying speed and then once airborne, it had to be able to climb safely in the event of one engine failing. In fact, the terrain at Malaybalay was sufficiently steep that the standard practice had to be to turn left immediately after take-off so that the ground fell away, an accepted method permitted by the World's airworthiness authorities, provided the terrain had been surveyed and the aircraft's flight path calculated and demonstrated. It was always my view that demonstrating engine failure procedures to potential customers was very difficult because in the parts of the World we tended to fly, the terrain had never been accurately surveyed. Consequently, we never actually stopped an engine and feathered the propeller during these demonstrations but merely throttled the engine back to a power which simulated a real engine failure. Real engine cut take-offs, feathering the propeller, were always reserved for certification flying since we never wished to create an emergency situation unnecessarily, certainly not with passengers on board. The airline did not always understand, at first, our refusal to stop an engine, thinking we were hiding something, but normally accepted our throttling back procedure after we explained the reasons to them.

My problem for this particular rescue trip was that after landing at Mactan we were going to pick up more passengers and then land at Malaybalay at maximum permitted landing weight, at dawn with the grass covered with dew making it a skating rink. Clearly, when planning the fuel I had kept our fuel load to a minimum but I had to ensure that we had sufficient fuel to get back to our next airfield, Cagayan, since there was no fuel at Malaybalay.

I considered all these problems as we approached Mactan and as Ben made a smooth landing on the enormous runway. It was still dark as we taxied in to the ramp. Eight more passengers walked across the hot tarmac to the airplane, looking very concerned and worried as they met their airline colleagues based in Manila. At last we began to hear what had happened. A Fokker F27 aircraft had landed at Malaybalay the previous afternoon on a demonstration flight with a lot of senior airline people from Mactan. The aircraft had been borrowed from an Indonesian oil company and flown by a Fokker test pilot. Apparently the aircraft had turned straight round after landing, taken off and crashed half a mile beyond the end of the runway, killing all on board. In taking the Accident Investigation team into Malaybalay I tried to look unconcerned, but I knew that our landing safety limits were not as great as I would have liked.

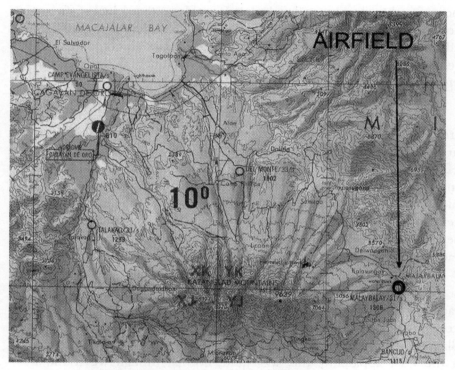

South Easterly approach to Malaybalay

Ben and I changed seats and I taxied out as the first glimmer of dawn could just be seen, taking my time as I did not want to be at Malaybalay until it was really light. The team wanted to be on the ground as soon as possible, since they were planning to go by foot to the scene of the accident to try to get some idea of what had happened and this would take most of the day. We took off and flew up the valley crossing the Del Monte pineapple plantations which made the airfield so important. Slowly we began to be surrounded by mountains rising to many thousands of feet above the airfield. I had subconsciously already made up my mind that the best way to land safely would be uphill, notwithstanding the proximity of the mountains. However, I had decided not to tell Ben of my intentions since he would understandably be very nervous, so I manoeuvred the aircraft around the airfield doing a left hand circuit as if I was going to land normally downhill. But I kept my altitude and did not start to descend until I was downwind for an uphill landing. The hills were uncomfortably close on our right but I could see that I had sufficient room to make a 180 degree turn. I selected landing flap and Ben suddenly realised what I was going to do. He made no complaint, put the landing gear down and we managed to touch down near the beginning of the runway going uphill.

We stopped without having to brake heavily and managed to turn around at the end of the runway though the strip was very narrow at this end, since no aircraft of any size had ever turned there before. We taxied to the downhill end of the strip and stopped at the ramp surrounded by all the local villagers, their dogs and some chickens; security was just not possible, with the village right next to the strip itself. The team got out of the aircraft and spoke at length to the local village elders and the army commander. Then a procession made its way up the hill towards the wreckage.

It was going to be a long wait and we had brought books to read. Apparently all the victims, about fifteen people, had been brought down the mountain the previous evening. We could see the villagers crowding around the mortuary which was open for all to see. In the East apparently this was quite normal though we found it strange.

Inevitably, I found myself wondering about the cause of the accident. It is a truism that accidents are always a collection of unexpected events, since aircraft are intrinsically designed and operated to make air transport as safe as possible; designers, regulators and operators try to allow for anticipated failures of men and machines. Being a pilot I knew how easy it was to make a mistake and it was clear that the Fokker pilot must have been under great pressure to demonstrate the excellence of the F27, since our aircraft had been operating very successfully during the first two months of its three month demonstration operation. There seemed little doubt that unless Fokker could make some special effort, the airline was going to replace all its F27s with Avro 748s and buy some extra aircraft for the Dakota operation.

I was convinced in my mind that the Fokker pilot would have worked out the Malaybalay terrain problem as carefully as he could but why the aircraft had crashed straight ahead instead of turning left was a mystery. I had a nagging suspicion that the pilot deliberately chose to fly straight ahead to show how powerful the aircraft was. I had no idea whether the aircraft was heavily loaded but, normally, on demonstration flights the weights tended to be unrealistically low.

It was a very long hot wait but finally the team returned. They told us that one of the propellers had been feathered before impact and apparently the villagers heard the change of note just after the aircraft took off. The view seemed to be that the pilot deliberately stopped the engine to show the capability of the aircraft and had not realised how steeply the ground rose beyond the runway. The truth will never be known but I wondered whether the F27 was like the Avro 748; the power of the Rolls Royce Dart engine was boosted in a hot climate by water methanol being injected into the engine and theoretically the boosted power was independent of the oil temperature of the engine. In fact, for the Avro 748 we had discovered that the actual power when using water methanol was very sensitive to the oil temperature so that we disliked doing take-off tests when the engine oil was hot. The crashed aircraft had landed, turned straight round and taken off, but even with the hot engine why did the pilot not turn left?

We departed at the end of the afternoon with a full load including one coffin, taking off uphill and turning left immediately as the wheels left the ground. We landed at Cagayan for fuel and returned to Manila. A sad day which, rightly or wrongly, confirmed to me the view that displays and demonstration flying seem inevitably to promote accidents.

We made the sale to Philippine Airlines but we would have done so regardless of the accident. We had flown all over their routes, into their worst airfields. We had been to Basco to the north on the Island of Bataan in the South China Sea with an airfield slope of 5% . We had been to the rice terraces of Baguio, to the bed of stones at Tuguegaro, to the short strip at Calaban with the cemetery at one end and the sea at the other, to the island of Jolo with the houses on posts over the water, to Tawi Tawi, a tiny grass strip at the western tip of Mindanao and to the flesh pots in Davao in the extreme south. We had flown everywhere the DC3 went but with more passengers and with single engined safety. The aircraft had performed flawlessly. I was so brown that when we had gone to some accident emergency at Legaspi by the perfect Mayon volcano, the local commander had spoken to me in Tagalog. The 748 was virtually already part of Philippine Airlines as our demonstration wet lease came to an end. To Dicky and I this had been a very interesting time and we had learnt a lot about the Philippines, the people and the way they lived.

Mayon Volcano

Legaspi

Jolo, houses over the water

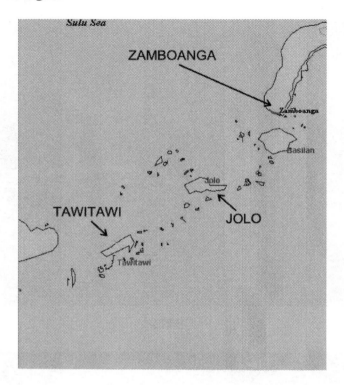

Sulu Archipelago

Tawi Tawi, airfield on right

Tawi Tawi village

No life jackets

In fact, there was a sequel to the sale of the 748 to Philippine airlines. When the airline started operating the airplane they had a spate of punctures and I had to go out to see what was the matter. Luckily the problem was easily solved. An aircraft operating on stones needs the tyre pressures to be as low as the tyre manufacturer permits

245

so that the stones press on as large a surface as possible. However, occasional punctures are bound to take place with such an inhospitable operating environment. Unfortunately, the airline started operating at normal tyre pressures and when they got punctures they raised the tyre pressure to try to minimise the problem. I persuaded them to lower the tyre pressures to the lower approved limit and it did not take long before the confidence of the airline in the 748 was fully restored.

Baguio Rice Terraces

***

During the years we were selling the Avro 748 we reckoned that, between us, we had been to all the world's worst airfields though, to be fair, we never demonstrated the aircraft in Russia or China. Jimmy Harrison flew into airfields in the Himalayas that before the advent of satellites were too secret even to mention. He had a terrible experience in the early days when our one demonstration aircraft did not have weather radar. The aircraft was flying from Bankok to Calcutta and went unexpectedly into the centre of a thunderstorm; somehow he managed to keep control and they were thrown out of the side of the storm at 31,000ft, well above the maximum altitude capability of the aircraft, such was the enormous power of the vertical up currents in the cumulo nimbus clouds.

For myself I flew across the great green greasy Limpopo river to Johannesburg and Capetown, to Lesotho and to Botswana. I flew right across Zaire from Zambia, while the riots were taking place in the Congo. I took ministers into the interior and came out with elephant tusks and copper bound spears. I flew over the Volcanoes of Indonesia and saw the smoke rising from Krakatoa, a century after the explosion. I saw the huge craters in Bali just as the brand new runway was being opened and the new hotels were being built. There, it was not uncommon for Zamrud airlines, the local airline, to lose contact with their aircraft flying in Papua for days at a time, as their pilots plied the aircraft for their own personal hire and reward. Somewhere at home I have lots of snake skins which I purchased in an Indonesian bar, together with a lovely carving which the airline gave me to protect its owner from the gods. In contrast, at home we also have a wooden dish given to me by our Brazilian agent as a reward for our labours with Varig; I suspect the gift was rather small in value compared to his commission..

I remember doing one trip to Australia to try to sell the 748 to the Royal Australian Air Force as a VIP transport and as a navigational trainer, The trip was unusual for me because I did not have an aircraft; I was just part of a marketing team. However, there was one thing the marketing people did not know until we got to Canberra; the Minister of Aviation, the decision maker, was a Peter Howson and he and I rowed together at Cambridge in the Trinity College Cambridge 2nd Boat. I managed to get in touch with him and he invited me to dinner in the Australian House of Commons. I arrived in the lobby area at precisely the agreed time and immediately

Howson's Personal Assistant saw me and took me up to Howson's Office. We had a pleasant dinner together and then his PA took me down to the bar where we continued talking. I remember a newspaper reporter appeared from nowhere saying he had seen me in the lobby and what was I doing there. I fobbed him off with some story but it made me realise how careful one has to be when there are keen journalists about. In the morning I was called to the de Haviland sales office to see the local head man, Rollo Kingsford Smith, son of Charles Kingsford Smith, the very famous Australian Aviator. He clearly did not welcome a junior member of a sales team having easy access to the decision maker and interfering with his marketing strategy. He asked me sarcastically how the dinner went and what advice I could give him. We did actually sell some aircraft to the RAAF but it was no thanks to my dinner with Howson; the aircraft happened to fit the RAAF immediate needs.

***

Martlesham Heath Landing Strip

Perhaps the most important sales demonstration we ever had was early in 1962, not to an airline but to the Royal Air Force. The R.A.F. needed a transport able to operate from short, rough airfields and the 748 seemed an ideal solution. It was a marvellous chance to get some Government money for the project but, very sensibly, before placing the order the RAF wanted to be certain that the aircraft really could do what we claimed and operate from rough, unprepared airfields. The RAF had a test rough landing strip at Martlesham Heath and we were asked to demonstrate the aircraft to a select audience of 'scrambled egg' Air Marshals with their entourage and lots of civil servants. Jimmy quite rightly decided to do this vital flying himself and asked me to accompany him.

We decided that we must have a practice on the strip since time spent on reconnaissance is seldom wasted. So on 22nd January we flew down to Martlesham loaded with spare wheels, aircraft jacks and shovels. In order not to make the demonstration too demanding we only had a small fuel load but we took six engineers plus some marketing people as passengers. As we made our first landing, we realised immediately that the strip was much softer than the airline strips we were used to. The airlines who bought the 748 generally had airfields which were covered with stones and very often were very slippery when wet, but the actual surfaces were normally quite firm. Martlesham however had very few stones but the surface consisted of recently ploughed earth which was very soft so that when we stopped there was liable to be a build up of earth in front of the wheels. This was fine for stopping but prevented the aircraft moving again when the throttles were opened for taxiing and take-off. Consequently, we were a bit despondent after our first landing, when we got out of the aircraft, to see that there was no way that we would be able to move. Luckily the shovels came into their own and all hands removed the earth from in front of our wheels.

We left all our passengers on the strip and, with the earth removed, we managed to taxi back to the start of the strip for take-off. However, we decided not to stop but managed to turn round and take-off. As a result of our experience operating from poor airfields we had developed a standard technique for rough field take-offs, which consisted of keeping the control column fully back as the speed increased to minimise the load on the undercarriage. We used this technique to try to prevent the nose wheels from digging in and spraying stones and earth all over the airframe and propellers; in addition, the technique reduced the weight on the main wheels as early as possible which, on a rough airfield, reduced the drag from the wheels. Then, just before the aircraft could be dragged into the air, we lowered maximum take-off flap and the aircraft would tear itself away from the rough surface and climb away. Speed was immediately increased and a normal take-off resumed with flap retraction and followed by landing gear raising as the speed increased. We used this technique at Martlesham and it worked extremely well, though we had to use take-off speeds below the minimum permitted in the Flight Manual to minimise the high frictional effect of the soft earth. Luckily we did not have any engine failures; had any occurred we would have had to close both engines and land straight ahead.

Bogged Down

Once we had realised that, at Martlesham, landings not take-offs, were going to be the critical operation because of the problem of the build up of earth in front of the wheels, we developed a procedure to try to reduce the amount of this earth as we came to a stop. The method adopted to prevent the earth build up was to use the absolute minimum of braking, applying any required early in the landing run, so that towards the end of the landing run no braking had to be applied at all and the aircraft would roll to a stop. I can't remember how many landings we made on that day or how many times the engineers had to dig us out, but I do remember that, by the end of our practice, we were pretty confident we could land and take-off without getting bogged down.

Another go

The great day arrived, 24th January 1962, and the weather was bad with poor visibility at Martlesham. Jim had decided not to preposition the aircraft at an R.A.F. station nearby, very unwisely in my opinion since our Managing Director was still Air Chief Marshal Sir Harry Broadhurst and, as a good R.A.F. Officer, he always liked to preposition if there was the slightest doubt. As before, we set off with as little fuel as possible to keep our weight down but with a selection of engineers and marketing people who, of course, would not be on board to increase our weight during the demonstration. The weather was extremely marginal but, somehow, we managed to find the strip, which was just as well for Jimmy who would, almost certainly, have lost his job if we had not been able to do the demonstration. We landed uneventfully before all the spectators arrived, unloaded all our gear and passengers and then waited for all the 'scrambled egg' to arrive.

Evaluation Team arrive

Ready to go

The actual demonstration passed off without a hitch. We did quite a few take-offs and landings and did not have to be dug out at all by the engineers. We chatted to the decision makers from the Procurement Executive and the Ministry of Defence over coffee and sandwiches and, hopefully, made it seem that operating from Martlesham was the easiest thing to do in the world. After the de-briefing we returned to Woodford feeling very pleased with ourselves. In due course we got orders not only for the Andover Mk.1 as a troop support aircraft but also for the Andover Mk.2 for use in the Queen's Flight.

Avro 748 G-ARAY at Martlesham Heath

***

After a few years we all knew the North Atlantic like the back of our hands. When we started in the early '60s the 748 did not carry as much fuel as it did in later years and we had to refuel at Stornoway before we could reach Iceland. We soon learnt that when the weather was good in England the depressions were tracking over Reykjavik and Keflavik. From there we had to reach Sondestrom in western Greenland and the first sight of Greenland's icy mountains on the Eastern shores by Kulusuk was unforgettable. From then on there was very little aid to navigation but unexpectedly we discovered a United States radar station, protecting the free world, sitting in the middle of the Greenland ice cap and, very fortuitously, it stood out like a sore thumb on our weather radar. We used to home overhead and looking down we could see the C130 transport aircraft arriving and leaving on skis. Invariably we would talk to the radio operators and they would spontaneously and unasked give us our position in latitude and longitude. Finally we would make Sondestrom and the United States radar station would insist, quite rightly, on giving us a Ground Controlled radar approach onto the 11,000 ft runway. From there we would go either to Frobisher Bay in Labrador or Goose Bay further south. The only navigation aids at that time were radio beacons and, on a good day, the human eyeball.

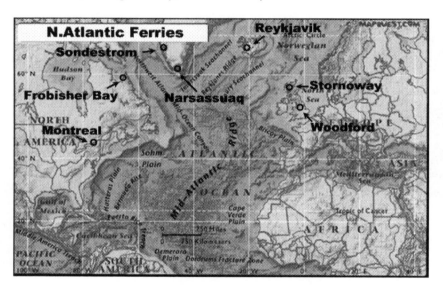

North Atlantic Ferry Aerodromes

In later years the extra fuel meant that we could, if we wanted, overfly Sondestrom. On the way home we had the option of landing in Narsassuaq on the southern tip of Greenland, but the weather had to be completely clear for this option and the airfield was not available at night, so using Narsassuaq could on occasions be time wasting. I was lucky enough to do the North Atlantic trip in the HS125 business jet on several occasions which, with one exception described in the next chapter, proved to be a much quicker and more comfortable experience.

Greenland's Icy Mountains

Sondestrom

Narsassuaq

We also knew the ferry route out to the Far East, since we had to deliver a lot of new aircraft as well as making demonstration tours. Rome was invariably our first port of call followed by Ankara and, in those days, Teheran. We used to love driving up the hill and staying in the Hilton looking down from the bar over the Town, not that we had much time going east as the clock was always against us. From there we would go either direct to Karachi or land first in the desert at Zahedan. The regulations in all these countries as we penetrated eastwards got more and more difficult so it was always with a sense of great relief that we rotated the aircraft at the take-off safety speed, V2, and left the place in question.

Going from Karachi to India was particularly difficult due to the uneasy peace between the two countries. We were never allowed to fly direct from Karachi to Delhi but had to follow some convoluted route to satisfy the military requirements of the two countries. From Delhi we had to refuel in Calcutta, but I always preferred to stop for the night in Delhi and spend the minimum time on the ground in Calcutta. In fact, I only night stopped once in Calcutta and experienced the drive from Dum Dum airport to the town. It was an unforgettable experience, seeing families who spent their whole lives on the road with all their belongings including their cattle, whilst the vultures flew overhead. After that journey up the road I never, ever forgot how lucky I was to be born into a sheltered environment where, most of the time we are protected from the truth, that life is about the survival of the fittest. Once we had left Calcutta life started to improve; Bankok had lots of first class hotels and lots of other facilities that some people found attractive. Then, if Thai Airways was not our destination, we went on to Singapore or Manila. I never flew to New Zealand but a lot of 748s made the journey.

Refuelling from 5 litre cans at Tabriz

One of my last trips home was after our three month demonstration in the Philippines. All went well with night stops at Singapore, Delhi, Karachi and Teheran. Margaret and our two children were with me plus Elvi Banaag, a well connected Philippine airline hostess. As we reached Teheran one of the Arab Israeli wars broke out. We had planned to land at Baghdad but that was clearly not possible. We could not make Ankara direct because of the head winds but the Iranian authorities kindly gave us permission to refuel in Tabriz. We got permission to land at Ankara and so we set off first thing in the morning having purchased the 'regulation' camel bells to hang at home. When we got to Tabriz we discovered that there was indeed fuel there but it was in five litre containers in the town and that the bridge from the airfield to the town was broken. We waited for the fuel all day; it eventually arrived and we made a human chain passing the cans up to the engineers who poured it into the wings. Everybody was very kind and it was an unforgettable experience. Our son managed to fall down the aircraft steps while we were waiting, cutting an eyebrow, but apart from that, all went well.

We took off for Ankara waving our farewells, but as we landed there, we were told to wait miles away from the terminal while the Shah of Persia met with the President of Turkey; Dicky calmed me down as I fumed impatiently until finally we were given permission to refuel and somehow we made Corfu that day, though rather later than planned.

We sold the 748 all over the world from New Zealand, through the Far East, the Middle East, Africa and in North and South America. Selling the aircraft was teamwork; as pilots we had to try and do everything that was required of us. But, however well the aircraft was flown, it was always necessary for the commercial experts to arrange the finance for the hard pressed airlines and for the salesmen, with their agents, to make sure the decision makers chose our aircraft against the opposition. In England we like to think that equipment choices are made without fear or favour but, in reality, in most places the decision makers expect to be rewarded for their efforts. All manufacturers have to use agents and all salesman will say that they are completely unaware of their agent's expenses. Unfortunately, this is the way of the world and when our newspapers periodically go for the high moral ground and try to expose 'bribery and corruption' they are in fact being unrealistic and making it even harder for our salesmen to succeed against the competition from the United States, the French, the Germans, the Dutch and all the other countries. Being successful in getting overseas contracts is a team effort, not only within the company making the equipment but within the UK. The Government has to set the business environment and everybody, including the media has a responsibility to help, not hinder.

CHAPTER 7

Howard Hughes

Courtesy Evergreen Aviation Museum, McMinnville, OR,USA

Howard Hughes in his Flying Boat

Howard Hughes was a legend in his time. He inherited immense wealth which he seemed to increase effortlessly. He was a film producer, a film director, an airline creator, a socialite and had many other interests. But perhaps above all he will be remembered as an aviator. He started the Hughes Aircraft Company and, after winning the 1934 Air Meet in Miami he built and personally test-piloted the world's most advanced airplane, the H-1. With this plane in September 1935 he set a new world's airspeed record of 352 mph and over the next two years he set two new transcontinental records. In 1938 he set a new round the world record flight in a modified Lockheed twin engined aircraft cutting in half Lindbergh's time for the New York to Paris flight. On the way he received the Harmon International Trophy as the world's outstanding aviator, he was honoured by President Roosevelt in the White House and he received a ticker tape parade down Broadway in New York.

Courtesy UNLV Libraries

Howard Hughes and H1

Besides being a world famous aviator his name was linked with many of the most beautiful women in Hollywood; he was the creator and owner of Trans World Airlines but then, in later life, sadly he became a recluse. Inevitably, he was always newsworthy and the mere fact that he wanted to be a recluse encouraged all the media to try to photograph him. Stories about him were countless. Many books were written about his life, long before our paths crossed but, in spite of this, all I knew about him was that he had been an aviator and had designed Jane Russell's brassiere for the film The Outlaw..

As I write this chapter and relate my meetings with Howard Hughes, I keep seeing television documentaries and newspaper articles all saying that Howard Hughes was virtually a vegetable in his declining years, a captive of his drugs but, in my view, this material must have been written by people who did not know the whole story.

Howard may indeed have been a captive, surrounded by 'keepers' who, by all accounts, tried to regulate his every communication with the outside world and, possibly, his intake of 'drugs'. However, I can attest that Howard, when we were together in 1973 in England, behaved as any normal elderly man would, who liked flying. My friend Jack Real has explained the actual situation surrounding Howard's later years very clearly in his book 'Asylum of Howard Hughes' (ISBN 1 902807 21 9) and Jack in fact was my introduction to Howard Hughes.

Jack Real

I first met Jack Real in April 1973. He had been steeped in aviation all his life having worked for Lockheed most of the time, and he was a first rate aeronautical engineer.

He had run the ill fated Cheyenne rigid rotor helicopter programme, killed by the Air Force, Jack told me, because they did not want the Army to have a helicopter which flew faster than their helicopters. He became a vice-President of Lockheed and grew very close to Dan Haughton who was chief executive of the Lockheed Corporation at the time. He seemed to know everybody in the world's aerospace industry. Not surprisingly he lived in the Los Angeles area not far from Lockheed's Burbank facility and for some time worked with Kelly Johnson in the famous Skunk Works where the F104, the

U2 and the SR71 were born. Jack had left Lockheed in 1971 in order to be Howard Hughes' Aviation adviser; Hughes was important to Lockheed since TWA operated the Lockheed 1011 and Hughes still had great influence with TWA so Dan Haughton welcomed Jack's new job.

Cheyenne Rigid Rotor

No one could have served Howard Hughes more faithfully than Jack; he gave him invaluable advice on all flying matters and, in my judgement, it was a pity that Howard did not take Jack's advice on a lot of other things.

I had become Chief Test Pilot of Hawker Siddeley Aviation at Woodford Airfield by the time Hughes, with his unusual life style, impacted on my life and the firm for which I worked. As already detailed, Hawker Siddeley were manufacturing the 748 twin turboprop airliner which was selling reasonably well around the world against its main competitor, the Fokker F27, winning whenever an airline had to operate from short unprepared airfields and still had pre war DC3s, Dakotas, which they had decided to replace.

As luck would have it, my tasks at Woodford had been widened and were no longer restricted to the Manchester factory's output, since the Group was becoming more and more integrated. Because of my experience testing, demonstrating and selling the 748, I had been appointed Project Pilot for the new HS146 100 seat feeder jet liner, which had the dubious distinction of having to have four engines since, at the time, there was not a big enough engine available to enable it to fly with just two. The aircraft was being designed and built at Hatfield where John Cunningham was Chief Test Pilot. However, it was the view in the Group's corridors of power that I would be the best person to lead the 146 from a piloting design viewpoint, because of my background with the 748 which served the markets to which the 146 was aspiring. In addition John Cunningham was approaching retirement and so would not be able to see the 146 through its development life into airline service.

Inn on the Park (now The Four Seasons)

At the time I became involved, Hughes was the sole owner of Hughes Air West but that was about all I really knew about him. It was, of course, common knowledge that he was meant to be a recluse and incredibly rich. Just before the previous Christmas he had landed at Gatwick in a Gulfstream 2 and was reputed to be staying downtown in London at the Inn on the Park Hotel near Hyde Park Corner. Stephen Ward, our contracts manager, called me one afternoon and asked me to accompany him to London on a mysterious trip associated with Howard Hughes.

We met Jack in the Hawker Siddeley headquarters in St. James. At the time Jack was probably just short of 60 years old, 6ft. 2in. Tall and thin. He never spoke Hughes' name when he had meetings though he relaxed his attitude as he and I got to know one another later. Jack always spoke of his Principal and he informed us that his Principal wished to start flying again. He told us that he had surveyed the local UK scene and had come to the conclusion that the Hawker Siddeley aerodrome at Hatfield, about 20 miles north of London, would be the ideal location. He also announced that he had concluded that the 748 would be the best aircraft for Hughes to use. Jack wanted to enter into a lease purchase agreement for one of our demonstrator aircraft, registration G-AYYG, so that Hughes could fly the aircraft with a Hawker Siddeley pilot 'to assist'.

It is probably worth remarking that Jack always worked on a need to know basis. It was not always easy to follow his ultimate goal since he frequently went off at a tangent before returning to the subject in hand. However, Jack did explain that the actual flying with Hughes was unlikely to be as straightforward as an airline scheduled departure. His vision, which he confided to us, was that we would position the 748 at Hatfield with a team of maintenance engineers, paid for, of course, by Hughes, and that these engineers would be on stand-by, day and night, to meet Hughes' wishes.

We finally agreed, after several hours, to Jack's request and undertook to prepare the necessary papers. We discussed at length how Hughes could enter the airfield without being seen and without the world's press knowing what was going on. We were joined by Tony Banham, a contracts man from Hatfield, who advised Jack of a back way onto the airfield and told us how the cars could then proceed to the hangar. During our discussions we went to lunch in the Cavendish nearby where I remember that Jack proceeded to discuss some technical aerospace points, not particularly related to our meeting, illustrating his points by drawing on the tablecloth. We all behaved as if this was the most natural thing in the world; I am not sure whether a new tablecloth was included in the bill.

After the meeting I had to grapple with a variety of quasi-legal problems that needed to be solved if we were to conduct the flying side of the agreement without breaking the law. Hughes, of course, had a valid United States FAA licence because, unlike a UK licence, an FAA licence does not expire but merely has to be kept current. However, if Hughes were to use this licence legally he would need to have check flights with US FAA approved examiners and there was no way that this could happen. We considered getting Hughes a UK pilot's licence but a UK licence, whatever the category, required a photograph and we knew that Hughes would never agree to that. A decision was therefore required, could Hughes legally fly the aircraft without a current or valid licence? The 748 Flight Manual clearly stated that two pilots were required to fly the aircraft but, luckily, the Manual did not specify whether the pilots had to be licensed or not and there could be no doubt that Hughes was a pilot.

I was very reluctant to have to advise Hawker Siddeley that under UK law we could not fly Hughes since, because he was the sole owner of Hughes Air West, I felt that this could be a great marketing opportunity for Hawker Siddeley and for Hatfield in particular, where the marketing team were looking for a launch customer for the 146. Consequently, I took the view that we were not breaking the rules of the Air Navigation Order. However, I insisted that we took great care to ensure that the contract conditions between Hughes and Hawker Siddeley ensured that there was no way that Hughes or his organisation could take legal action against us should an accident take place and we were later judged to have an improperly constituted crew.

The next problem I had to grapple with was the choice of pilot to fly Hughes. From Jack's roundabout description of the requirements, it was clear that the designated pilot, whoever he was, would have to hold himself available full time to minister to Hughes' needs, which clearly was going to be very inconvenient. However, Hawker Siddeley was not only about to manufacture the 146 but was also considering re-engining the 748 with jet engines and, of course, they were always looking for customers for the 125 business jet. Rightly or wrongly I decided to take on the commitment to fly Hughes myself because I considered that this was a fantastic marketing opportunity to get the 146 a launch customer. Anyway, since it was my decision to take on the commitment, it seemed unfair to hand it on to another pilot.

We got the aircraft lease purchase signed very quickly but now we met for the first time a Hughes idiosyncrasy that Jack was aware of from the beginning but chose, understandably from his viewpoint, not to share with us until he had us signed up and committed to his schemes. Hughes would never fly an aircraft he owned or was buying. Jack, faced with the near impossibility of explaining this situation to us, likened the situation to a man who would not wear his best suit since it would then wear out and no longer be his best suit.

I discovered later talking to people at Vickers, from whom Howard bought a Viscount, that it was not unusual for Howard to buy aircraft, isolate them but pay people to service them. Jack told me that there was a hangar somewhere in the States which had several Lockheed Jetstars. In the case of the 748 which Howard had bought, Avro's tucked it away in the corner of one of the flight hangars and Jack arranged for George Larsen to come to England with his wife and son to supervise the handover of the aircraft and arrange regular servicing. George was employed to keep an eye on Howard's immobile fleet of aircraft.

It became quite clear that what had seemed a simple lease purchase agreement had now become impossibly complicated. Jack wanted us to provide our other demonstrator, G-AZJH, for Hughes to fly, but this aircraft had numerous commitments already, including being away at the Paris Air Show. Bill Tull, our marketing director, agreed that Hughes could fly the aircraft the following week, but after that it was not available.

For the next week or so I flew down to Hatfield regularly in our communications aircraft, an old de Haviland Dove, and the maintenance crew had the 748 ready each day. Apparently, Hughes could never make his mind up whether he was going to fly or not and so my daily telephone calls with Jack got more and more frustrating for both of us. All the onlookers wondered why I had to go to Hatfield every day, though my work on the 146 design was a convenient smoke screen. Sometimes, I stayed overnight in the Esso Motor Hotel at Potters Bar or the famous Comet Hotel next to the airfield and then travelled up to Woodford for the day when Jack called the flying off.

After putting up with this disruption to my normal life for a bit I decided to spend a week-end with my family at Woodford, but had the foresight to leave the Dove ready on the Tarmac and not inside the Hangar. The ground crew were not so lucky and had to stay with the 748. It was a Sunday and a glorious English Summer's day;

after lunch I was cutting the hedge when Jack called and said 'the man was getting dressed to go and fly'; I believed him and broke the speed record between Woodford and Hatfield. I called Jack from the operations room at Hatfield, one hour after his phone call to my home. Jack said that all was going as planned and that they would be in the car park of the Comet Hotel at Hatfield in about an hour. Apparently they were well practised in getting Hughes down the Service Elevator of the hotel so that no one would see him getting into his car and, sure enough, Hughes arrived on time.

I was with Tony Banham in his open sports car waiting in the Comet Hotel car park. When the long black Daimler arrived, we led it through an unmarked gate which I unlocked and from there we drove through an old and decaying farm onto the Hatfield aerodrome perimeter track. The Daimler followed a long way behind to avoid, we learnt later, the dust we were kicking up. I got out of the car and positioned myself by the hangar door controls. The Daimler drove into the hangar and I shut the hangar doors. There was complete silence, with the engineers standing way back out of the way.

After a few minutes Jack got out of the back of the car and confirmed all was in order. A man of medium height and running to fat got out of the car; I found out later that his name was Levar Myler, a member of the Summa Corporation that managed Hughes' business affairs; it soon became clear that he was acting as male attendant to Hughes. He opened the car door and helped Hughes out of the car.

Hughes was 68 years old, over six foot tall and rather frail. He had grey hair, a small grey beard but no moustache. He was wearing an open necked shirt, blue trousers and some rather flimsy sandals. He spoke slowly but firmly. He walked unsteadily to some steps at the bottom of the front entrance door of the aircraft where Jack introduced me to him. He paused and looked at the 748 and straightaway commented on the mushroom rivets on the fuselage. We discussed the need for flush rivets on such a slow aircraft; I explained Avro's view, which was that on a slow aircraft like the 748 flush rivets should only be used when it really mattered aerodynamically and that therefore flush rivets were used only on the top surface of the wing and the tailplane. Hughes agreed reluctantly to the logic of the design

267

and then slowly ascended the steps. Having briefly inspected the flight deck he decided to make himself comfortable before the flight; he knocked his head on a temporary antenna tuning unit in the roof of the aircraft as he was going to the toilet but made no comment. Jack and Levar sat in the back.

Hughes soon got tired of my calling him 'Sir' and told me to call him Howard as I helped to strap him into the left hand seat. I wanted him to wear the shoulder harness as well as the lap straps but he would not agree to this. I conceded to his desire, even though it was fundamentally unsafe, because I had another more important difficulty to deal with, one which I just had to win in connection with the wearing of headsets. Unlike United States registered aircraft, it was necessary for pilots in UK registered aircraft to wear headsets and use a boom microphone when taking off and landing, though the headset could be taken off in flight providing loudspeakers and hand microphones were installed; this rule was enforced because it was considered that the wearing of headsets would ensure much better crew communication in the case of an emergency. In fact on this aircraft there were no loud speakers and knowing that Hughes would not be too keen to wear a headset I had provided him with a brand new one for his special use. He regarded the whole procedure with some mistrust but once I had persuaded him to put the headset on, life became a lot easier since he could hear me perfectly and I had no need to raise my voice. He was probably high tone deaf, like most aviators of advancing years, and the directed sound into the ears compensated for this even though the noise was not boosted. It is worth remarking that once he had got used to the headset he treasured it and Jack had to keep it available at all times.

I started briefing Hughes on the 748 and he had clearly done some studying of the manuals which I had sent to him via Jack. One of the strengths of the 748 was its simplicity and he obviously did not expect any problems. I carried out the pre-starting checks and then shouted out of the front door for the ground crew to come out of hiding and tow the aircraft out of the hangar. I closed the door, got into the right hand seat and, once we were outside, started the engines. At 7.10 PM, two hours after leaving home, I got permission to taxi the aircraft from the control tower, waved the chocks away and I opened the throttles for Hughes to taxi the aircraft.

268

The 748 had a very poor nosewheel steering system with only one control on the left hand side of the aircraft which meant that I was unable easily to help Hughes in pointing the aircraft in the right direction. There was a large amount of backlash with the nose wheel steering control in the centre of its travel, but as the tiller came out of the dead area the control was extremely sensitive. We always tried to prevent the pilots of potential customers from discovering how bad the nose wheel steering was, but there was no way I could hide the problem from Howard. We zigzagged all the way to the runway but, to be fair to Howard, he soon started to get the better of the system. He lined the aircraft up for take-off and I did the pre take-off checks. I opened the throttles slowly and we accelerated down the runway weaving from side to side; when I called 'rotate', Howard slowly rotated the aircraft into the air, thirteen years after his last flight I later discovered.

I had arranged to keep another Hawker Siddeley airfield open, Bitteswell about 40 miles north of Hatfield and we had got clearance from air traffic to fly over Luton towards Bitteswell. My problem was getting Howard to fly at the assigned altitude and airspeed since he was not used to our instruments and we were in controlled airspace. He slowly improved and we arrived at Bitteswell after about fifteen minutes. I demonstrated my idea of a typical take-off and landing, but soon realised that the demonstration circuit was far too tight and close to the airfield for the job in hand, which was to get Howard to land the aircraft after not having flown for all this time; a wider circuit with much smaller angles of bank was clearly required. Howard took off without too much difficulty, turned downwind and then, when further away than I would have liked, turned onto the final approach. It had become quite clear by this time that Howard had no intention of touching the throttles, leaving that menial task to me, whilst he manoeuvred the aircraft as he thought fit. In effect, I was his automatic throttle, which perhaps was not a bad thing since the aircraft was very speed stable on the approach so that, if the speed did vary, quite large changes of stick forces were required to control it. Howard started to descend lower and lower and I kept on having to pull the stick back to prevent us landing in the undergrowth well short of the runway. We made several approaches with the same thing happening each time but Howard was determined, if he possibly could, to land on the first inch of the runway if not before. In spite of the aircraft being new to Howard and in spite of the fact that he had not flown for many years, he clearly knew exactly where the ground was but, unfortunately, he did not care what speed he had when the aircraft touched down; he regarded landing up the runway as 'sloppy flying'.

We made several circuits, landing each time and taxiing round for the next take-off. I adopted the strategy of taking over control of the aircraft at the bottom of the downwind leg and putting it in such a high position that Howard just could not get down to his favourite undershooting position before touch-down. By this time it was getting dark and Bitteswell was not equipped for night flying. I got permission for us to go to East Midlands airport close-by because Howard was completely engrossed in trying to master the 748 in the circuit. When we arrived he soon noticed the two sets of Visual Approach Slope Indicators which, by showing either white or red, aided the pilot in getting onto the right glide slope visually. We discussed these lights at length and, of course, I pointed out that, in order to get the correct white/red colours for landing, the aircraft had to be immeasurably higher than the almost suicidal approach paths that Howard was adopting.

The Control Tower started to complain of our low approaches and the M1 motorway seemed very close each time as we approached to land. He grunted at one stage 'I guess you're not the first guy who has criticised my landings. I like to land at the beginning of the runway. Anything else is sloppy'. Of course I pointed out that airspeed was just as important as position but I don't believe he was convinced.

As it got really dark he soliloquised that perhaps he should not be flying on instruments without being in practice but, in fact, he was starting to accept that if he wanted to land the aircraft without my interfering he would have to land further up the runway. After one or two more landings he agreed that he had done enough. As we waited for take-off, another aircraft was coming in to land; I had inadvertently left on our landing lights and they were shining towards the incoming aircraft. Howard noticed my mistake and asked me to turn them off to avoid confusing the pilot, which made me realise that he was beginning to get back into practice.

We headed home to Hatfield. On the way back he said how much he was enjoying the flying and he remarked that he had a 125 in the States. He was delighted when I offered to fly it to England but made it clear that he was going to fly it in England, not me, though I might accompany him. At last Hatfield came into view and Howard made a pretty reasonable landing 3 hours 10 minutes after leaving. We were both delighted and he taxied in feeling justifiably pleased.

I left my seat, only then remembering that Jack and Myler had been in the back of the aircraft the whole time; Jack look relaxed but Myler looked shaken. He helped Howard back into the car. I suddenly felt hungry and noticed some sandwiches and coffee which had been brought on board for Howard. I pointed these out to Jack, hoping that I would be the recipient but he rushed back and to my horror he collected the food and took it with him to the car.

Anti-climax set in. I rang my wife and then went back with the engineers to the hotel. We had a beer and some food and then I went to bed. The following morning I flew the Dove back to Woodford and life returned to normal for a few days.

We were back on stand-by next week-end, Bill Tull having reluctantly given in and allowed Howard to use the aircraft. I flew the Dove down to Farnborough on the Friday; Margaret came with me and we went to a cocktail party at the Royal Aircraft Establishment, Farnborough that evening. I rented a car and we met up with Jack for dinner; his wife Janet had just come over from California and we were joined by Wilbur Thain, one of Howard's doctors and his wife. After dinner Margaret and I drove back to the Queens Hotel at Farnborough. On Saturday morning I flew to Hatfield; Howard never showed and we flew back to Woodford on Monday.

***

Janet and Jack spent the week-end in Cornwall and, while they were away, I started getting phone calls from the Inn on the Park asking for an aircraft to take Hughes overseas. Someone had suddenly realised that Howard needed his visitor's permit renewed or, more likely, someone from the UK immigration authorities had called to find out what were Hughes's intentions. Apparently the immigration authorities had agreed that all that was required for the visa renewal was for Hughes to land outside the UK but the team had problems; they could not or would not tell Jack what was happening because Jack always stood aloof from Howards' team, making clear his dislike of the whole setup. It was Jack who always arranged the flying. The team wanted to show that they could manage without Jack.

We were having our problems getting hold of an aircraft since, as usual, Howard would not fly his own 748 sitting in the hangar at Woodford. We finally found one we could charter in France and then things started to deteriorate.

The people in the Inn on the Park said that the trip would take place on the following day Wednesday 27th June leaving at 10 am. Bob Stubbs our operations manager made all the necessary arrangements with the French airline for the aircraft to land at Hatfield at 9 am. Tony Banham was trying to make certain that the immigration and customs authorities would be present so that we could fly straight to an airfield somewhere close-by in Europe and return. I left home at 4.30 am and drove down from Woodford arriving at Hatfield at about 8.30 am only to find that the Hughes people had cancelled the flight. I called them to be told that it was off for the day. My guess at the time was that they did not want to be seen smuggling Hughes out of the hotel in broad daylight with photographers trying to get some exclusive pictures. In addition, the factory would be working during the day with too many people about.

I drove back to Woodford only to be told by Bob that the trip was on again but that the Rousseau aircraft could not be at Hatfield before 2200 hours. I was feeling irate by this stage and realised that I would be very tired by the end of the day; I retired home to bed but could not sleep. When I got back to my office I called the hotel and found to my great relief that Jack was back from holiday and very cross with the 'amateurs' trying to arrange the flight. I told him that as far as I was concerned the trip was only on if I could bring Bob with me. I knew he would have a job getting Howard to agree but that was his problem. True to form on being told that I was insisting on having Bob on board Howard said 'Jack, your one job to-night is to make certain that this man does not see me'. But Howard had to agree that Bob could come; it was the only good decision I made that day.

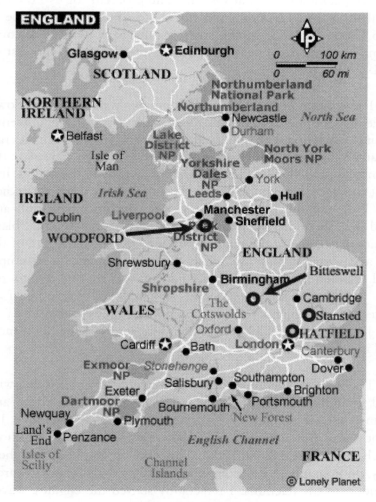

Howard's airfields

Memory can be very capricious but I can remember everything about that night even though it was many years ago, not because Howard was famous, not because he was erratic, not because wereof the publicity but because of the weather, which could not have been worse. A warm sector was lying across Southern England with very low cloud, rain and poor visibility. I called Jack again trying to cancel the flight but Jack was very reluctant to cancel, now that everything was set up. Luckily Belgium looked as if it would be all right so we planned to land at Ostend. The problem for us now was that Banham had told us that the customs officers would not agree to come to Hatfield in the evening so we would have to clear customs and immigration both ways at Stansted, about 50 miles to the east of Hatfield.

There was nothing further we could do. We were flown down to Hatfield in another 748 seemingly powerless to influence events. Everything happened a lot later than planned. The French aircraft landed at 22.55 hours and Howard with his entourage arrived at the same time. By now, the weather was getting worse and the aircraft had only just managed to get in to Hatfield, using the Instrument Landing System. Bob met the French pilots, signed the documentation and arranged for them to be taken to a hotel. The two long black limousines, glistening in the rain, arrived through the back gate of the airfield and drove up to the plane. Once the aircraft was empty Howard climbed slowly out of the car and up the steps into the aircraft. Jack and I settled him into his seat and the other four passengers from Hughes' staff plus Bob strapped themselves in behind; Jack had brought Howard's own headset from the hotel and I plugged it in for him .

The weather was by now impossible and I remonstrated with Howard, pointing out that now was not the time to be flying and suggesting that we should leave the operation for another day. He would not hear of it, even though I said we would probably finish up in Manchester to the delight of the World's photographers. 'Let them take my photograph, I don't care. Let's go and fly' was Howard's contribution to my dilemma. I reluctantly started the engines, waved the chocks away and Howard taxied the aircraft out to the runway. With only one nosewheel steering tiller I felt very uncomfortable as Howard only just kept within the taxiway.

The air traffic controller passed us the Stansted weather, 100 yards visibility with cloud base indeterminate and asked me for our intentions. I told the Hatfield tower that we were going to try to land at Stansted. I felt I was being trapped into an impossible situation, already tired, and with all the ingredients for a spectacular disaster in the making.

We lined up for take-off and for the last time I asked Howard to give up but his mind was made up. He was in position and determined to go. We could only see a few hundred yards down the runway and the wipers were steadily, but ineffectively, trying to remove the rain. There seemed nothing else I could do but open the throttles. Manchester was still a good diversion, so we were not really in any danger providing I kept to the approved weather minima. Unwisely, my marketing instincts kept reminding me that Hughes was more than just a lonely eccentric billionaire; he was the sole owner of Hughes Air West which needed new aircraft and I was the project pilot of the new HS 146 which urgently needed a launch customer.

We slowly gathered speed, the runway lights appeared and disappeared in the gloom and I called out to Howard to rotate the aircraft. As we left the ground we went into cloud. I immediately took over the controls, put the autopilot in and set course as cleared to Stansted. I spoke to Stansted air traffic; the weather had not altered. I was given permission to make an approach and I coupled the auto-pilot to the ILS. Howard said nothing and watched the proceedings with great interest but unable to help.

It is a truism that in life you have to be lucky. I suppose I was well equipped for what was to follow in the next few minutes. Very fortuitously, we had been carrying out trials in a simulator at Hatfield to try to determine the minimum visibility in which it is possible to land an aircraft manually. Not unexpectedly, the minimum visibility for landing varied with the approach speed of the aircraft and I had established to my own satisfaction that a 748 needed about 200 yards to get sufficient guidance from the runway lights to be able to touch-down and to keep straight after landing, providing that the aircraft was lined up on the ILS system as the lights came in to view. The other point was that I had carried out all the testing necessary to install the autopilot on the 748 so I knew that with a good glide slope the aircraft would not go unstable under autopilot control but would remain on the glide slope until about 50ft above the ground. Consequently, I felt it was reasonable to continue the approach to my approved minima of 200ft above the ground. However, the aircraft was designed to be operated by two crew to monitor the instruments and Howard was unable to help.

I selected the landing gear as we reached the glide slope, throttled the engines back to approach power and we settled onto the glide slope. I tried to watch the altimeter and look out at the same time since I had no one to call out the height. We went below 1000 ft, 800ft, 600ft, 400ft and there was no sign of anything. I saw 200ft briefly as the loom of the approach lights lightened the murk below and unwisely, like many foolish aviators before me, decided to carry on a for a few seconds. I saw something ahead, decided I had better disengage the autopilot and reduce the rate of descent and to my slight surprise and unmitigated relief found that we were on the ground. I selected ground fine pitch on the propellers and managed to keep straight on the runway. We came to a stop in the middle of the runway because there was no way I could see to taxi the aircraft. We could see nothing but the next runway light 50 yards away.

The tower sent out a follow-me van and Howard taxied slowly to the ramp, though I encouraged matters by judicious use of my brakes to augment what in my view were Howard's slow responses. The team trooped out of the aircraft and Howard remained seated. Bob took the ship's papers to the customs' and immigration office which could barely be seen a few yards away. The very bright amber lights. on their tall masts, illuminated the gloom below.

Feeling a bit shattered I told Jack that enough was enough and that I needed to be in the left hand seat and that I needed Bob in the right hand seat. Howard would have to be a passenger for this trip. Jack dutifully took the message back to Howard and for the next 40 minutes whilst the ground officials looked on with amazement Jack, Howard and myself negotiated the next move. Howard's staff were encouraging my stance whilst Howard started making counter offers. His first suggestion was surprising, bearing in mind his aversion to being seen; "Let Tony's man sit in the jump seat, I'm learning a lot watching Tony". To be fair I think he was enjoying the experience which was more than we were. At this stage I went back into the aircraft and tried to explain that the weather required that two qualified pilots needed to be sitting in the seats; it was not the night for pilot training.

He was unconvinced and Jack had another go after I left the aircraft again. Finally Howard conceded defeat and Jack turned two of the passenger seats round and made a bed for Howard. He reluctantly vacated the left hand seat and Bob and I took our places. The follow-me van obligingly led us back to the runway and we took off for Ostend not knowing where we were going to finish up. Jack, the perfect organiser, had contacted the drivers at Hatfield, and, planning for success, told them to position the cars at Stansted.

Once again we were swallowed up by the cloud as soon as we rotated and we set course for Ostend. We flew at 11,000 ft and suddenly we were in the clear, the English Channel below and the lights of Belgium ahead. Bob and I had already decided that we would just do a touch and go, obviously not wishing to have to clear all the formalities in Belgium. Unlike the British officials, they might have wished to see the legendary Mr Hughes. I declared a hydraulic emergency and asked for a clearance back to Stansted. We orbited the airfield without touching down and, after receiving our clearance, we headed west for another approach to Stansted.

It was just getting light as we started our descent but nothing else had changed. Bob called out the heights as the autopilot made a perfect approach down the glide-slope. 200ft above the ground came and went but maybe I was better prepared or in better practice; I just had enough visual clues to close the throttles and pull the stick back and we made a good touch-down. The follow-me van appeared out of nowhere and I taxied back to the ramp where the passengers got out. The cars had arrived from Hatfield to Stansted, though even that must have been difficult in the fog, and they drove onto the ramp. As Hughes was helped into his car my last words to Jack were 'Do you think he will ever forgive me?' 'Not tonight he won't ' was the instant reply and off they all drove, in time for a picture by a reporter to be taken in London of Howard's car with all the side and back windows covered with newspapers.

We left the aircraft for the French crew and I slept most of the way back to Woodford in the back of one of the ground crew's car. I told the story to Margaret feeling very depressed, as I felt a great marketing opportunity had been lost. It was by far the worst weather in which I had ever landed and I learnt later from more simulator trials that the weather was just about the limit of what was possible. Had I been fresher I might have been able to let Howard stay in the left hand seat but, as it was, I had had no alternative. Margaret as usual summed it up perfectly 'If Hughes can't see that you did the right thing, then you are well out of it'. Two days later Jack called - 'Howard said you were right and how about Tony flying with me in a 125?'

10	HS 748	EA2JH	SELF	H HUGHES	Circuits
11	DOVE	GARHH	SELF		Hatfield & Return
13	VICTOR	KL232	SELF	HAWKES	Initial
14	DOVE	GARHH	SELF	1	Hatfield
15	DOVE	GARHH	SELF		To Farnborough
16	DOVE	GARHH	SELF		Farnborough - Hatfield
17	DOVE	GARHH	SELF		Hatfield - Woodford
23	VICTOR	XL231	S ELF	HASEFIELD	P.F.T.S.
27	HS 748	FBRE	SELF	H HUGHES	Hatfield - Stansted
		F BRSU	SELF	R. DIXON-STUBBS	Stansted - Osland - Stansted
29	VICTOR	XL231	SELF	FISHER	P.T.S.

Log Book extract 748 flying

I had taken the precaution some time previously to get the Hawker Siddeley 125 on my licence. I had done this for no particular reason except that I was working more and more at Hatfield, where the aircraft was designed and flown, and I had flown on several transatlantic delivery flights with the Hatfield pilots. The 125 was actually built not at Hatfield but at another Hawker Siddeley factory at Hawarden, Chester. My opposite number at Hatfield, John Cunningham, controlled all the 125 flying. I telephoned him and explained that Howard wanted me to fly him in the 125 and John, to his great credit, made no difficulties even though my experience on the aircraft was quite small. He arranged for Don Lucey, one of his pilots, to check me out on the HS125 Mk600, the latest variant which I had not flown and the one that we were going to use to fly Howard.

True to form Howard kept me waiting around for two or three weeks. On 13th July we had to change 125s to an earlier model and by the end of that week I told Jack that, unless we flew very shortly, we would have to take a rest from continually preparing for an event that never happened; in addition we were fast losing credibility with Hawker Siddeley management. Jack relayed this message to Howard who decided to appear on 17th July at 1630 hours. He was able to do this during a working week because we had positioned the 125 on the compass swinging base, which was at the far side of the airfield near the back entrance which Howard was using.

HS 125

The flight was a great success. The weather was fine and we went to Stansted again. It was difficult to believe that this was the same airport we had landed at in the 748 a few weeks earlier, in rain and fog. Hughes still tried to land right at beginning of the runway, but we were able to discuss the matter and he gradually started to land further up the runway. He extolled the flying qualities of the 125 comparing the 748 to a truck, though he had the good grace to apologise to me for criticising one of my aircraft. The truth was that Jack had quite rightly chosen the 748 for Hughes to start with because it was so slow, but the problem with the 748 was that the control forces were very high which made it difficult to fly on the approach.

The 125 on the other hand had much lighter controls and, probably for Hughes, this was the critical factor.

Howard's object, in any flying that he did, was to do as many take-offs and landings as possible. I tried to avoid this by getting him to land each time, taxi round and then take-off again. However, Howard soon tumbled to this; he suggested that we did 'touch and go' landings and so each time we touched down I raised the flaps, retrimmed the elevator and then opened up the throttles so that we did not have to stop each time we landed. Howard was delighted with the way things were going, though I still had to do all the throttle handling myself.

146 Mock Up

We started talking about other things and I mentioned we were considering re-engining the 748; he was singularly unimpressed. I then started talking about the HS146 and pointed out that as far as we could see it would be an ideal aircraft for Hughes Air West. He expressed annoyance that he had not heard about the 146 and immediately called Jack, who was with us in the passenger cabin, up to the flight deck to express his displeasure. Jack, of course, had sent Howard all the information on the aircraft but Howard's 'bodyguard' had chosen not to deliver the material to him. I invited Howard to visit the mock-up the next time he came to Hatfield and he was very keen to do this. 'Jack, you arrange this.'

The three of us went back to the passenger cabin and sat down. I broached the idea of the possible use of the Club House at Woodford and clearly Howard liked the idea of getting out of the hotel and living on the airfield, very convenient for flying. I undertook to show him the Club House next time we flew. 'Jack, you arrange that.' As we spoke I realised that, despite what I had been told, Howard had not the slightest difficulty with his hearing. He could clearly hear whatever he wanted to hear. The flight had lasted 2 hours 20 minutes and he left with Jack, very happy.

I had previously discussed with Humphrey Wood, the Manchester General Manager at the time, the possibility of Howard using the Club House. He was most unhappy at the idea though I pointed out that Howard's track record was that he always helped people who helped him. I finally got Humphrey to agree that Howard could use the Club House for two to three weeks only, but he felt that it would be a great inconvenience since the Club House was needed for important visitors to the factory. Humphrey felt that it would be Hatfield that would get any benefit from being nice to Howard and pointed out that Hatfield had a similar facility, an Elizabethan Manor called Nast Hyde. I knew about Nast Hyde since we had already entertained Dave Hinson, then owner of Midway Airlines and later FAA Administrator, to dinner and told him about the HS146. The place would indeed have been ideal for Howard to stay. However, Jim Thorne, Hatfield's General Manager, when I had approached him, did not want Howard in his 'Club House'. I found his approach incredible bearing in mind the need to find a launch customer for 'his' aircraft. My view, which I tried to express very politely, was that we were missing a great marketing opportunity to launch the 146.

Woodford Clubhouse

The next week-end I went to our holiday house on the river at Dartmouth in Devon, about 240 miles south west of London. On Tuesday 26 July Jack called and said we were to fly the next day. I caught the Golden Hind express train from Newton Abbott, picked up a rental car from Paddington station and went to Hatfield. Jack confirmed on the telephone that it was 'all systems go' for the flight and Howard turned up at 1630 hours. As I saw the car coming towards the aircraft I could not help contrasting the problems we had had scheduling the first flight in the 748 and this one; instead of a reluctance to 'bite the bullet' and 'go flying', Howard was obviously keen to leave the hotel and fly some more.

We were airborne at 1730 hours and flew straight to Woodford. We taxied to the ramp and Howard looked at the building through the flight deck windows. He seemed taken with the place, but though I had made plans for him to see inside the building, he decided not to get out of the aircraft.

We took-off and went to Stansted and after more circuits than I care to remember we returned to Hatfield in a rain shower just as it was getting dark. While we were flying round and round Stansted we spent most of the time discussing the merits of Howard's method of landing vis-à-vis mine and he was beginning to concede that my method might not be so sloppy after all. I was also getting him to take an interest in the Collins Flight System which was fitted to the aircraft.

When we finally got out of the aircraft we drove over to the HS146 mock-up and, because it was getting cold, I lent Howard my jacket since as usual he was only wearing an open necked shirt. Tony Banham turned on the lights in the Hangar and Howard, Jack and I crawled all over the mock-up. Howard's chief worry was the landing gear geometry with the high wing configuration. Jack being an ex-Lockheed man with the C130, 141 and C5, all high wing airplanes, could not see the problem. Howard conceded that our design kept the bulges on the fuselage to a minimum and therefore the associated aircraft drag, but he still pondered over the landing gear weight penalty in the fuselage by having .a high wing configuration.

17	HS 748	DARSE	SELF	MMHES	F 13
17	HS 125	FAYOS	SELF	H.HUGHES	Circuits, Stansted
27	HS 125	FAYOS	SELF	H. HUGHES	Hatfield . Woodford – Stansted PP

Log book extract 125 flying

The visit went very well and Howard waved goodbye, wearing my jacket, so I grabbed Jack's coat as he got into Howard's car. I followed them to the hotel in my car and felt a little bit out of place in the lobby of the Inn of the Park with Jack's sports jacket and my definitely 'not matching' trousers. Jack gave me back my suit jacket, we had dinner in the hotel and, as we had done on many occasions, I stayed the night on the 9th floor that Howard and his entourage had taken over. I kept the suit for many years without wearing it, realising it was the last jacket Howard ever wore. In the end I gave the jacket to the Evergreen Aviation Museum where the Spruce Goose is now kept, along with lots of Hughes' other memorabilia.

In the morning I returned to Dartmouth. Hughes was now stronger and much more active than he had been when we first started flying and it looked as if most of my holiday was going to be spent flying with him. But alas, it was not to be. Jack called me and told me that Howard had apparently slipped getting out of the shower and fractured his hip. I never saw Howard again. The Arab/Israeli Yom Kippur war broke out and caused a fuel shortage causing power cuts in the hotel. Howard left London for the Xanadu Princess Hotel at Freeport in the Bahamas; England was far too wrapped in other problems to even notice. He left behind three aircraft which he owned and never flew; an HS748 at Woodford and a HS125 at Cambridge. He also had a 125 which was being modified so that he could get into the aircraft and fly it, broken hip and all.

Whilst Howard was still in the UK, I tried to persuade Jack to come to the Society of Experimental Test Pilots Symposium in Beverley Hills that September. Jack used to go regularly before he joined Howard and was keen on the idea; the plan was for Margaret and I to stay with him and Janet. However, Howard virtually forbade Jack to go and apparently told him that having friends to stay was a bad idea. He told Jack to arrange for us to stay as his guests in one of his hotels in Las Vegas after the symposium. I was busy at the time on HS146 business looking at engines and equipment but Margaret and I did find time to spend two nights in a Hughes hotel but I cannot remember its name. However I do remember that we were looked after by John Seymour who took us to a show and that we gambled one quarter in a slot machine!

Jack also kindly arranged for me to fly in a Lockheed 1011. I went up to Palmdale to fly the aircraft from Los Angeles and Bill Weaver, Chief Test Pilot of Lockheed's, kindly let me do some flying including some landings. It was a particularly interesting flight as the plane was fitted with the latest integrated automatic flight system which John Gorham, who I knew from Avro days with the Vulcan automatic landing system, had helped to design.

***

During the period I was involved with Howard in England, I met quite a few people who were close to him and inevitably formed some views of the way he was living. In my view his only real friend was Jack. The only other Hughes' supporter I met was Larry Chafin, the doctor who had looked after him in the past when he had had his spectacular flying accidents. Larry, who lived to be over 100 years old, seemed to have known and looked after every Hollywood actor and actress in the past. Margaret and I got to know him quite well and we would meet regularly at the Los Angeles Country Club when I was attending the Society of Experimental Test Pilots annual symposium. Larry arranged for Margaret, who taught teachers of the deaf, to be taken round the Tracy Clinic which she found very instructive and interesting.

Unfortunately Howard would not take Larry's medical advice with regard to his damaged hip. Howard seemed to have a rotating team of doctors in London and, unfortunately, Larry was not one of them and the lack of specialist treatment which Larry prescribed reduced Howard's chance of recovery.

My impression was that Howard was surrounded by a team of people who seemed to be responsible not to him but, apparently, to Bill Gay in Encino, California, the headquarters of the Summa Corporation, the company that controlled all Hughes' assets. The people in London seemed to be freeloading at Hughes' expense. I had occasion to visit Jack Real in Freeport at least twice while Howard was staying in the hotel with all his minders. Nothing seemed to have changed except that Howard was no longer mobile because of his fractured hip. His 'guards' still seemed to be freeloading and consuming alcohol freely though I had understood that Mormons were meant to be teetotal; in fact I have always understood that was why Howard chose these guards. After his death I read about the drugs he was supposed to have been taking, but certainly I never saw any sign of this.

As far as I was concerned Howard was always quiet and courteous. He was a lonely man and I felt very sorry for him. I have included a picture of him in his famous Flying Boat all alone on the Flight Deck of the huge aircraft. To me this picture epitomises the man as I knew him, alone on the bridge. Howard himself lived frugally and never wasted money. As I said at the beginning of this story, if only he could have brought himself to trust Jack and have listened to his advice, things might have been very different.

***

People used to ask me if Howard left me anything in his will and the answer, of course, was always in the negative. However, Howard's three aircraft, the 748 and two 125s, needed to be sold, and I got permission from Jack, who was charged with disposing of the aircraft, to do the selling on behalf of the Summa Corporation. With an aviation friend of mine we sold the 748 to Mount Cook Airlines and also we found a buyer for one of the two 125s. The income taxation in UK was punitive at the times, being 87%, so the deals did not make our fortune.

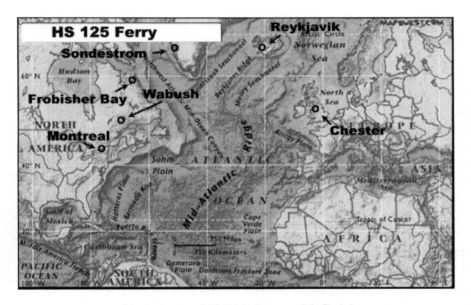

Christmas HS125 Ferry Airfields

Summa then decided that they would keep the other 125, and the final episode in the Hughes saga, as far as I was concerned, took place when I delivered the last of the 125s to Las Vegas. The aircraft had been on the ground in Marshall's fixed base operation at

Cambridge for several years and they delivered it to Hawarden near Chester for overhaul and bringing the mandatory modifications up to date. The aircraft was declared fit by the Hawker Siddeley flight test organisation a week or so before Christmas 1976, and the challenge for me was to deliver the aircraft and be back in time to be with the family for the holiday.The head of the Summa Corporation flying operations, Bill Bush, came over to fly with me to Las Vegas.

I stayed the night with Margaret's family close-by in the Welsh Hills and met up with Bill in the briefing room at Hawarden. The weather was going to be a problem; an active front of rain, sleet and snow was moving across the Canadian Eastern seaboard heading for Frobisher Bay and Greenland, right over our intended track. It was imperative to get away quickly to beat the front but as usual on these occasions, the aircraft was not ready for an early start. We did not get away until midday and headed for Reykjavik, arriving 3 hours and 40 minutes later where it was dark already. We refuelled quickly and I climbed up onto the wing to put oil into the engines since the early 125s used Viper engines with a 'total loss' oil system. Our next stop was Frobisher Bay and we climbed up to 39,000ft; after we had been there for about 45 minutes or so the starboard engine started to lose rotational speed, rpm, and it clearly had fuel filter de-icing problems; I tried everything to clear the problem to no avail. We slowly lost altitude and I had to request flight level 170, 17,000ft, from Gander Control over the HF as we were out of VHF communication with Keflavik. We crept slowly over the Greenland ice cap in the dark and did a radar let down into Sondestrom. I began to feel that the fates were against us.

I was in two minds what to do; if we stayed where we were we were unlikely to get proper maintenance and the weather was scheduled to be closing in. If we carried on we would still have fuel filter de-icing problems. I elected to go on, filing flight level 170 for Frobisher Bay where we were expected and where there might be some engineering assistance. We took off in the dark and made for Frobisher Bay where the wind was getting up ahead of the front; the temperature was -30°C and the wind was already blowing up to 30 knots. The only good news was that, though there was slight snow, we had flown through the main front and would probably escape a significant fall overnight. However, at Frobisher Bay there was bad news in spades. Firstly, the Eskimo ground crew were nowhere to be seen and we discovered them later paralytic in the bar, celebrating the arrival of Father Christmas himself, presumably using their reindeer. Secondly, there was no chance of any maintenance to the engines. Thirdly, I realised that if we did nothing overnight the engine oil would be so cold in the morning it would be impossible to start the engines from the internal batteries.

I decided that the only thing to do was to plan to carry on flying in the morning at relatively low altitude, so that the engines would not ice up, but this meant of course that we would not be able to make Montreal non-stop where we could have proper maintenance. Thank goodness Shell were still around and arranged refuelling for 7am the following morning and they also alerted Wabush as an intermediate stop. The Royal Canadian police, the Mounties, gave us a lift to the hotel and we had a swift meal and went to bed. At midnight I called the Mounties and asked for their help to take me out to the aircraft to run the engines and keep them warm. They stayed for the 20 minutes or so the operation took and took me back to the hotel. I repeated the whole operation at 4am and got up at 6am to prepare for the next leg. I called the meteorological office from my room and the weather was forecast to be good. Bill and I went out to the aircraft, courtesy once more of the Mounties and in the howling gale I had to clamber onto the wings to add the engine oil. Even though I was wearing all the correct cold weather clothing I still got slight frostbite on my cheeks since, at the time, the head cover of the RAF winter clothing that we used did not project far enough forward ahead of the face.

We got into the aircraft and the Shell truck miraculously appeared. I got out again, checked the filler caps were closed correctly and paid for the fuel. At 17,000 ft the fuel filter icing started again and more out of hope than anticipation I pressed the fuel filter ground test button. There was a horrifying roar and suddenly both engines were working correctly. I re-filed our flight plan to flight level 390 and climbed up thankfully without any further incident. I rapidly calculated that we would be able to make Montreal after all and cancelled our stop at Wabush. When we landed at Montreal the weather was clear, no wind but the temperature was only 0°F; we got out of the aircraft and it felt like a spring day.

We had breakfast and proceeded uneventfully to Lethbridge, South of Edmonton, and thence to Las Vegas; Jack had asked me to make Las Vegas our first port of call in the USA to simplify customs procedures. It had been a very interesting delivery and my reward from Jack for my efforts was the latest HP25 Hewlett Packard Calculator. When I got home, just in time for Christmas, Margaret took one look at my frostbite and the calculator and remarked that she thought that the Summa Corporation had got the better of the ferry deal.

CHAPTER 8

The Avionics Revolution

After 22 years with A.V.Roe and flying for 29 years, I decided to make a career change but to remain closely involved with aviation, piloting and the modern flight deck. It had always been my view that, as a pilot gets older, there comes a time when the increased experience is counterbalanced by the inevitable decline in physical ability and mental flexibility. Eyesight is the most obvious example of the effect of old age, not only in the need to wear corrective glasses, but also in the vital but less obvious effect of the increased time taken to change focal length from the instrument panel to the far horizon. In my experience also, I was aware that older pilots were not able to adapt to change and new ideas nearly as quickly as younger pilots. There was no reason to believe that I would be any different in ageing from anyone else, so when I had the opportunity to retire and start a new career in aviation on the Aerospace Board of Smiths Industries, I welcomed the chance. Smiths specialised in producing many different types of auto-pilots, instruments and head-up displays for military and civil aircraft, so I knew a lot of the engineers from the work we had done installing and developing their products.

During my twenty two years with A.V.Roe, advances in electronic technology had invaded the aerospace industry in every way, from computerising aircraft design to automating a lot of the flight deck functions by integrating sensors. My function in Smiths Industries, initially as Technical Operations Director, was to advise on the likely changes to the way the pilot interfaced with the control of the aircraft as a result of the new displays and systems. Inevitably, these changes would mean that the conventional products obtained from the instrument manufacturers would need to be replaced with more modern, technically advanced equipment.

Avionics, as the electronics on the flight deck soon became known, enabled, amongst many other things, the engineers to present information to the pilot in a way which was easier to assimilate and, therefore, to take the correct action from all the displayed information more quickly and in a more accurate and therefore safer way. The real revolution in displaying information was started by the Boeing Company in the early '80s with the new Boeing 757 and 767 aircraft displaying the critical flight instruments on 'TV' tubes. Up to that time the pilot had to rely on the basic T for information, with airspeed, attitude, altitude and direction, all displayed on separate dedicated mechanical instruments. With the new 'digital' aircraft, the necessary information could be integrated and displayed on cathode ray tube displays together with the navigation information shown as a map.

The proponents of new technology always claim that its introduction makes for efficiency and greater safety. Certainly, as a result of the new displays on the flight deck, the integration of the navigation information, the introduction of inertial navigation systems and, most importantly, the ability to display and control the aircraft systems from the flight deck, meant that the number of flight deck crew required to cross the Atlantic finally dropped to two pilots from the five crew required twenty years earlier. This reduction of numbers on the flight deck definitely resulted in economic savings for the airlines, but whether it had actually increased safety was, for a time anyway, a debatable point. However, I think it is now accepted that the reduction of crew to two pilots has not significantly affected the accident rate though there have been certain accidents which might well have been avoided had there been a third pilot or a flight engineer on the flight deck, for example the British Midlands Boeing 737 trying to do a single engine landing at East Midlands Airport in January 1989 when the crew diagnosed the wrong engine as faulty.

In fact, my first job with my new firm was to go to Japan to try to get colour cathode ray tube displays specially manufactured for my company, which were even larger than the displays being used by Boeing. The tubes were to be used, initially, on the so called Advanced Flight Deck being developed at Weybridge. The symbology to be used on the displays was even more advanced than that which Boeing was using and the initial aim of the programme was to fly the new displays on the Ministry of Defence BAC 111 research aircraft. Boeing on their 757 and 767 airplanes used the displays, made by Collins, just to replace the mechanical attitude indicators and horizontal situation displays currently in use. On the larger eight inch displays there was room to display not only the attitude and horizontal displays but also the airspeed and altimeter information.

292

Fortunately for us, Toshiba agreed to manufacture these large tubes and the research programme and flight trials which resulted were a great success. However, the UK never got any real commercial benefit from the work. John Wilson, who I had met for the first time at Wunstorf in Germany many years earlier, and with whom I had worked laying out the British Aerospace 146 flight deck, was the very innovative designer of the new symbology, but since British Aerospace was slowly going out of the aircraft manufacturing business, there was no home for the new displays.

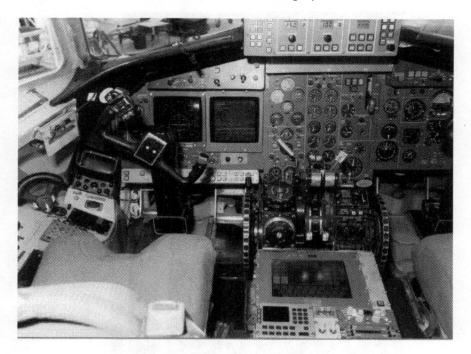

BAC 111 Instrument with two 8" displays

Both John and I were members of the United States Society of Automotive Engineers S7 Flight Deck Committee, which included test pilots and engineers from Boeing and Airbus, technical pilots from all the main airlines and engineers from many of the avionic manufacturers like Collins and Honeywell. The Committee met every six months in different locations world wide and when we met in England the members were able to see the work that was taking place at Weybridge, so that all the innovative ideas were absorbed, in one

way or another, on to the Boeing and Airbus aircraft. My firm tried
hard to take advantage of the work, since Smiths Industries engineers
carried out all the intricate programming work which enabled John's
symbology to be displayed. However, we were unable to persuade any
of the world's aircraft manufacturers to buy from us, perhaps
understandably, since the airlines were more comfortable with their
established suppliers, Collins and Honeywell. In fact I accompanied
the BAC 111 when it made a demonstration tour to the USA visiting
Douglas at Long Beach and Boeing in Seattle, all to no avail.

**Sperry (Honeywell) Flight
Management Computer**

The digital revolution on the flight deck was not just related to the display devices being used on the flight deck. Digital computing enabled processing of all the sensor information at very high speeds, doing a lot of the work that the pilot would previously have had to do in his head. This in itself was a real contribution to safety, bearing in mind the increased speed of jet aircraft, enabling the pilots to spend more time monitoring other important and critical aspects of the flight. It was perhaps in the area of navigation that the new technology was of the greatest benefit. For the first time, all the various navigation sensors could be integrated with the flight performance of the aircraft so that it was possible to display not only very accurate real time positions but also accurate predictions for the rest of the flight. The aerospace industry decided that there should be a box called the Flight Management Computer, FMC, to do all this computation, which would receive all the navigation and sensor data and then output position and other relevant information. The specification was called AIRINC 706 but it proved to be a very imprecise specification. The AIRINC concept of having different manufacturers meeting a standard equipment specification, so that the airlines could have a competition between manufacturers for a particular piece of avionics, was never reached in the case of the FMC since the specification was ignored by the avionic manufacturers in detail design. It was never possible to have interchangeability of FMCs between Sperry and Smiths, who at the time were the only manufacturers of the FMC.

The FMC was seen as 'an all can do' box by the technical pilots of the key airlines of the time and they asked for some very advanced features to be included in the box, right from the initial design stage. The avionic manufacturers' engineers agreed to implement these ideas only to find that the software programming work required was much greater than they had anticipated. Consequently, the development of the FMC took much longer than planned, both for Sperry and for ourselves, and initial deliveries of aircraft had only a small part of the FMC's planned capabilities working. At the time, I remember thinking of a favourite remark of my old boss at Woodford, Humphrey Wood, 'it's taking longer than I thought it would, but then I thought it would'. I used to think the remark was amusing until I got personally involved with the FMC program and realised the horrendous financial implications.

Nevertheless the concept of the FMC was correct. The box took airspeed, altitude, attitude, inertial position, radio bearing and distance along with many other items of information and presented to the pilot his actual position, his time to destination along the desired track and the estimate of the total fuel required to the diversion airports. It could also do 'what if' calculations to help the pilot deal with unexpected changes of flight plan. At first the limitations of digital computing speed resulted in the computer taking a long time to calculate these functions, the problem being compounded by the limited amount of 'database' information that could be stored, such as the position of airfields and radio facilities. However, the advances of technology gradually enabled the engineers to pack more and more capacity and calculating power into the same size box so that, in the end, the airlines got what they wanted.

Smiths Industries was successful in selling their FMC to many of the Airbus airline customers in competition with Sperry, who was in the fortunate position of being the sole FMC supplier to the new Boeing airplanes. In fact, my membership on the S7 Committee enabled me to help considerably in effecting the sales. However, the Smiths Industries Cheltenham facility found the development of the box very expensive and time consuming, made infinitely worse by the specification being continually changed by Airbus, as they learnt of new ideas and problems from working with their launch customers who had specified the competing Sperry Computer. It became very clear to the managers at Cheltenham that the cost of developing the FMC was going to be far greater than they had budgeted for but, unfortunately, they did not confide their difficulties to senior management in London until the programme was in real trouble. Something clearly had to be done to keep the programme costs under control and I was sent to take charge of the project at Cheltenham.

I soon discovered that the FMC program had a superb engineering team but were woefully short of the equipment they needed. In addition, there was a lack of project control. I was able to make some immediate management changes and, once the senior management of Smiths Industries were informed of the test equipment requirements, sanction was rapidly given. Slowly the FMC got back on to a recovery path. The project was a fascinating but a very difficult one. The computing capability of the box, as initially designed, was completely inadequate for the task the computer had to do but, luckily, new high density components were becoming available which enabled changes to be made so that the required performance standards were achieved, albeit at a significant cost penalty. It was a great relief when the first customer delivery to Kuwait Airways was made on time, though only the navigation function of the box was delivered on day one. Gradually more functions were added so that in the end the box worked very well.

Before leaving the subject of managing complicated software projects, I should explain that I would never have been able to understand the engineers, and control the project, if I had not been operating and programming my own small computers at home. I always said that I experienced in miniature what the Smiths Industries engineers were experiencing on a large scale in their development programs. The machines never worked quickly enough, there was not enough memory, there were bugs in the software, a later release was needed and, of course, new and later hardware was always required. Any computer I had at home always needed replacing almost immediately I had purchased it, and the same seemed to be true in the labs of Smiths Industries. I don't think the financial controllers of Smiths Industries ever came to terms with this unpalatable situation, though downstream profitably did help to heal the wounds.

I mention the FMC project in some detail because it showed how important and difficult it was then, and is now, to judge the development cost of an advanced piece of electronics. Quite apart from software development, which is definitely not an exact science, the hardware still has to be integrated and made to work. Consequently, there are two key things which an avionics manufacturer must consider when bidding for a new project. The first is to estimate the recurring cost of manufacture correctly so that money is not lost on every delivery. The second challenge is to estimate the cost of developing the product. In my time at Smiths Industries, I often saw the operating units underbid the true cost of development in their eagerness to be awarded a contract, despite all the efforts of senior management in trying to prevent this occurring. Luckily however, the calculations of recurring costs were generally about right which helped to keep the firm solvent.

There was a book written about this time by John Newhouse called 'The Sporty Game', which discussed how the large airframe and engine manufacturers were always betting the future of their companies when bidding to supply new aircraft and engines to the airlines. The same thing applied equally to the avionics manufacturers, even though the gross financial numbers were considerably smaller. Interestingly, Sperry Phoenix always seemed to be our main competitor and usually, when they beat us, we never could understand how their prices were so low. In retrospect, perhaps they bet too heavily in order to win the programmes, because they ran into financial problems and were bought out by Honeywell and then, again, Honeywell were bought out by Allied Signal.

In earlier years, both airframe and avionic manufacturers could recover some of their costs by selling spares, but new aircraft and new equipment had become so reliable that there was very little opportunity to do this. Only the brake and tyre manufacturers could rely on selling spares but, even here, the competition was such and the new materials were so good that the opportunities for financial recovery were greatly reduced.

When the Flight Management programme at Cheltenham was back on the rails Hugh Pope, my new boss who had been recruited from Dunlops, asked me to take over the role of Marketing Co-ordination between our various sites. There was never any question within the aerospace group of having a Marketing Director directly responsible for all company sales, since each operating unit was responsible for its own marketing, winning new business and getting the required budgeted profit. However, there was some product overlap between the various units and my job was to try to prevent units bidding against one another and confusing the customer. In addition, there were certain marketing functions which were central to the Aerospace Group like arranging representation at various exhibitions, notably the SBAC exhibition at Farnborough and the Paris airshow at Le Bourget, which alternated each year.

In the latter function I was helped enormously by David Bainbridge, who we had recruited from British Aerospace. He knew the business backwards and made the mechanics of designing the company stand in the main exhibition hall, arranging the chalet and organising the catering support seem extremely straightforward though, in fact, a tremendous amount of hard work was required to make everything go smoothly. We always reckoned that our stand and chalet were absolutely first class. I was always very proud on the first day of the show to come to the stand and admire all the hard work that had been put in to building it. Each day I would go to the chalet for the daily briefing of the marketing staff and have some coffee. David and I would then look at all the acceptances from the guests and work out, with the various salesman, the seating plan for lunch.

It was always difficult to judge whether the considerable sum that was required each year to take part in the aerospace shows was really worthwhile but it would have been commercial suicide to have withdrawn. Sales were rarely made at the Show but the discussions that took place there with the potential customers were absolutely vital and the deals were often consummated when the customer next visited the manufacturing sites. In retrospect, I think we might have given ourselves a slightly easier time had we had exhibited less hardware at these shows. The effort required to get new products to the shows was expensive in time and money and, of course, it was necessary to have engineers to support the products which very often became temperamental in the adverse operating environment of a display booth. On the other hand, it was useful to get the opinions of the pilots and engineers who came to the shows.

Another central marketing function which we had was the contracting of our various agents around the world. This was a very important task and, normally, the selection of the agent was undertaken by the operating unit which was selling into the area. In many countries it would be quite impossible to sell to the airline or the defence force without inside specialist customer knowledge. Furthermore, the decision makers as often as not wished to be rewarded for their selections and this delicate task had to be undertaken by the agent, since it was very important for any Western firm selling in this situation not to talk directly to the customer discussing possible rewards. Consequently, the commission that an agent got paid often seemed remarkably high to an ill-informed spectator. The amount of money that was paid out to an agent in avionic marketing was chicken feed compared with the sums of money involved with the sale of the airframes and engines but, nevertheless, we had to take part in the commission process and comply with the purchasing expectations of the key decision makers in the countries in which we were selling, in accordance with local practice.

People unfamiliar with the incredibly difficult and competitive task of selling aerospace products overseas, or at home for that matter, often condemned the practice of rewarding the purchaser for choosing one's product. However, not to have done so would have made every day seem like Christmas to the French and United States firms with whom we were competing. The important thing was not to get financially involved with the airline decision makers, as Lockheed did once in selling 1011s in Japan. Incidentally, if people imagine that rewards are not paid in the Western World then they are very naïve, though nobody likes to discuss the subject. The fact is that the rewards are not necessarily financial ones and salesmen are always looking for ways to influence their customers to their advantage, not necessarily by the price and performance of the products.

A typical advantage we had when selling to Boeing was the fact that the Boeing engineers loved coming over to the UK to supervise the development of the products they had purchased; it was much more fun than visiting the frozen wilderness of the mid-West of the Continental United States in Winter or the blinding heat in the Summer. No money changed hands but the engineers were always looked after extremely well and this situation was well known at Boeing. We were also well aware that Boeing management liked to buy some UK products, as it helped to justify the UK airlines buying their aircraft instead of Airbus.

Occasionally, I did get involved with the actual selling and one case I found particularly demanding and, eventually, rewarding was when the British Aerospace Hawk was sold to Abu Dhabi Air Force. Smiths Industries had given the navigation/attack flight deck avionics to British Aerospace for installation on their Hawk demonstrator for free, in return for the equipment being made basic fit when sales were made to foreign air forces. Abu Dhabi was the first Hawk customer but their Air Force used French Mirage fighters. Consequently, when the Hawk was chosen the customer insisted on being given more time to decide whether to have the basic Smiths Industries equipment or have French avionics more compatible with the Mirage. I remember discussing the problem with the then head of B.Ae marketing Mike Turner at the Dubai Air Show; he told me it was up to us to sell the product to Abu Dhabi.

British Aerospace Hawk Trainer

Fortuitously, the head of the Air Force was a young, well connected man who let it be known that he did not believe in agents and would not allow them to be used. I had a specialist Arab salesman working for me, a United States citizen of Armenian extraction and immediately we made it clear to our local agent in Dubai that, in view of the Commander's edict, he could no longer be in the game. We then asked for a meeting with the Air Force, which we had a day or two later. I had checked with Cheltenham that the prices for our equipment and not been determined with B.Ae and so I was able to offer the Abu Dhabi Air Force a discount on all spares prices which they purchased.

The Air Force did not give us an immediate decision but, a few weeks later I was told that, subject to some adjustments, our offer was accepted and Smiths Industries had been selected to provide the avionic equipment on the flight deck of the Hawk. I returned to Abu Dhabi and signed two copies of the agreement, one which they kept and one which was Smiths' copy. The confidentiality of the agreement was clearly written in the contract and stressed by both sides. I returned back to London feeling pleased with the way things were going and I gave our copy of the contract to Alan Smith, the Company solicitor.

Unfortunately, winning the equipment selection with the United Arab Emirates Air Force was not as beneficial as it should have been. I was a bit disappointed when I learnt shortly afterwards that Cheltenham had concluded a deal with B.Ae Warton on the prices of the Hawk avionics which did not take real advantage of the deal we had struck. Prices had been agreed which resulted in very little profit on the spares, after the Abu Dhabi commission had been paid.

Some months later when Cheltenham were in the middle of the production development of the avionics, we learnt that the head man at Warton had got hold of a copy of the Abu Dhabi agreement and felt that we were in fact loading our prices to B.Ae to pay our commission to Abu Dhabi; in effect he felt B.Ae were paying for the selection of our equipment. B.Ae was a big customer of ours and there was some nervousness in our senior management, who wondered whether we should have concluded such a deal. I think I managed to convince everybody that it was a very good deal indeed and kept us in the Navigation/Attack business. A lot of Hawks were sold and Cheltenham business would have suffered very badly if we had not won the initial customer.

My only concern in the matter was to check that the B.Ae copy of the agreement had not come from Smiths Industries.

Cheltenham had, of course, got copies of the agreement and the leak could have come from there. B.Ae had the courtesy to send us a copy of their copy and it was a great relief when I compared their copy with ours and found that they did not match. Clearly, Abu Dhabi had given a copy of our agreement to B.Ae in order to conclude a similar deal with them!

The final act of this saga was in fact very similar to the problem on the Airbus Flight Management Computer, where I had helped with the sale of the computers to a lot of airlines through my contacts on the SAE S7 Committee and then had to go to Cheltenham and take over the project. Cheltenham got into difficulties developing the avionic kit for the Hawk and were in real trouble commercially with B.Ae. I was asked to go down and sort it out. Once again I had to institute improved programme management but, in addition, this time I had to renegotiate contract details with Mike Clifford at B.Ae, Warton. Again I was lucky, this time because the Chief Engineer at Warton had ambitions to take back the software development on the single seater version of the Hawk and do it 'in house'. In fact it was this development that was giving us so much trouble but, in defence of Cheltenham, it was not their fault because the requirements were not defined adequately. I reluctantly agreed to let them take over the software task but was able to charge them for certain hardware development tools which were our property.

Once the software task on the single seat Hawk was no longer our responsibility, the Hawk programme became a lot easier to manage and, in the end, it was a very successful one for Smiths Industries. I left the Company fairly soon after I had concluded the amended deal with Mike Clifford at Warton and I felt pleased that everything was sorted out in the end. Afterwards I felt the problem was very similar to the FMC problem; not enough money had been budgeted for development and headquarters had not been told the true cost of developing the product.

***

One of the jobs I did enjoy doing was visiting other firms when Smiths Industries were considering purchasing them. From the moment Hugh Pope arrived, he wanted the Aerospace Company to expand and we were continually considering possible acquisitions. When Sperry at Phoenix, Arizona came on the market the first time we became very excited, since they were our chief competitor, certainly in the Flight Management business. However, the asking price if I remember correctly was in the region of $1B and it was pretty clear that we could not afford such an adventure. Hugh Pope paid a solo visit to Phoenix, but we were not a serious bidder. As already mentioned, Honeywell bought the Company but judging by the fact that Honeywell itself changed hands sometime later, perhaps Sperry was not all that profitable after all and Smiths was well out of it.

However, we had another chance to buy a significant avionics company in the USA. Forstmann Little had bought the whole of Lear Siegler and was clearly interested in selling off bits. A large team went to visit some of the sites, Florham Park NJ, Grand Rapids MI, and Lear Astronics in Los Angeles CA. The Aerospace Group was particularly interested in the Grand Rapids facility, since it made FMCs for the Boeing 737 and was stamping out computers in large numbers. I persuaded the Chief Executive that we should visit the Lear Siegler marketing site and so Gerry Mortimer and I went on to visit the Stamford facility in Connecticut. We soon realised that this unit was making very large profits indeed by marking up the spares prices of the equipments they bought from their own operating units and then selling to the end customer. Furthermore, one of the Lear Siegler divisions, the Power Electronics Corporation which was not on our shopping list, was contributing enormously to the profits.

I left to go on holiday only to find on my return that the whole purchase project had stagnated. I suspected that we were finding it difficult to afford the total price and, at Gerry Mortimer's instigation, I rapidly wrote a report justifying buying three of the units but not Lear Astronics. This report seemed to have the desired effect and Gerry Mortimer was authorised to start again trying to conclude a deal. Meanwhile Ron Howard, Chief Executive of Marconi Avionics, our great UK competitor, was also trying to buy Lear Siegler and I remember meeting him at the Paris Air Show and listening to him recounting how well he was doing with the purchase of the whole company, clearly not knowing that Gerry Mortimer was about to close the deal.

Gerry had realised that Forstmann Little was desperate to sell and offered them a now or never deal. Gerry's plan worked and Hugh Pope and Alan Hornsby the financial director went out to sign the deal. We were all delighted, but the next morning when I was sitting in my office Ron Howard came on the phone absolutely thunderstruck saying 'what about the pension problem' and 'what about the taxation' etc. etc. He clearly had had the cream taken from his saucer. I hope I sounded undisturbed; in fact I was confident that Cyril Miles our tax expert had considered everything and thought the purchase was an opportunity and a risk worth taking.

In fact, the purchase of Lear Siegler by Smiths Industries proved to be a great success and moved the company into the big avionics league. Sadly, the whole deal could have been even more successful since the Power Electronics Corporation was still for sale and I knew how much profit it was making. I got agreement to visit the plant with Mike Townsend, the Aerospace financial controller, and wrote a report on my return pointing out what a wonderful deal was available for us alone, since only we, of the possible purchasers, knew how much money was being made on PEC's behalf by the Stamford division. Hugh I'm sure agreed with me but Smiths Industries did not want to spend any more money, not facing up to the fact that by not buying PEC the spares profit stream, which in part justified the purchase of Lier Siegler, would inevitably be lost. And so it came to pass. Lucas bought PEC and the profit from Stamford steadily declined.

Gerry Mortimer and I went round looking at many other companies for possible acquisitions and I think we both enjoyed it. One could learn so much from wandering around factory floors and listening to the manner of the presentations. I was interested in the technology and Gerry the finances but we always agreed in the end on whether a company would be good for SI or not. Unfortunately, even if we both wanted to buy a company, our wishes were very rarely granted, either because the price was too high or Smiths Industries had some other reason for not wanting to do the deal.

***

I left Smiths Industries after fifteen very enjoyable years to retire to Devon but, thanks to Brian Trubshaw, who had led the flight development of the Concorde, I was asked to join the Board of the Civil Aviation Authority as its Technical Member. At the time, the Chairman was Christopher Chataway, ex Olympic athlete and Member of Parliament.

I well remember my interview for the job. I was asked to lunch on the top floor of the Authority's offices at the bottom of Kingsway. The building was interesting in itself as it was a circular one going up fifteen stories. Christopher's secretary ushered me into a private dining room and we introduced ourselves. Christopher was as pleasant as I expected from watching him on television but Tom Murphy, the Managing Director of the Authority and a retired oil company executive, looked slightly less friendly. I kept to my tomato juice at lunch time and looked down at the magnificent view over the Thames and Waterloo Bridge. After the normal pleasantries we sat down and the interview, as well as the lunch, commenced. It was explained to me that this lunch was one of several to enable the new Technical Board Member to be selected.

The content of the lunch has not stayed in my memory since, as is normal on these occasions, so much concentration is required to answer the questions and frame suitable replies that eating becomes entirely automatic. I usually found after such a meal that I had eaten far too much in the excitement. As requested, I had sent a curriculum vitae in advance so that they could see that I was very familiar with safety and certification issues. My weakness, it seemed to me at least, was my lack of knowledge of the Air Traffic Control function of the CAA which, certainly in financial terms, was about 75% of the budget. As a pilot one tended to take the excellent service provided by Air Traffic for granted.

As luck would have it, that very day the developers of the Stock Exchange embryonic settlement system called Taurus had finally had to admit that the software development had got out of control and the whole project had to be abandoned. This was indeed very serious for the Stock Exchange and for the international reputation of the City of London which suffered a serious blow from which, in my opinion, it has never really recovered. I was able to hold forth at length on the difficulties, dangers and costs of software development, a subject which is difficult to understand fully unless one has had practical experience. I thoroughly enjoyed the whole discussion and left feeling I had acquitted myself quite well.

Weeks went by and nothing happened and I resigned myself to having failed the interview. However, after having adjusted to the dashing of my hopes, our daughter, who was living in our apartment in London, opened a formal looking letter and read it over the phone to me down in Devon; I was being asked to join the Board of the CAA. It was an important moment for me and I knew I would have to expand my knowledge and experience considerably.

My first dealings with the CAA was when I was invited to visit the new Air Traffic Control Centre, then under construction at Swanwick near Southampton. It was a terrible day, pouring with rain and my umbrella kept on being blown inside out. I was soaked between getting out of the train and getting into the only taxi at Bursledon station and got even wetter getting from the taxi to the site manager's hut. However, when I caught up with Christopher and the team I was glad to see that there were quite a few faces I knew from my past dealings with the Ministry of Defence and Aeroflight at Farnborough. The visit was interesting as I was able to see the vast size of the building being erected on the site of a disused brick works, which introduced an environmental dimension to the surrounding area. I mentioned to Christopher that I thought my appointment had taken a long time. He laughed --- apparently it was the fastest appointment they had ever made.

The CAA was nominally an independent body but, in fact, the Board was appointed by the Department of Transport and the Chairman of the CAA had to follow government policy very closely. The Chairman recommended the Board members to the Department and invariably they accepted the Chairman's wishes, as had happened in my case. At the time the CAA had three functions; Firstly, to provide the National Air Traffic System for the UK, NATS; secondly, to regulate the safety of civil aviation and thirdly to regulate certain economic aspects of airlines and airports. In fact, the ever increasing influence of Brussels and the EU had removed a lot of the actual responsibility for airline regulation from the UK, but the economists in the CAA still produced a mountain of statistics which they fed to the Department of Transport. The main economic regulation that was left for the CAA dealt with the airports and the way the traffic and freight was handled.

We used to have Board meetings of the Authority seven or eight times a year and the spread of expertise of the Board members covered every aspect of the CAA's responsibility. Air Traffic was clearly the most important part of the CAA and sometimes I felt the Director of NATS grudged the time spent on other matters at our meetings. Certainly criticism of NATS was not welcome and on one occasion, when I had the temerity to mention that software was clearly the biggest issue on getting Swanwick operational on time, it was made very clear to me that NATS had the situation well under control. Unfortunately, time proved that this confidence was unjustified, and it was to take many years and millions of pounds before Swanwick became operational..

The regulation of civil aviation safety was carried out from a relatively new building close by Gatwick Airport and, amongst other things, the Safety Regulation Group looked after aircrew licensing, airline operations, airline maintenance and the issuing of aircraft type certificates. Here again the ever increasing effect of European standardization was removing the power and independence of the SRG and, during my four years with the CAA, I became increasingly disturbed by the diminution of expertise within the SRG.

One prime example of the effect of European influence was in connection with the initial approval of a new type of aircraft on to the UK register. The SRG not infrequently, when certificating an aircraft, had a habit of requiring 'special conditions' to be introduced by the airframe manufacturer where it was felt that the aircraft failed to meet the certification requirements of the UK British Civil Airworthiness Requirements, BCARs. This seemed to happen very often when a new US type was approved by the FAA and there was a shortfall in meeting not only the CAA's requirements but, surprisingly, also the FAA's own requirements. For example, it was deemed necessary for the Douglas DC9 to have automatic stick pushers fitted, in order to meet the BCAR stalling requirements and thus be approved to go on to the UK register. The airlines used to complain at having to pay for these extra modifications but, generally, there was a lot of justice in the SRG's special conditions and there was little doubt that it made the aircraft safer. However, the regulated airlines invariably complained about the regulator, since safety is a difficult thing to sell to fare paying customers who are always looking for the best deal.

Of course safety is not a black or white concept. It is all a matter of degree and judgement whether a thing, in this case an aircraft, is safe enough. Nevertheless, for many years the UK managed very well with SRG regulation. However, in 1971 the concept of European Joint Airworthiness Requirements, JARs, was discussed and agreed so that an aircraft being flown in the EU would be acceptable from a safety viewpoint to all countries in the EU. I was the project pilot on the HS146 at the time and we worked to JARs for the first time, as well as to BCARs. The concept was eminently reasonable and loved by the airlines but, as frequently happens, there were unexpected side effects. The European countries formed an organisation so that new aircraft were no longer certificated by each country but by a committee drawn from all the countries, the Joint Aviation Authority. From that point the capability of the SRG started to decline. Inevitably, the composition of the certification team depended, to some extent, on 'buggins turn next' rather than who was best equipped to certificate the aircraft. Furthermore, however well the certification was carried out, the SRG just could not know all the details of a new aircraft since it would only have been dealing with part of the certification, perhaps the engines.

There were three effects of this European certification situation. Firstly, the managers of the SRG had difficulty in justifying and maintaining the size of their technical staff and therefore their expertise. Secondly, if an accident occurred to an aircraft on the UK register, the Aircraft Accident Investigation Branch, AAIB, could only ask questions of the SRG and they, in their turn, would not necessarily know the answers since the aircraft system concerned might have been carried out by some other expert in some other country. This meant that if there was any political covering up taking place due to national issues, the SRG would not be aware of the situation. The third effect of European standardisation was the drive to get the UK to remove any special certification requirements which had been imposed only by the UK.

The airlines, of course, leapt at the chance of getting the special modifications removed and got the Department of Transport to pressurise the CAA Chairman to give orders to SRG to go ahead to amend the requirements. In fact, the situation was complicated by the existence of a truly independent body called the Airworthiness Requirements Board, of which I became a member. This body supervised the SRG in a non-mandatory way and expressed a view of its performance. In the case of the removal of special conditions, the ARB objected to their removal but, just before I joined the ARB, the Chairman of the CAA attended a meeting of the ARB and persuaded them, albeit reluctantly, to acquiesce in the removal of a large number of the special conditions. In my view, no technical justification had been made for their removal and a considerable number of the ARB's members were unhappy with the situation. During the rest of my tenure on the ARB there was a continual battle to remove the remainder of the special conditions, which some of us resisted. The point we always made was that only after millions of flight hours and by assessing any accidents as they occurred would it be possible to judge whether the extra modifications demanded by the UK authorities were necessary to meet the required safety standards. While we were arguing the case for keeping our special modifications, it was not at all clear legally whether, if the UK refused to remove the special conditions, we would be breaking EU laws.

I have described the story of the special conditions at some length because it shows so clearly how Europe is removing the power of safety regulation from the UK. Like most European issues, there are divergent views within the UK but certainly I felt, and still feel, very unhappy with any diminution of the powers and expertise of the SRG. In fact, the ARB has now been disbanded and the EU has created a European Aviation Safety Agency to be the equivalent of the FAA. How this will work bearing in mind that there is not a United States of Europe remains to be seen; without an independent body such as the ARB there must be some concern about the safety maintenance of standards and the influence of politics.

The other matter which concerned me during my time with the CAA was the desire to privatise the Air Traffic System and remove it from the CAA. However, before dealing with that issue, there was another matter which caused me great concern, was extremely important and did not bring great credit to the CAA. The Swanwick centre was completed on time structurally and clearly was going to be a delightful place to work. However, the software to run the system was in trouble. As mentioned earlier, in my initial interview with Christopher Chataway I had underlined the risk of the programme overrunning, not from any particular knowledge at the time, but just because the program size was so large that the chances of its being completed on time were extremely small. At one of my early Board meetings when the subject came up I expressed my views, but it was quite clear to me that, despite the nature of my employment on the Board and my not inconsiderable experience of running software programs, there was no way that the then executive director of the Air Traffic System was going to allow me to get an educated view of the progress of the software. Furthermore, it was clear that Christopher was not going insist that I be allowed to learn more about the problem.

In fact, the software development situation deteriorated more rapidly than even I had anticipated because the design organisation charged with Swanwick software development, the IBM Federal Systems Division, was sold first to Loral and then to Lockheed Martin. The Division was already losing money on the project and the new owners were faced with having to continue to pour money into the black hole since, politically, it was quite unacceptable to pull the plug on what was in effect a UK national program. I often wondered whether either of the new owners had carried out a proper due diligence survey and were really aware of the situation before they bought the division. From a technical viewpoint, each change of ownership inevitably lengthened the program. I remain convinced that the management of the CAA and NATS did not really face up to the issues early enough and a lot of time and money was wasted. Fortunately, Swanwick is now functioning and, no doubt, will go from strength to strength as more functions are added.

The software problem at Swanwick gave ammunition to the proponents of privatisation, particularly to the then Conservative Government who believed that private ownership must, by definition, be superior to public ownership. A year or two before I joined the Board, the CAA, after a review by Brian Trubshaw who was a Board member at the time, came to the conclusion that the responsibility for regulating the safety of the NATS operation should be with SRG. NATS would still be responsible for ensuring the safety of the UK air traffic system, but the way they did it would be examined by SRG. I believe that at the time NATS was not enthused with the change but there can be little doubt that it was entirely the correct thing to do. The difficulty the CAA had then was that it was the regulator, as well as the provider of the air traffic system and this was clearly not desirable.

Increasingly, it was becoming clear that there was no real justification for having NATS within the CAA and the argument that 'if it ain't broke don't fix it' was not a sufficiently compelling reason for the status quo. I took the view that NATS should become an independent body, but the Treasury did not like that concept because they considered that all NATS borrowing requirements would still count against the UK national spending, the Public Spending Borrowing Requirements. They wanted private investors to pick up the tab for all future capital requirements. Having already had to carry the expense of Swanwick, the Treasury did not want to have to carry another large expense which was the building of a Scottish Air Traffic centre; this new centre was needed as a technical back-up to the Swanwick centre, so that either centre could control the whole of the UK airspace should there be a catastrophic failure due to an accident or terrorism.

The pressure from the Department of Transport to privatise was irresistible and Christopher, an ex-conservative MP and a banker, was clearly wholeheartedly behind the idea. We had a Board meeting and approved the plan, I regret to say unanimously even though I was not keen on the idea; in my defence I did point out that, in my opinion, a privatised NATS should not be allowed to search for new business overseas; I considered this wholly undesirable and dangerous. A monopoly provider is always searching for sources of unregulated income to increase the profits, but experience proves that in going for the new business the provider very often underestimates the technical and management challenges involved. Now, an organisation like NATS will always be very short of both technical and management skills so that any resource that is needed to rescue a difficult programme will be at the expense of the core business. In my view, the compelling need to increase the timely flow of air traffic safely in UK controlled airspace would always mean that technically and managerially NATS would be stretched to the limit. There would never be any time to deal with new outside business without risking NATS outstanding safety record.

In truth, one of the reasons I did not challenge Christopher at the Board meeting was that it was nearly time for my term on the Board to be renewed and I was keen to remain on the Board. I was concerned that if I made too many waves my Board tenure would not be renewed. My opposition would have made no difference, except to remove my voice from the Board. Rightly or wrongly, I judged I would be more use in place. This, of course, was no excuse but, like many others in similar positions to myself at the time, I kept quiet rather than voice my true feelings. There was no real excuse and I do not make any.

After Christopher left the Board and Malcolm Field took over, there was a general election and New Labour was swept to power. Privatisation was put on the back burner. However, to everyone's surprise Gordon Brown decided that the money from privatisation was worth having and so privatisation was schemed under another name, thus ensuring that the money rolled in. I became more and more convinced that what was being done was fundamentally wrong but I realised that New Labour, increasingly sensitive to the pressures of big business, would go ahead notwithstanding the reservations of many Labour MPs and all the unions. It is to be hoped that my concerns will prove to be unfounded. The ATC System will be a lot more secure if and when the Scottish Centre is built, especially with the new threat of terrorism.

I enjoyed my four years in the CAA enormously with my office overlooking the Strand and the National Theatre. It was not, of course, a full time job. I generally travelled up to London from Devon once or twice a week. For me it was a fascinating experience and it confirmed my view that governments tend to make changes happen for all sorts of reasons, but seldom consider the law of unintended consequences.

CHAPTER 9

Then and Now

When I started flying, technology was a worthwhile end in itself. For example, it seemed self evident to the UK and French Governments that to build the Concorde was an admirable thing to do since aviation was all about speed. It was true that the UK had second thoughts on the project and wanted to stop it but that was because of the cost of the project, not because the value of the objective was being questioned.

As a test pilot I was involved in testing aircraft, their systems, meeting regulations and meeting safety standards whilst at the same time always selling the products of the companies for which I worked. My firm was not at the forefront of scientific knowledge but the work that we carried out contributed to our success in finding customers, which was vitally important to the United Kingdom, our company, for the continuation of our jobs and, therefore, to me personally.

During my test flying years we developed the Vulcan, the Shackleton, the Nimrod, the Victor Tanker, the Avro 748 and initiated the design of HS146. Development was always an iterative process and we were continually updating the aircraft as more capable equipment became available. We had to meet not only the performance requirements of our customers but also the safety requirements of the regulatory authority, be it military or civil. One of the greatest changes that took place during my working life was the acceptance by the test pilots and the engineers that an aircraft, or any piece of equipment for that matter, need only meet the safety requirements, nothing more was needed. Safety was always vitally important, then as it is now, but safety always has a price and we soon learnt the lesson that we would be uncompetitive if we made an aircraft or a system too safe. For the older test pilots this concept took a little time to sink in, but certainly one of the main contributions that I felt I made whilst I was at Woodford was to bring home to the test crews that we had to be cost effective in everything we did.

When I first moved into Industry I had yet to learn about not gilding the lily and was guilty at first of striving for perfection. We were all encouraged in this particular pursuit because that was the way the military customer was thinking at the time, before the budget purse strings were tightened. We were allowed to talk the customer into 'nice to have' modifications. Slowly things started to change but the real break through on the military front came in the search for efficiency when Hawker Siddeley at Manchester won the contract to build the Nimrod Mk.1 on a fixed price contract. We delivered the aircraft on time and on budget and one of the reasons for this success was, in my opinion, that we were responsible for the design of the complete navigation and attack system, with the Elliotts' engineers, the navigation system designers, being based at Woodford, working with us all the time. All the unimportant changes we wanted to make to the Comet flight control system and flight deck were quite rightly vetoed; the Nimrod could have been a much pleasanter aircraft to fly but it did not matter.

If the Nimrod was an eye opener on how things should be done, the Avro 748 was even more of a cultural change. Here all the money being spent was Hawker Siddeley's and, by that time, Hawker Siddeley under John Lidbury had tight financial control on the operating units such as Manchester/Woodford. Shortly after my becoming Chief Test Pilot Humphrey Wood, the new managing director, appointed me to the management board of Manchester and so I became aware of the wider business scene, because every three months we had to go to Kingston and report on the progress of our major projects and on other key matters affecting the total business such as industrial relations.. This was my first experience of strict financial management and John Lidbury showed us all how it should be done. Humphrey would take us down the night before the meeting to stay in some ruinously expensive hotel and over dinner rehearse ad nauseam what was to be said and, more importantly, what was not to be said, the following day. The next morning the meeting always started bang on time and during the meeting Sir John always seemed to find the sensitive subjects which Humphrey did not want discussed. The probing was remorseless but perfectly structured so that we always finished at the published time. Managers like John Lidbury are vital to successful businesses but hard to come by.

***

The safety of an aircraft depends on good design. The design of the structure is obviously vitally important and a lot of the tests are static which can be done using rigs on the ground. However, dynamic tests such as flutter have to be done in the air and during my time it was necessary to increase speed in small steps, carry out the flutter tests, land for analysis and then try again at a faster speed. Unfortunately, this step by step approach did not always work and I remember an early Victor having a disastrous accident due to flutter. Nowadays, with data being transmitted to the ground in real time with immediate analysis, flutter checks can be carried out very quickly. Impending problems can be spotted immediately.

Handling qualities were another area in the past where a lot of flight testing was required. There were no flight simulators and a lot of time was spent checking whether the handling of an airplane met the certification requirements. The situation was complicated because different countries had different rules which were often nominally the same but tended to be interpreted differently. Dai Davies was the chief test pilot of the now defunct Air Registration Board when I started and his experience certificating the first British Overseas Airways Corporation Boeing 707 highlighted the problem. Dave would not accept the directional behaviour of the aircraft without modification even though the US Federal Aviation Agency had pronounced itself satisfied. Boeing, I suspect, probably agreed with Davies but they did not want to pay for the modification and delay the aircraft; they seemed miraculously and instantaneously to have a modification ready to solve the problem but because the FAA had certificated the aircraft, the modification had to be paid for by BOAC. Of course, once the modification had been cleared, Boeing applied it to all future aircraft though I am not clear whether it was free of charge.

In fact there are other examples of the FAA not applying their own regulations properly to US built aircraft. It may be relevant in this context to remember that until 1996 the FAA had a mandate to support US industry as well as certificate all civil aircraft. The CAA has never had such a mandate which is as it should be, because there must be a uniform standard of safety applied to all aircraft regardless of where they are manufactured. Of course, we suspected that the ARB pilots were harder on UK aircraft than overseas ones; this was strongly contested by the Board but we were never convinced.

It is probably worth remarking that sometimes the firm's pilot had the greatest difficulty convincing his own firm that a particular characteristic of an aircraft was not satisfactory, since changing the design of an aircraft and introducing modifications could be very expensive. Furthermore, as already mentioned, there is an enormous interplay between the performance of an aircraft and its handling. The decision whether an aircraft has satisfactory handling qualities can be very subjective. Luckily, firms' test pilots and certificating pilots generally agree on these critical issues and the firm has to go along with certificated speeds and making changes to the aircraft handling, accepting any consequent changes to the performance if it is necessary.

However, handling qualities no longer play quite such a prominent role in aircraft certification. Since the advent of simulators, the handling of an aircraft can be checked early in the design and then critical handling tests explored on the ground. Such a luxury was not available during the time I was flying, though I was able to help adjust the lateral control of the HS146 on the Hatfield flight simulator. This development has been a boon to designers and has undoubtedly saved a lot of development time. From a test pilot's point of view, the first flight of an aircraft is much more predictable than it used to be.

So far I have mentioned structural strength and handling qualities as key features in assessing whether an aircraft meets the safety requirements. But now the advent of modern technology has introduced a new dimension, because of the introduction of very advanced systems into the latest aircraft to make them competitive. These systems have to operate flawlessly and, furthermore, in the event of a malfunction, the remedial action required by the crew must be minimal and instinctive. As already remarked upon, it was only a relatively short time ago that the slow transatlantic airliners had five crew members to deal with the very elementary systems on these aircraft. Now two pilots have to control the aircraft for the whole flight and deal with any emergency or malfunction. It must be remembered that modern airliners can be unstable in certain flight conditions and the effects are hidden from the pilot because of the fly-by-wire system; it is obviously important that the any system malfunction does not cause the aircraft to be uncontrollable. Consequently, the judgement of whether an aircraft is safe enough has become much harder in recent years because of the complexity of the new aircraft systems. Judgement has to be made by the certificating authorities on whether system design, including the action required by the pilots, is satisfactory. In the past this was not a real problem; nowadays it is absolutely critical with only two crew members. Flight Deck layout and the design of the systems is just as important to safety as the aircraft's handling qualities and certification speeds. As mentioned before, the design of an aircraft's flight deck must ensure that it can be flown safely in an emergency by the airline's worst pilot.

Safety is a matter of probability. The certification regulations try to make an aircraft safe enough so that it does not have many accidents during it's life. It is not uncommon to hear some interviewers on the television or the radio questioning an expert after an accident and asking, belligerently, 'is the aircraft safe or not?' Safety as a concept is not that simple and, hopefully, this point is getting better understood.

***

I have mentioned accidents several times in my story. Accidents are undesirable, often tragic affairs, which statistically seem bound to happen regardless of the regulations which are imposed. What is absolutely vital is that the lessons from accidents are learnt and that the regulations are changed to prevent them re-occurring.

The only way to prevent accidents is to stop flying and this is not going to happen. The general public mostly believes that the chances of an accident happening are so slight that the risk of flying as a passenger on an airline is worth taking. This view is, of course, a tribute to the regulation standards that have been developed during the years and, as long as the standards are maintained, mass commercial aviation will continue to flourish.

Flight Testing to Win

Accidents these days are never simple because most of the obvious causes of accidents have been removed. For a start, aircraft are much easier to fly than in earlier days. Aircraft designers are able to design aircraft which make much less demand on pilots' flying skills. An obvious example is that fifty years ago many aircraft had tail wheel undercarriages. All airliners now have nosewheel undercarriages so that, for example, a cross wind landing is less likely to result in an accident than heretofore. Even the simplest aircraft is likely to have ILS and GPS receivers plus a radio, so that in bad weather a landing can safely be made at a well lit airport. Why is it then that accidents continue to happen? Unfortunately, the problem is that there will always be unexpected circumstances which have not been foreseen and for which the flight crews will not have been trained. Furthermore, there is probably a limit to the ability of the pilot to remember all the sophistications of modern aircraft.

When things start going wrong the pilot may take an incorrect action which results in a disaster. We have to be very careful in these circumstances before blaming the pilot, because sometimes the pilot's actions are due to imperfect design in the airframe manufacturer's system and the associated action required in the event of faults. It is for this reason that the cause of each accident, wherever it happens in the world, needs to be clearly understood and a matter of public record. It is absolutely vital that an accident is rigorously examined by an organisation that is completely independent of the regulatory authority and of the aircraft/engine manufacturer. There should never be any secrecy or any suggestion that something is being covered up. We have to remember that there is always the problem of competition between airframe/engine manufacturers and that perhaps an accident will reflect unfavourably against the design of a particular aircraft or engine. The investigator must not be influenced by any of the concerned parties be they the pilots, the airframe designers, the engine designers, the certificating authorities or the air traffic control authorities, to name but a few. The full, unexpurgated result of all accident investigations should always be published.

Accidents can occur anywhere in the world and usually the airliner concerned will be a type that is used by all the world's airlines. It is bad luck that an accident happens and pure luck where it happens; it is usually chance which country is the aircraft's country of registry but the whole worlds' aviation community is likely to be concerned, whenever and wherever there is an accident, like it or not. An accident investigation team will normally come from the country where the accident occurs assisted by the country where the aircraft is registered; the aircraft and engine manufacturer are often called in to help. It is important that these accidents, which may happen a long way from the centres of the industrial world, should be fairly examined. It is sometimes very tempting to dismiss an accident as pilot error when, in truth, the aircraft is so complicated that a normal pilot cannot be expected to understand all the systems and, therefore, the action required in the event of a malfunction. Aircraft designers are now very alert to this problem; the modern aircraft, however sophisticated, must be capable of being flown, as mentioned frequently before, by the airline's worst pilot and this is a real challenge.

Certain accidents have made landmarks in the pursuit of safety. The accident to the 737 at Manchester airport in August 1985 contributed to the introduction of features to help passengers on the ground escape from an aircraft in an emergency. The Air Inter A320 accident hitting the mountains approaching Strasbourg emphasised the need to carry Ground Proximity Warning Systems to protect against human fallibility. There was an accident to a British Midlands 737 at Kegworth where one engine vibrated very badly and the pilot stopped the good engine; easy to blame the pilots but perhaps more scrutiny was required as to why the pilots did get confused. There have been some accidents and incidents to early Airbus aircraft which have resulted in auto-pilot modifications. There are accidents to aircraft that have not been explained, like the accidents to Boeing 737s, possibly due to full rudder being applied unexpectedly, for no understandable reason. All these matters are very complicated and only unceasing and independent scrutiny will ensure that the travelling public is fully protected.

The International Civil Aviation Organisation has an Annexe 13 dealing with the investigation of accidents to try to ensure that each accident is investigated very thoroughly, so that the maximum benefit is obtained from the investigation to try to prevent that particular type of accident being repeated. In Europe, the regulations

321

now insist that each country has its own accident investigation branch to prevent the regulatory authority influencing the investigators. Perhaps if Europe gets more and more integrated, other changes to accident investigation will take place with a new body more like the United States National Transportation Safety Board being formed. Airlines always pressurise the regulator for being too tough, but the accident investigation organisation must try to make the regulator force improvements to aircraft if they are considered necessary.

As a test pilot and as a director of an aerospace avionics manufacturer I was being regulated; as a Board Member of the Civil Aviation Authority and as a member of the Airworthiness Requirements Board I was a regulator. There was always a difference of approach between being regulated and being a regulator, but everybody concerned made safety paramount and commercial issues were always secondary. Nothing has changed. This is still the situation to-day with competition even keener. Legal claims and settlements from accidents are continually increasing. Accidents, when they occur, put great pressures on the manufacturers and the airlines, since there are huge financial implications from insurance claims and from the effects accidents have on success in the marketplace. Consequently, the unbiased investigation of accidents is absolutely vital and care must always be taken that this is taking place.

**

All civilizations feel that they are living in times of change. They feel that the pace of change in past centuries has been very slow compared with what they are currently experiencing. Certainly to-day we look at the monuments and churches of the past, wondering how people had the time to build them. In my lifetime, it is clear that the industrial revolution of the 19th century, with its emphasis on heavy engineering, has been replaced by the industrial revolution of the 20th century with the silicon chip and the dawn of software engineering. The technological rate of change is accelerating and it must be debatable whether human society can adapt quickly enough in the 21st century to manage this change and keep our civilization stable, without destroying ourselves.

I consider myself very lucky both in the time and the place where I was born. The advances in technology enabled enormous strides in communication and transportation. Space exploration was just beinning and, when I started to earn my living, computers were only just visible on the horizon. It was into this rapidly developing scenario that I entered and chose by pure chance to get involved with aviation. Now, over fifty years later and only a hundred years after the Wright Brothers' first flight, it is interesting to look at the way aviation is developing.

When I started flying the jet era was still in its infancy. Inevitably, military developments forced the pace though it did not take long for the aircraft designers to see the possibilities and attractions of jet commercial air travel. In fact, manned military fighter aircraft using air breathing engines have probably reached the limit of their capability with regard to speed, due to the limitations of the human body. Unmanned aircraft and missiles are being used more and more for military purposes. Military airplane development is now concentrated on making the aircraft invisible to the radars and other sensors that try to detect them. Space development has enormous attractions and the world now has the use of the Global Positioning System and the Internet. Let us hope that the human race does not spoil the technical advantages of space exploration in the way it has tended to spoil other developments with unwanted military side effects.

The civil marketplace is concentrating on cheap air travel. The Concorde was a wonderful achievement, but the air breathing subsonic aircraft will always be more efficient than the supersonic aircraft and in reality, though it may not be universally accepted, the Concorde was not in the mainstream of air transport development. Airplanes are getting larger and larger to reduce the costs of a passenger seat mile, which has the side benefit, in this age of mass air travel, that the total number of passengers travelling at an airport increases for a given number of aircraft movements; this is extremely important when so many of the large airports are already at their maximum number of aircraft movements per day.

Flight Testing to Win

Of course, the changes in new aircraft, both civil and military, are only occurring because of the increasing power and capability of airborne computers. The transistor, followed by the silicon chip, has enabled aircraft designers to introduce facilities undreamt of when I first started flying. Perhaps one of the best examples is the modern airliner, designed to be efficient by being unstable aerodynamically and with only electric wires connecting the pilot's control column to airborne computers and from there to the flying controls. It is vital that safety and risk assessments are taken by the regulators, both in military and commercial applications, to ensure that the advantages being enjoyed using the new technology have not introduced any unforeseen dangers.

The unpalatable facts are that statistics demonstrate that aircraft always have accidents; the bigger and more complicated the aircraft, the more devastating the accident when it occurs. It is just not acceptable for a fully laden aircraft carrying upwards of 600 passengers to crash and for all on board to be killed. It can be argued therefore that for the large new airliners there surely needs to be a step change in both the safety regulations and, probably, in the way aircraft are operated. Perhaps both the design and the operating rules must be tightened significantly to try to ensure that the probability of a fatal accident occurring will be statistically at least ten times less likely than at present. Most accidents occur during the take-off and landing phases of flight when the unpredictable human being is in the loop; perhaps the operating rules will have to be changed so that the auto-pilot must be used for these phases of flight with the pilot acting as a manager. Furthermore, these large aircraft in particular need visual systems which enable pilots to see the airfield, even in thick fog, both in the air and on the ground. Possibly there should be three crew instead of two on the flight deck to help monitor the systems.

***

There has to be, of course, a downside to mass air travel due to there being a finite limit to the amount of fossil fuel on our planet. The situation is getting more acute as the wealth of India and China increases dramatically and the huge populations of these countries are wanting to travel. The price of fuel is rising quickly which will encourage exploration for more of the world's oil reserves but sometime there will have to be a discovery of a new source of economical fuel for aircraft or there will be a decline in air travel and airplane manufacturing. However, so far, there seems to be a reluctance to consider the consequences of this fact. The airframe builders race ahead building more and more aircraft, not just to replace the old aircraft that are wearing out and to improve efficiency but to cater for the steady increase in the world's population available for travel. It is true that these new aircraft have a lower fuel burn per passenger but the number of passengers travelling far outweighs the improvement in efficiency.

There seems to be no connection between the politicians who advocate taking measures to prevent global warming and conserve the earth's dwindling fuel reserves, and the same politicians who encourage the building of aircraft to maintain employment and technical capability. Similarly, there seems to be no connection between the plan for increasing the size and the number of airports and other necessary infrastructure to accommodate more and more passengers, and the possible consequent damage to the fragile environment in which we live. The air transport industry keeps announcing the expected percentage increase each year in passenger air miles, but there is no corresponding response from Governments saying that these increases are unsustainable.

The time change from starting the design to the first flight of a new airliner is relatively short but the time to build all the new facilities on the ground to accommodate the aircraft always takes much longer. It must always be remembered that the advent of the larger airliners affects not only the aircraft manufacturers and the airlines but also the airports and ground infrastructure to support these enormous aircraft. There is always a long delay in making the necessary ground preparations for new aircraft because of the inevitable political problems involved in making the changes; there is the inconvenience which is caused to the local population who cannot see any advantage in what is happening, and there is the financial problem of finding the money to fund the infrastructure. Airports all over the world are continually being changed to be able to service the demands of new aircraft. Ground transportation to these airports has to be enlarged to deal with vast numbers of people involved, 'meeters and greeters' as well as travellers.

Perhaps it is time that there is a critical analysis into what should be the correct direction of commercial airframe development; perhaps it is time that consideration should be given to whether it is really acceptable to manufacture more and more aircraft, to provide more and more passenger seats, to consume more and more fuel, to pump more unwanted gases into the atmosphere and to cover the world's surface with more and more concrete to support the aircraft.

To complicate matters still further, there is unfortunately another relatively new aspect to air travel which requires yet more regulation but which precludes designing on a well proven scientific basis; this is the threat of terrorism from suicide bombers or from missiles fired at aircraft as they take-off or land. Airport checks are becoming more and more stringent, which is absolutely necessary if these dangers are to be overcome. However, a failure to prevent terrorist attacks could have a real effect on air travel. Vigilance, on the ground and in the air, cannot be relaxed and already new systems are appearing in aircraft including one to enable the flight crew to observe the passenger cabins, but will they have the spare time to monitor the displays? Hopefully aircraft will not need to be fitted with active defence against missiles but this problem is unlikely to go away, quite the reverse.

***

I have been incredibly lucky in the time in which I have lived and the work I have been able to do. Technology has spawned inventions at an amazing rate so that the crystal set with its one 'transistor' sixty years ago has been replaced with silicon chips with millions of transistors in a space minute compared with the crystal. What is almost unbelievable is that these huge integrated circuits have an amazing reliability, so that they can be used in flight critical computers for flying round the world or into space.

Technology has also changed materials so that aluminium and its alloys are almost disappearing in favour of carbon fibres with their advantages of weight and rigidity.

Technology has enabled the development of satellites and the internet. Together they have enabled global communication. The world is no longer split into small compartments. Information can no longer be controlled, parcelled by governments to their citizens as desired. Satellites and the internet ensure that anybody, anywhere in the world, can listen to information, from hundreds of different sources.

During my working life I was able to take advantage of a lot of this technological development and I was also able to visit parts of the world where this new technology was vitally needed. The transformation that has taken place, especially in the third world countries where I did most of my demonstrations, has been enormous. Many of the airfields still leave a lot to be desired but global communication has reached the inhabitants of almost every part of the world. As I remarked at the beginning of this book, I have never looked back --- there is always another challenge waiting, but I do feel that I was very privileged to have had the opportunity to witness many parts of the world before the impact of 'civilisation'.

The rapid growth in aviation and technology has not been an unmixed blessing but change has always been inevitable. How far our Governments succeed in managing change is one of the major problems of our time, but that is for the future.

I have been extremely fortunate during my working life; my company had good products and I was lucky to have been involved with enthusiastic pilots, engineers and sales teams. Ronnie Millsap had it right in his song ---

"I wouldn't have missed it for the world".

A Wonderful World

ALB September 2005

Flight Testing to Win

FLIGHT TESTING TO WIN

No aircraft is absolutely safe. This book is about Aviation, from learning to fly, becoming a test pilot, flight testing, demonstrating on some of the third world's worst airfields, then specializing in Avionics and finally joining the Board of the UK Civil Aviation Authority, helping to formulate the regulations that the author had spent so many years living by. The book makes the point that flying is inherently risky, that regulations always try to quantify acceptable risk, that safety is a cost, and that test pilots have to sell their aircraft and should not try to make an aircraft safer than the rules require. It emphasizes the almost unbelievable changes in aviation in one working lifetime, whilst painting a picture of a much simpler world, now gone beyond recall. Many stories are told, including flying with the legendary Howard Hughes when the world thought him a mad recluse, and testing many aircraft including all three V Bombers, an almost unique experience.